the booke of Richard the 3 in the yeare 1647

The true Portraiture of Richard Plantagenest, of England and of France King Lord of Ireland the third King Richard

THE HISTORY
of the Life and Reigne of
RICHARD
The Third.

Composed in five Bookes
By GEO: BUCK Esquire.

Honorandus est qui injuriam non fecit, sed qui alios eam facere non patitur, duplici Honore dignus est.
Plato de legibus. Lib. 5.

Qui non repellit a proximo injuriam si potest, tam est in vitio quam ille qui infert.
D. Ambros. offic. Lib. 3.

LONDON,
Printed by *W. Wilson,* and are to be sold by
W. L. H. M. and *D. P.* 1647.

RICA

THE

Com…

By Geo…

The Argument and Contents of the First Booke.

The Linage, Family, Birth, Education, and Tirociny of King *Richard* the third.

The Royall house of Plantagenest, and the beginning of that name; What Sobriquets *were: The antiquity of Sirnames;* Richard *is created Duke of Gloucester, his marriage, and his issue; His martiall imployments; His Iourney into Scotland, and recovery of Barwick; The death of King* Edward *the* 4th. *The Duke of Gloucester made Lord Protector, and soone after King of England, by importunate suite of his Barons and of the People, as the next true and lawfull heire.* Henry Teudor *Earle of Richmond practiseth against the King; He is conveyed into France. The Noble Linage of Sir* William Herbert, *his Imployment; He is made Earle of Pembrooke. King* Edward *the* 4th. *first, and after King* Richard, *sollicite the Duke of Brittaine, and treat with him for the delivery of the young Earle of Richmond his Prisoner. The successe of that businesse. The quality and title of the Beauforts or Sommersets. The Linage and Family of the Earle of Richmond. The solemne Coronations of King* Richard, *and of the Queene his wife, his first at Westminster, the second at Yorke. Nobles,*

Knights and Officers made by him; Prince Edward *his Son invested in the Principallity of Wales, and the Oath of Allegeance made to him; King* Richard *demandeth the Tribute of France; His Progresse to Yorke; His carefull charge given to the Judges and Magistrates; He holdeth a Parliament, wherein the marriage of the King his Brother with the Lady* Gray *is declared and adjudged unlawfull, their children to be illegitimate and not capable of the Crowne: The Earle of Richmond and divers others attainted of Treason; Many good Laws made; The K. declared and approved by Parliament to be the only true and lawfull heire of the Crowne. The King and Queene dowager are reconciled; He hath secret advertisemēts of Innovations and practises against him; Createth a vice-Constable of England. His sundry treaties with Forraigne Princes. Doctor* Morton *corrupteth the Duke of Buckingham, who becometh discontent, demanding the Earledome of Hereford, with the great Constableship of England; He taketh Armes, is defeated and put to death by marshall Law.*

The

THE

FIRST BOOKE OF THE HISTORY OF *RICHARD* THE THIRD, OF *ENGLAND*, AND OF *FRANCE*, KING, AND LORD OF IRELAND.

RIchard Plantagenet, Duke of Glocester, and King of England, and of France, and Lord of Ireland, the third of that name, was the younger sonne of Sir *Richard Plantagenet*, the fourth Duke of Yorke of that Royall Family, and King of England, designate by King *Henry* the sixth, and by the most noble Senate, and universall Synod of this Kingdome, the High Court of Parliament. The Mother of this *Richard* Duke of Glocester, was the Lady *Cecily*, Daughter of Sir *Ralph de Neville*, Earle of Westmerland, by his wife *Ioane de Beaufort*, the naturall Daughter of *Iohn Plantagenet* (alias) *de Gaunt*, Duke of Guiene and Lancaster, King of Castile and Leon, third Sonne of King *Edward* the third, for in that order this Duke is best accounted, because *William* of Hatfield, the second Sonne of King *Edward* the third dyed in his infancy, and this Duke of Yorke, and King designate, was propagated from two younger sonnes of the same King *Edward* the third, whereby he had both Paternall and Maternall Title to the Crowne of England and France: But his better and nearer Title, was the Maternall Title, or that which came to him by his Mother the Lady *Anne de Mortimer*, the Daughter and heire of *Phillippa Plantagenet*, who was the sole Daughter and heire of *Lyonell Plantagenet*, Duke of Clarence, and second Sonne of King *Edward* the third, according to the account and order aforesaid.

The House and Title of *Yorke*.

And this Lady *Phillip* was the Wife of Sir *Edmond de Mortimer*, the great and famous Earle of March, and that Duke *Richard*, King designate, by his Father *Richard Plantagenet*, Duke of York (sirnamed also *de Conningsborrough*) issued directly, and in a masculine line from *Edmond Plantagenet*, alias *de Langley*, the first Duke of Yorke, and the fourth Sonne of King *Edward* the third, who was the most renowned and glorious Progenitor to those Princes of Yorke and Lancaster, and the first King in a Lineall descent from that great *Henry*, sirnamed *Plantagenet*, famous for his great Prowesse and many victories, King of England in the right of his Mother the Empresse *Matilda*, or *Maud*, daughter and heire of King *Henry* the first, and stiled *Anglorum Domina*, sometime wife of the Emperour *Henry* the fifth, by which he was also sirnamed, *filius imperatricis*: The French men called him, *Henry du Court Manteau*, or Court Mantle, because he wore a cloake shorter then the fashion was in those times. By his Father *Galfride*, or *Geoffry Plantagenet*, he was Earle or Duke of Anjou (for then *Dux*, *& Comes*, and *Ducatus & Comitatus*, were Synonomies & promiscuous words,) he was also Earle of Maine, of Torraine, and hereditary Seneschall, or High Steward of France, and by his marriage of *Elianor* Queene of France Repudiate, Daughter and heire of *William* Duke of Gascoigne and of Guiene, and Earle of Poictou: He was Duke and Earle of those Principalities, and Signiories, also by the Empresse his Mother Duke of Normandy: He was Lord of Ireland by Conquest, and confirmed by Pope *Adrian*. But these were not all his Seigniories and Dominions; for after he was King of England, he extended his Empire and Principate in the South to the Pyrenean mountaines, (The Confines of Spaine and France) in the North to the Isles of Orkney, and in the East and West with the Ocean, as *Giraldus Cambrensis*, *Gul. Neubrigensis*, *& Ioannes Sarisburiensis*, grave and credible Authors affirme, who stiled him, *Regum Britannia maximus*; and doubtlesse he was the greatest King of Brittaine since King *Arthur*.

The Linage of Edward 3.

The Empire of K. Henry 2.

Girald. in Topog. Hibernie. Sarisbur. in Pol. Newbrig. Lib. 2.

But it is controverted amongst the Antiquaries and Heralds, which Earle of Anjou first bare the sirname and *Sobriquet* of *Plantagenest*, or *Plantagenet* after the vulgar Orthodoxe, by what occasion, and for what cause it was taken and borne, and from what time and age it had beginning: Some would have the forenamed *Geoffry Plantagenet*, Father of this *Henry*, the first Earle of Anjou, which bare it. But we shall finde stronger reasons to derive it from a much more ancient Earle of Anjou, and better causes then can be found in him, if we step but a little backe to their stories, and compare the men and their times. *Geoffry Plantagenet* being a man of a gallant and active fire, disposed to the Courts of Princes, to Justs Turnaments, &c. and to the Courtship of faire Ladies, those of the highest ranke, and had so amorous a Star, That *Philippe le Grosse* K. of France, suspected him for too familiar commerce with his bed. But it was of better influence when he archieved and married the Empresse *Matilda*, by which we may very well calculate, he neither had, nor would be intent or at leisure for such a mortified and perilous Pilgrimage to Jerusalem. But if we would know the man, let us looke upon the first *Fulke*, Earle of Anjou,

Fulk Earle of Anjou.

Anjou, who lived about an hundred yeares before the Norman Conquest of England, and was Sonne of *Godefray*, or *Geoffry Grisegonell* the first Earle of Anjou (according to *du Haillon*) Ancestor and Progenitor to the foresaid *Geoffry Plantagenet*, some seven or eight degrees in the ascending Line, as *Paradin* accounteth, a man raised upon the foundation of a great courage and strength (two of the best Principles when they have good seconds, and make too a glorious man, where they serve his vertues, not affections, as in this Prince they did) whose disposition on the other side being let out into as vaste an ambition and covetousnesse, ne're looked upon the unlawfulnesse of his desires, how horrid soever (which amongst the many rest) run him upon the shelves of wilfull perjury, and murder; the one for defrauding & spoiling a Church of certaine Rights, and the other for contriving the Tragedy of his young Nephew, *Drogo*, Earle of Brittaine, to make himselfe Lord of his Countrey and Principallity. The secret checke and scourge of those crimes had a long time to worke upon his conscience, and of a great sinner made a great Penitent, being old and having much solitary time, and many heavy thoughts (which naturally accompany old age, and suggest better considerations of our former and youthfull sinnes.) he opens the horrour of them, and his afflicted mind to his Confessor, (as great *Constantine* to *Ægyppius*) who enjoyned him to make the same confession before the holy Sepulcher, at Jerusalem, which Pilgrimage the Earle performed in all lowly and contemptible manner, passing as a private and unworthy person, without traine or followers, save two of his meanest, which he tooke rather for witnesses then servants, whose service was, when they came neare Jerusalem, the one with a cord (such as is used for the strangling of Criminals) thrown about his Masters neck, to draw or leade him to the holy sepulcher, whilst the other did *acoustre* and strip him as a condemned person, and with extremity scourge him untill he was prostrate before the sacred Monument where he gave evidence of his unfained contrition and sorrow. Amongst other devout expressions, uttering this, *Mon dieu & Signeur recoy a Pardon le perjure & homicide & miserable Foulque*; And after this pilgrimage he lived many years of prosperity in his Country honoured of all men. To justifie this, there be many Examples of other Princes and Noble Persons, who lived about the yeare of our Lord one thousand, and somewhat before, and in three or foure ages after, who under-went the like Pilgrimages imposed under base and mechanicke nick-names and persons, as of a Carpenter, a Smith, a Fisher-man, a Mariner, a Shepheard, a Woodman, a Broome-man, &c. In my Inquiry after that of *Plantagenet*, I met with an ancient Manuscript, that afforded me a large Catalogue of many such, by the French called *Sobriquets*, from whence I have transcribed these few for a taste.

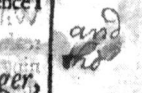

Acoustre in criminall & condemne Paradin.

From this example *Henry* 2. submitted his body to be scourged by the *Monks* of *Canterbury* for the death of *Tho. Becket.*

Berger,

Sobriquets.

Berger, Shepheard.	*Hapkin*, Hatchet.
Griſegõnelle, gray-coat	*Chapelle*, Hood.
Teſte de Eſtoupe, Head of towe.	*Sans-terre*, Lackland.
Arbuſte, A Shrub.	*Malduit*, Ill taught.
Martell, A Hammer.	*Geffard*, *Jeuvencas*, or *Heyfer*.
Grandebœuf, Ox-face.	*Filz de Flean*, Son of a Flaile.
La Zouch, Branch upon a Stem.	*Plantageneſt*, the Plant or ſtalk of a Broome.
Houlette, a ſheep-hook.	

After this manner and long after K. *H.* 2 the heire and ſucceſſour of this Earle, *Fulko* was injoyned by the Pope to go to the *Holy-Land*, and to fight againſt the Infidels, and *Hoveden* *Rival.* &c.

And under the name and habit of a Broome-man our Pilgrim performed this Penance, and tooke the *Sobriquet* of *Plantageneſt* from wearing a ſtalke of Broome, or plant of *Geneſt*; this is generally received, but the time and reaſon neither ſet downe nor rendred by any of our Heralds and Antiquaries, French or Engliſh; for the time when he performed this, I obſerve it about the yeare of our Lord, one thouſand certainly. But for the particular relation, this Count had to chuſe the *geneſt* plant, or Broome-ſtalke before any other vegitall or thing, I ſhall lay downe that opinion which is mine owne noting for a circumſtance by the way, that the Broome in Hieroglyphicall Learning is the Symbole of humility, and the Poets, particularly *Virgil* the beſt of Poets, give it the Epithet of *humilis*, *humilis geniſta*; and the Etymologiſts derive it from *genu* the knee, the part moſt applyed, and as it were dedicate to the chiefe Act of Reverence, kneeling, to which the naturall Philoſophers ſay, there is ſo mutuall a correſpondency, and ſo naturall a ſympathy between *genu* and *geniſta*, that of all other plants or vegitals, it is moſt comfortable and medicinable to the paines and diſeaſes of the knees. *Pliny* a great Maſter amongſt them ſaith, *Geviſta tuſca, cum,* &c. *genua dolentia ſanat*.

Leon. Fuchius.

Plin. Lib. 24. cap. 9.

But the conſiderable reaſon is, as I conceive it, from the uſe he was conſtrained to make of the twigges of Broome when he came to be ſcourged at Jeruſalem, the place neceſſitating the uſe of them to that purpoſe, being (as *Strabo* relates) a ſtony, ſandy, and barren ſoyle, only naturall and gratefull to the *geneſt*, as the watry and moiſt to the Birch, Willow and Withy, of which there could be none there, for that reaſon. And from hence it muſt moſt conjecturally take the beginning of that Honour, which afterward his Princely and Noble Poſteries continued for their ſirname, who became Dukes & Princes in

Strabo, Lib. 16.

ſundry

sundry places, and some of them Kings of England, France, Scotland and Ireland; and (as the pious people of that Age verily beleeved by their observation) were the more prosperous and happy for his sake. *Du Haillon.*

For the continuance of the Name, some (who pretend to see further and better in the darke then others as cleare sighted) would have it taken of late time, and not used by the Kings and Princes of England, of the Angeume race. But there are many proofes to be adduced against them; Let us looke into Master *Brookes* genealogies of England, we shall find nothing more obvious and frequent in the deductions of those Princes of the House of Anjou, then the addition and sirname of *Plantagenet*; *Edm. Plantagenet*, *Geo. Plantagenet*, *Iohn Plantagenet*, *Edward Plantagenet*, *Lyonell Plantagenet*, *Humphry Plantagenet*, &c. In the French Historians and Antiquaries, *Ion de Tillet*, *Girard du Haillon*, *Claude Paradin*, *& Iean Baron de la Hay*, we shall often meet with *Geoffry Plantagenet*, *Arthur Plantagenet*, *Richard Plantagenet*, and diverse the like, all of the first Age, when the Angeume Princes first became English, and some before. Master *Camden* also in his *Immortall Britannia*, mentioneth some very ancient, as *Richard Plantagenet*, *Iohn Plantagenet*, &c. And witnesseth, that the forenamed *Geoffry Plantagenet* used to weare a Broome-stalke in his Bonnet, as many Nobles of the House of Anjou did, and tooke it for their chiefe sirname. It might be added, that these Earles of Anjou were descended out of the great house of Saxon in Germany, which hath brought forth many Kings, Emperors and Dukes; and that they were of kindred and alliance to the ancient Kings of France, and sundry other Princes. But I will close here for the high Nobility of King *Richard*, as the good old Poet did for another Heroicall Person:

In his Catalogue of Honour.

——— *Deus est utroque parente.* Ovid. *Deus. i. Rex.*

And come to the other matters of his private story. And first for his Birth and native place, which was the Castle of Fotheringay, or as some write, the Castle of Birkhamsteed, both Castles and Honours of the Duke his Father, about the yeare of our Lord 1450, which I discover by the calculation of the Birth, Raigne, and death of King *Edward* his brother, who was borne about 1441, or 1442. and raigned two and twenty yeares, dyed at the age of one and forty, *Anno* 1483. The Dutchesse of Yorke their Mother had five children betwixt them, so that *Richard* could not be lesse then seven or eight yeares younger then King *Edward*, and he survived him not fully three yeares.

This *Richard Plantagenet*, and the other children of *Richard* Duke of Yorke, were brought up in Yorke-shire, and Northampton-shire, but lived for the most part in the Castle of Midelham in Yorke-shire, untill the Duke their Father, and his Sonne *Edmund Plantagenet* Earle of Rutland were slaine in the battell of Wakefield, *Anno Dom.* ~~1641,~~ 1460

1460 ~~1641~~, upon which the Dutchesse of Yorke their Mother (having cause to feare the faction of Lancaster, which was now growne very exulting and strong, and of a mortall enmity to the House of Yorke) secretly conveyed her two younger sonnes, *George* and *Richard Plantagenet* (who was then about some ten yeares old) into the Low-Countries, to their Aunt the Lady *Margaret*, Dutchesse of Burgundy, Wife of *Charles* Duke of Burgundy and Brabant, and Earle of Flanders. They continued at Utrich, the chiefe City then in Holland, where they had Princely and liberall education, untill *Edward* Earle of March their eldest Brother had revenged his Fathers death, and taken the Kingdome and Crowne (as his right) from *Henry* the sixth, when he called home his two Brothers, and enters them into the practise of Armes, to season their forwardnesse and honour of Knighthood which he had bestowed upon them; and soone after invests *George* into the Dutchy of Clarence, and Earledome of Richmond, which Earledome he the rather bestowed upon him, to darken the young Earle of Richmond, *Henry Teudor*. *Richard* had the Dukedome of Glocester, and Earledome of Carlile, as I have read in an old Manuscript story, which Creation the Heralds doe not allow. But whether he were Comes thereof after the ancient Roman understanding, that is, Governour, or Comes, or Count, after the common taking it by us English, or others; that is, for a speciall Titular Lord, I will not take upon me to determine, but affirme I have read him, *Comes Carliolensis*.

Lib. manus. in quarto apud D. Rob. Cotton.
Comes, i. Praefect.

And after the great Earle of Warwicke and Salisbury, *Richard de Neville*, was reconciled to the Kings favour, *George* Duke of Clarence was married to the Lady *Isabell*, or *Elizabeth*, the elder Daughter of that Earle, and *Richard* Duke of Glocester to the Lady *Anne*, which Ladies by their Mother the Lady *Anne de Beauchamp*, Daughter and heire of Sir *Richard de Beauchamp*, Earle of Warwicke, were heires of that Earledome. But *Anne*, although the younger sister, was the better woman, having been a little before married to *Edward Plantagenet*, Prince of Wales, and Duke of Cornwall, only Sonne of King *Henry* the sixth, and was now his Princesse and Dowager, by whom Duke *Richard* had a sonne called *Edward*, created Prince of Wales when his Father came to the Crowne.

The imployment of this Duke was for the most part in the North, as the Countrey of his birth, so more naturally affected by him according to the Poet:

——*Natale solum dulcedine cunctos mulcet*. Ovid.

And there lay his Appanage and Patrimony, with a great Estate of the Dutchesse his Wife, of which the Signiory of Penrith, vulgo, Perith in Cumberland was part, where he much resided, and built or repaired most of the Castles, all that Northerne side generally honouring and affecting his Deportment, being magnificent, (to apply

Camden in Cumberland.

Sir

Sir *Thomas Moore* something above his ability: which he exprest most in his hospitality. And surely, if men are taken to the life best from their actions, we shall find him in the circle of a Character (not so commaculate and mixt, as passionate and purblinde pens have dasht it) whilst we squint not at those vertues in him, which make up other Princes absolute; His wisedome and courage, had not then their nicknames and calumny, as now, but drew the eyes and acknowledgment of the whole Kingdome towards him; and his brother had a sound experience of his fidelity and constancy in divers hazardous congresses and battels, through which he had faithfully followed his fortune, and return'd all his undertakings successefull: as at Barnet, where he entred so farre and boldly into the Enemies Army, that two of his Esquires, *Thomas Parr* and *John Milwater* being nearest to him were slaine; yet by his owne valour he quit himselfe, and put most part of the Enemies to flight, the rest to the sword. With the like valour he behaved himselfe at the battell of Exon, Doncaster, St Albans, Blore-heath, Northampton, Mortimers Crosse, and Tewkesbury. And it was then confest a very considerable service to the State, his taking of the famous Pyrate, *Thomas Nevill*, alias, *Faulkonbridge*, Earle of Kent, with whom complyed Sir *Richard de Nevill*, Earle of Warwicke, a neare kinsman to the Earle of Kent his naturall Father, which held him up in the better esteeme, and whetted him to any Attempt. For this haughty Earle, who had drawne him from the House of Yorke (to which he had done valiant service not long before) to the party of *Henry 6.* and his Lancastrian faction; and fearing what forces and aid King *Edward* might have from beyond Sea, provides a warlike Fleet for the narrow Seas, of which this *Faulconbridge* was appointed Admirall, with Commission to take or sinke all Ships he met, either of the Kings friends or Subjects; who did not under act it, but made many depredations on the Coasts, and put many to the Sword becoming an Enemy, the more considerable, King *Edward* finding (as the case stood then with him) his Attemps by Sea would be of too weake a proofe to surprise him, which the Duke of Gloucester contrived by an advertisement he had of his private stealth into severall of the parts, sometimes where he had recourse to some abetters of that Faction, and comming too shore at *Southampton*, by a ready Ambush seized and apprehended him, from whence he was conveyed to *London*, so to Middleham Castle, and after he had told some Tales, put to death. And whilst he continued in the Northern parts, he governed those Countries with great Wisdome and Justice, preserving the Concord and Amity betweene the Scots and English, though the breaches were not to be made up with any strength and continuance, the borders living out of mutuall spoyles, and common Rapines, ever prompt for any cause that might beget braules and feuds. And in the last yeare of the Reigne of the King his brother, the Quarrels grew so outragious and hostile, that nothing could compose them, but the Sword and open War

Sir *William Haward.*

purblind *Quasi* pareblind.

The Bastard *Faulconbridge.*

An Army sent into Scotland under the D. of Glocester. arising from an unjust detaining the Tribute, King *Iames* was yearly bound to pay, as *Polidore* thus writeth.

King *Edward* tooke it very ill at the hands of *Iames* fourth King of Scotland, that he refused to pay the Tribute whereunto he was bound by Covenant; And therefore resolved by Armes to compell him to it: But King *Edward* being distracted with a jealous care and watching of France, neglected that businesse of Scotland, and in the meane time *Alexander* Duke of Albany, Brother to King *Iames*, pretending earnest businesse in France, makes England in his way, and instigates King *Edward* to put on Armes against his Brother, promising to returne shortly out of France, and raise a power in Scotland for his aide: Hereupon the King resolved it, and sent the Duke of Glocester with a good Armie into Scotland, who marched master of the field neare to Barwicke, having a little before sent thither *Thomas Stanley* to besiege it, and soone after tooke it himselfe. But the Duke of Albany failed him, and had underhand strooke up a peace with his Brother of Scotland; yet *Richard* of Gloucester accomplished the expe-
Anno 24. *Ed*. 4. dition very honourably and happily: Thus *Polidore*. But to enlarge what he reporteth desertively, and abridgeth; King *Edward*, notwithstanding that negligence (noted by him) levied strong forces (the King of Scotland being as vigilant in that businesse) and made the Duke of Glocester his Generall, under whom went Sir *Henry Peircy* Earle of Northumberland, the Lord *Stanley* after Earle of Derby, the Lord *Lovell*, the Lord *Gray* of Grestocke, the Lord *Scroope* of Bolton, the Lord *Fitzhugh*, Sir *William Parre* of Rose a noble and valiant Gentleman, Father of the Lord *Parr* of Rose, Kendall, and *Fitzhugh*, and Grandfather to Sir *William Parr* Earle of Essex, and Marquesse of Northampton, Sir *Edward Woodville* Lord *Rivers* Brother to the Queene *Elizabeth*, with many other of Eminency and Noble quality. The Duke marched first with his Armie to the borders and frontieres of Scotland, giving the overthrow to such as resisted, then made up to the strong Towne of Barwicke, which at that instant the King of Scotland possessed by the surrender of *Henry* 6, and had the like successe with those Troopes of the Enemies he met and found about the Towne. After a short siege the besieged upon Summons and Parlee (finding themselves too weake to make good the opposition) were easily perswaded to be at quiet, and safely rendring the Towne and Castle upon very slender conditions, as is recorded in the Chronicle of
Chron. Croy. *Croyland*. Having plac't a Governour and Garrison in the Towne, he continued his march towards Edenborough, with a purpose to besiege and sacke it, but was met in the halfe way by Embassadours from thence, who (after a favourable audience and accesse craved) in the name of their King and Nation implore a League, or at least a Truce betweene the Kingdomes, offering so faire conditions for it, that the Generall after a deliberate consultation, granted to suspend or intermit all hostile proceedings, with a faire entertainement to their persons, and a publike Edict throughout the Army, that no English should

ſhould offer any violence or offence to any Scot or their goods, and by this provident truce, that ruddy ſtorme (which ſeemed terrible to impend) was diverted and made a calme preface to the famous League, afterward concluded by him when he was K. and *Iames* the 4th of Scotland. But whilſt theſe imployments ſtaid him there, newes arrived of King *Edwards* death, and was muttered very doubtfully by ſome who had confidence and ground to ſuppoſe it haſtened by treachery. The Nobles at London, and in the South parts ſpeedily call the Duke home by their private letters and free approbation, to aſſume the Protection of the Kingdome, and two Princes committed unto him by the King. *Rex Edwardus 4. filios ſuos Richardo Duci Gloceſtriæ, in tutelam moriens tradidit*: as *Polidore* teſtifieth.

The doubtfull death of K. E. 4 *vid. lib. 4.*

The Duke of Glouceſter made Lord Protector.

The Army and affaires of thoſe parts diſpoſed, he came to Yorke, where he made a few daies ſtay to pay ſome religious Offices and Ceremonies to the manes and exequies of the deceaſed King, ſo haſtned to London, having in his Traine (beſides his owne ordinary Retinue) ſixe hundred voluntary Gentlemen of the North parts, brave Horſemen and gallantly mounted, upon the way he diſpatched certaine ſeguall meſſengers to the young King (who was then at Ludlow Caſtle in Wales) to provide for his honourable Conduct of London where he arrived not long after the Lord Protector, and was magnificently received and lodged at the Biſhops Pallace; his Brother the Duke of Yorke was then with the Queene Mother in the Pallace at Weſtminſter, who out of a pretended motherly care (rather indeed her pollicy) would not let him ſtirre from her to ſee the King, who had deſired his company, but inſtantly takes Sanctuary with him in the Abbey. The Lord Protector ſollicites her by ſome Noblemen to ſend or bring him to the King, which ſhe peremptorily ſtood againſt, untill Cardinall *Bourſer*, Archbiſhop of Canterbury, was made the Meſſenger, who ſo gravely and effectually perſwaded with her, that ſhe delivered him the Duke: After ſome dayes reſpite in London-Houſe, the King (according to ancient cuſtome) was to remove Court to the Tower of London, the Caſtle Royall, and chiefe Houſe of ſafety in the Kingdome, untill the more weighty affaires of the State, and ſuch troubles (if any hapned, as often interceeds the alterations of Raignes were well diſpatched and compoſed (ſome threatning evils of that kind being diſcovered and extinguiſhed before the Protector came to London.) And untill all things proper to his Coronation were in preparation and readineſſe, the Lord Protector ſtill being neere unto him with all duty and care, and did him homage, as Honourable *Phillippe de Comines*, *Le Duc de Gloceſter avoit fait homage à ſon Nepheu Comme à ſon Roy & ſouverain Seigneur*; but this Teſtimony being avoucht by one who loved not the Protector may leave more credit; who ſayes, when the young King approacht towards London, the Lord Protector his Unckle rode barehead before him; and in paſſing along, ſaid with a loud voice to the People; *Behold your Prince and Soveraigne*, to which the Prior of Croyland, who lived in thoſe dayes, reporteth,

Phil. de comines in Lud. 11.

Sir *Tho. Moore*.

Chronic: *Abbat. Croy.*

Richardus

Richardus Protector nihil reverentiæ, quod capite nudato, genu flecto aliove quolibet corporis habitur insubdito exigit, regi nepoti suo facere distulit aut recusavit; And why should these services and his constancy be judged lesse real to the Son then to the Father, his care & providence looking pregnantly through all turnes that concern'd him and his State; and therefore timely remov'd such of Danger as were vehemently suspected for their Ambition and insolent assuming Power and Authoritie not proper to them, and so stood ill-affected to their Prince, and turbulent Maligners of the Government. And thus his strict justice to some, begat the envie of others, as it fell out in the time of King *Edward*, betweene those of the blood Royall (with whom the ancient Barons sided) and the Reginists, who being stubborne, haughty, and incomputable of the others nearnesse to the King, stir'd up Competitions and turbulencies among the Nobles, and became so insolent and publique in their pride, and Out-rages towards the people, that they forc't their murmurs at length to bring forth mutiny against them: But finding the Kings inclination gentle on that side, they so temper'd it, as they durst extend their malice to the Prince of the blood, and chiefe Nobilitie, many times by slanders and false suggestions, privately incensing the King against them, who suffered their insinuations too farre, whilst his credulitie stood abus'd, and his favour often alienated from those, whose innocence could understand no cause for it. The Engines of those intrusions and supplantations, were the *Grayes*, the *Woodvills*, and their kinsmen; who held a strong beliefe, to have better'd their power with the young King their kinsman, and then they might have acted their Rodomontades and injuries in a higher straine, remov'd the Prince of the blood, and set up what limits they pleased to their Faction and Power during the minoritie of the King, and after too, whilst the Queene Mother could usurpe or hold any superintendency upon the Soveraigntie, or her Sonne. These things, and the mischiefes that seem'd to superimpend the State, equally poiz'd, and consulted, by the Lord Protector, and others of the principall Nobilitie; it was resolv'd, to give a timely remedy or period unto them; all which Sir *Thomas Moore* acknowledgeth, and confesseth, the Nobles of the Kingdome had reason to suspect and feare the Queenes Kindred, would put their power more forward when their Kinsman came to be King, then in his Fathers time, although then their insolencies were intollerable. And this Author further acknowledgeth there had bin a long grudge & heart-burning betweene the King and Queenes Kindred in the time of King *Edward*; which the King, although he were partiall for the Queenes Faction, was earnest to reconcile, but could not: And after he was dead, the Lord *Gray*, Marquesse *Dorset*, the Lord *Rich. Gray*, and the Lord *Rivers*, made full accompt to sway the young King; and having learn'd, it was best fishing in a troubled streame, threw all occasions of dissention amongst the great men of this Kingdome, that so, whilst the other Nobles were busie in their owne quarrells, they might

The insolency of the Queens Kindred.

Sir *Thomas Moore*, in *Edward* 5. *Rich.* 3.

might take an opportunitie to assault and supplant where they hated. And for provision towards the Designe, the Marquesse had secretly gain'd a great quantity of the Kings treasure out of the Tower, and the *Woodevills* made good preparations of Armes; of which, some were met with by the way as they were conveighed close packed in Carts. It was therefore high time for the Protector and ancient Nobilitie to looke circumspectly about them, and fasten on all occasions that might prevent such growing Treacheries, which could be no way but by taking off their heads. Which being resolved, the Marquesse of *Dorset*, the Lord *Richard Gray* their Uncle, Sir *Anthony Woodeville*, Lord *Rivers*, and some other of that kindred and Faction were apprehended, and at Pomfret executed (onely the Marquesse, by some private notice given him, fled, and tooke Sanctuary) At the same time the Lord *Hastings* (who much favoured the Queene and her partie, especially the Marquesse (therefore the more to be suspected dangerous) was Arrested for High Treason, and in the Tower upon the Greene had his head chop't off, an Act of more strange and severe appearance then the other, having the esteeme of a good Subject, and generally supposed much affectionate to the Protector, and the Duke of *Buckingham*. And Sir *Thomas Moore*, reporteth, that the Protector was most unwilling to have lost him, but that he saw him joyning with their Enemies, and so his life had ill requited them and their purpose; this was a *Dilemma*; But what that purpose was, and what they had in Agitation at that instant is not disertly said, onely from other places of the Story. And those which follow Sir *Thomas Moore*, it may be conceiv'd, they doubted him for his affection of the Soveraigntie, & some practice against the King and his Brother, for those be the charges they presse upon him, although it is neither said, nor made good by any direct and just proofe. But admit he was now growne jealous of him, and sent Sir *William Catsby*, a man in great credit with the Lord *Hastings*, to sound what opinion he held of that Title and Claime he might lay to the Crowne, who (presuming upon *Catsbies* gratitude and trust that had beene advanced by him) without circumstance, and even with indignation exprest an utter mislike thereof, and engaged himselfe, his uttermost power and abilitie against it, peremptorily adding, he had rather see the death and destructions of the Protector and Duke of *Buckingham*, then the young King deprived of the Crowne: Which reply *Catseby*, (being more just to his employment then honour in this poynt) returnes the Protector, who layd hold upon the next occasion to seize his head, which is the greatest and bloodiest Crime that brings any proofe against him; and yet not so cleare, but that there may be some other State-mistery or fraud suspected in it. Let us leave it upon that accompt, and but consider how much more wee forgive the fames of *H.* 1. *E.* 3. *H.* 4. *E.* 4. *H.* 7. because they had their happy Starres and successe; and then, *Prosperum scelus virtus vocatur*, there is applause goes with the Act and Actor: *Iulius Cæsar*, was, and ever will

Lord *Hastings.*

Sir *Thomas Moore.*

will be reputed a wise and a great Captaine, although his Emulation cost an infinite quantitie of excellent humane blood, and his Nephew, *Octa. Augustus*, never ceased proscribing banishing and massacring, untill he had dispatched all his proud Emulators: *Julius Cæsar* thought it, *Crimen sacrum vel crimen Regale*; or, *Crimen sacrum. Ambitio*: whose rule was,

Cic. lib. 3. de offic. & Suet. in vitâ Julii Cæsaris.

Si violandum est jus, regnandi gratiâ
Violandum est, aliis rebus pietatem colas.

If right for ought may e're be violate,
It must be only for a Soveraign State.

Drawing it from that rule (though *Apocrypha*) in *Euripides*.

Eurip. in Phœnissis.

Εἴπερ γὰρ ἀδικεῖν χρὴ τυραννίδος πέρι
Κάλλιστον ἀδικεῖν τ' ἄλλα δ' εὐσεβεῖν χρεών;

Si injuste agere oportet, pro tyrannide (aut regno) pulcherrimum est injuste agere, in aliis pietatem colere expedit.

And *Antonius Caracalla*, alledged the Text to justifie the killing of his Brother *Geta* his *Collegue*, in the Empire. *Polynices*, the Brother of *Eteocles* was of the same Religion, and said, A Kingdome could not be bought at too high a rate, put in Friends, Kindred, Wife, and Riches: *Via ad potentiam est tollere Emulos & premere Adversarios*, which the great Master of Axiomes allowed, hath beene countenanced by many great examples of State-reason, and policie in all times, even since the Ogygian Age for an old observation, and generall in all forraigne Countries saith,

Axiom. Polit.

Senec. in trag.

——————*Regnum furto*
Et fraude ademptum antiquum est specimen imperii.

So King *Atreus*, by his owne experience could say;

——————*Ut nemo doceat fraudis & sceleris*
vias, Regnum docebit.

But what those Ages call'd Valour, Wisedome, and Policy, in those great Schollers of State, who with credit practised their *Artes Imperii*, and rules of Empire, comes not under the license or warrant of our Christian times; yet we may speak thus much for *Richard* (to those who cry him so deepe an homicide) that he had either more conscience or lesse cruelty then they attribute to him, that by the same Act of power could not secure himselfe of others he had as just cause to feare, especially *Iasper* Earle of Pembroke, his Nephew *Richmond*, and

Artes imperii.

and the subtill Doctor *Morton*, who was extreamly his Enemy, and the Chiefe Instrument that secretly mov'd against him. And although the King had no certain notice which way his Engins wrought, yet he knew enough to suspect him for, and to remove him from the Councell-Table unto the custody of the Duke of *Buckingham*, the man he had reason to suppose nearest to his trust, though his expectation leaned on a broken Reed there; for the Duke was now secretly in his heart defected from the King, and become male-content; *Morton* but toucht his pulse, and knew how the distemper lay, which he irritated into such sparklings as gave him notice where his constitution was most apt and prepared; yea, so subtilly mastred it, that he had leave to steale from Brecknock Castle to Ely, so for good store of Coine found safe passage into France whither his desires vehemently carried him, in hope to fashion the Earle of *Richmond* to his Plot; and under pretence of a Lancastrian Title, to stirre him to take up Armes and invade England, with the Assurance of many mightie friends here, which would make the Designe of an easie and quick dispatch; nor forgot he how much Artificiall and Eloquent perswasions adde to the Blaze of Ambition, knowing the Earles temper like other mens in that, and observing him with a kind of pleasure listen, he gave such a studied glosse and superlation to the Text, that the Earle was now so full of encouragement and hope for the invasion, that their purposes spread as well into England as in France. The Protector having also certaine intelligence of some particular Designes, disposed himselfe in his actions more closely, and knew what Friends and Confederates had engaged themselves to *Richmond*; who yet kept a face of love and fidelitie towards him, as did the Duke of *Buckingham*, and the Countesse of *Richmond*, who appeared at this instant an earnest Sutor to reconcile her Sonne into favour; and that the King would bee pleased, to bestow on him any of King *Edward* the fourth his Daughters. But this took not the vigilancy of his eye from him and his partie, the cause being of greater danger and apprehension now, then in King *Edwards* time; for the Earle had drawne unto him many of the English Nobilitie and Gentry; and some Forraigne Princes had in favour to him promised their aydes. But in the time of King *Edward*, his Title and he, was so little understood by his blood of Lancaster, that the better judging-sort of the English Nobilitie and Gentry, King *Lewis* the eleventh of France, *Francis* the second Duke of Brittaine, and other Forraigne Princes looked very slightly upon it. And yet, as *John Harding* observed, the King might be jealous of him, being given out for an Heire of the House of Lancaster, and Nephew to *Henry* the sixt: With this he considered, that some Forraigne Princes stood not well-affected to him; or that some at home, envying his House and Posteritie, would catch at any sparke to trouble his peace, and kindle a Sedition; therefore he had good reason to thinke, that as his libertie might make these beginnings more popular, so their ends more dangerous and in-

grate-

gratefull (the vulgar tasting all things by the eare, and judging by the noyse) which he sought earely to prevent. For *Phillip Comines* reports, When he first came to know this Earle, he was then a Prisoner in Brittaine, and told him, he had beene either in Prison, or under strict command from five yeares old, which is not unlikely; for I find him but young when he was committed to the custody of Sir *William Herbert*, Lord of Ragland Castle in Montmouthshire, where he continued not long; for *Iasper*, Earle of Pembrooke, who was Uncle unto Him (being then in France, whether he had fled after the overthrow of the Lancastrians at Tewkesbury, (as *Iohn Stow*) having advertisement that his Nephew was under Sir *William Herberts* custody, with whom he had Alliance and friendship, came secretly out of France into Wales, and at Ragland Castle found onely the Lady *Herbert*, her Husband being with the King; in whose absence, the Earle practised so cunningly with her, that he got his Nephew from thence, and conveighed him to his owne Castle of Pembrooke, (the young Earles native place) presuming upon the strength of it and the peoples affection, but over-weaned in his opinion and hope. For so soone as the King received notice of the escape, Sir *William Herbert* was commanded to Levie Forces, and make towards them, a man of a wise and valiant disposition, descended from *Herbertus*, who was Chamberlaine and Treasurer of the Kings, *William Rufus*, and *Henry Beauclerke*, and was created Earle of Pembrooke afterward; from this Noble *Herbertus*, are descended the *Herberts*, Earles of Pembrooke and Montgomery; and many other Welch Gentlemen of that Sir-name and Family.

The flight of *Richmont* with his Uncle *Pembrooke*.

The Earle of *Rich*. borne in Pembrooke Castle.

The two Earles being informed of his approaches and strength, distrusting their owne, fled by night, and posted to the Port of Timby, where they kept close untill a fit opportunitie, offered them transportation for France, intending to see the Court there, where the Earle of Pembrooke had not long before received a very favourable entertainment. But a violent storme diverted their course, and runne them upon the coasts of Little Brittaine, which fell out as a sad disaster, and crosse to them and their Designe for a long time after, the Duke of Brittaine being no friend to it; but at the Port of St. Malos they must land. What successe they met with in this flight (and other Noble Englishmen which followed the unluckie partie of *Henry* the sixt, being constrained when he was overthrowne by *Edward* the fourth to fly) will fall into our discourse hereafter: there is this memoriall in the Stories of Brittaine.

This flight of theirs was in *Anno* 11. *E*. 4. *Iohn Stow*.

Plusieurs du Seigneurs d'Angleterre qui tenoyent la partie du Roy H. 6. sen fairent par mer hors du Royaulme & entr' autres le Conte du Pembrooke faisant sauué un jeune Prince de Angleterre nommé Henry Conte du Richmont.

Whilst these Earles made some stay in Saint Malo to refresh themselves, *Francis* the second, Duke of Brittaine had notice of their landing, who sent as speedily a Command to the Governour to arrest

Earle of *Rich*. Prisoner in Brittaine.

rest them both into safe custody, an act, as it appeared, both strange and injurious, being subjects to a Prince with whom the Duke had league. But for a better glosse, he had found a considerable clause to detaine the Earle of Richmond untill he had received satisfaction of him for usurping and holding the Title and Estate of Richmond, belonging to the ancient Dukes of Brittaine (whose heire and successor he was) though diseised by the space of thirty yeares, now he would expect either restitution or compensation for it; and the better to assure himselfe, he conveyes them with a good guard to the Castle of Vanes, where himselfe often resided, continuing a more cautious and strict eye upon the Earle of Richmond, as Nephew to *Henry* the sixt, and he that laid claime to the Title and Crowne of England, by the bloud of Lancaster: For which he made their imprisonment more honourable, as *Philip Comines* saith, *Le Duc les traicté doucement pour Prisonniers*. And *Jean Froisard* cals it, *Prison Courtoise*; for the Duke had well considered what expectation and use he might raise by them, and knew the newes could not be distastefull to the King of England, whose Throne had been threatned so much by the Earle of Richmonds liberty; and therefore, from hence he hoped an answerable benefit, and to contract the King in a firme amity and acknowledgment unto him; nay, which is further, (if we may beleeve *Iac. Nyerus*) he thought by this occasion to beare the reines so hard upon King *Edward*, as that he should not dare to make any breach with him, *propter Henricum Richmontiæ Comitem non audebat Anglus ab amicitia Brittani discedere*.

The last D. of Brittaine, who was Earle of Richmond, & possessed of the Earledome, was *John de Montfort*, who flourished *An. Dom.* 1440, & had sons, but not Earles of Richmond, as *Rob. Glou.* writeth, & now this *Francis* I. renewed the claime which was about 30 yeares after *John de Montfort*, Duke of Brittaine.

Jac. Nyerus in Annal. Fland. lib. 17.

Nor was this Author much mistaken, for the King would have accorded to any reasonable thing to purchase the Earle into his hands, and it was no little perplexity to him when he heard of their flight, but was the better calmed when he understood where they were, the Duke of Brittaine being his friend and Allie, in whom he supposed so neare an interest (set off by some other conditions) that he saw a faire encouragement to demand and gaine them both; whereas had they falne into France, he must have expected the greatest disadvantage could have been contrived out of such an occasion. For *Lewis*, though he were then in truce and league with him, was meerly a Politician, and studied only his owne ends, yet feares him as a King famous for his Prowesse and Victories, and as ably supplyed in his Coffers for all undertakings: But (which did equally quicken the hate aswell as feare of France) had threatened to enter it with fire and sword, for the reconquest of the Dutchy of Normandy and Aquitaine, the Counties of Poictou and Turaine; wherefore we may beleeve that beares the credit of an Oracle, which good *Ennius* said:

King *Edward* treateth for the delivery of Richmond.

——*Quem metuunt oderunt,*
Quem oderunt, periisse expetunt.

Ennius apud Cicer. in Offic.

And doubtlesse in his heart he was favourable to any chance that might have ruined or infested England, and could have wisht the Earle of Richmond and his Title under his Protection. King *Edward* seasonably prevented this, that such attempts, though at first they appeared but like the Prophets Cloud, might not spread after into spacious stormes. And to prevent all underhand Contracts with the Duke of Brittaine, dispatcht Letters unto him, further interpreted by a rich Present, and richer promises. The Duke receives both with as Honourable Complement, protesting none could be more ready to doe the King of Englands Commands then he. But where he treated for the delivery of the Earles, he hoped to be lawfully excused, being an Act would cast a staine and scandall, not only upon his credit and honour, but upon all Princely and hospitable Priviledges, and could appeare no lesse then a meere impiety to thrust such distressed persons as fled to their protection, into the Armes of their enemies; and it was his opinion, if any malice or violence should be acted upon them, the guilt must reflect on him. But that the King might beleeve he was forward to come as near his desires, as in honour could be, he engaged himselfe to keep so carefull and vigilant a watch upon them, that they should have no more power to endanger him, then if they were in strict Prison. This being returned, though not agreable to the Kings hope and wishes, yet bearing such a Caution of Honour and Wisdome, he remained satisfied; and so it paused for the space of eight yeares, (as I conjecture) for the King made this demand in the twelfth yeare of his Raigne 1472, all which time he was very intent to preserve the League with good Summes of Mony, and costly Presents. In the twentieth of his Raigne 1480, he received intelligence, that the Earle of Richmond had stird up fresh Embers, and new friends in the French Court to blow them, and that the French King had dealt by solicitation of the Earle of Pembrook, and others privately, to get the Earl of Richmond, and offered great Sums to the Duke of Brittaine. This gave new disturbance, and the King must now by the best meanes he could, renue his former suite to the Duke of Brittaine; for which employment, he intrusts Doctor *Stillington* Bishop of Bath, his Secretary, a man of a Wise, Learned, and Eloquent endeavour, of good acquaintance and credit with the Duke of Brittaine, who gave him an honourable and respective entertainement. The Bishop (after he had prepared him by the earnest of a very rich present) tenders the Summe of his Employment, not forgetting what he was now to Act, and what to promise on the Kings part. And (for a more glorious insinuation) tells him how the King had elected him into the noble Society of St. *Georges* Order (as the most honourable intimation he could give of his love;) to qualifie all exceptions too, and jealousies, assures him, the King had no intent to the Earle of Richmond, but what was answerable to his owne worth, and quality of the Kings Kinsman; having declared a propensity and purpose, to bestow one of his daughters upon him. The Duke well mollified and perswaded, delivered the Earle by a strong Guard to the Bishop at

K. E. 4 sends for Richmond.

Hist. de Brit.

D. Stillington sent for Richmond.

Saint

St. Maloes Port: a change of much passion and amazement to him, whose sufferings tooke hold upon the affable disposition of the Noble *Peir de Landois* Treasurer to the Duke, who had the Earle in Charge and Conduct, to St. Malo. He urges the cause from him of his so altered and present condition, with Protestation of all the aide he could: The Earle thus fairely and happily provoked (and perceiving the sparkles of his sorrow had lapt into a tender bosome) freely exposed himselfe, and with such an overcomming Countenance, of teares and sighes, framed his own Story, and prest *Landois*, that it so wrought upon his temper, he perswaded the Earle to put on clearer hopes, assures him there should some meanes be found to shift the Tempest; thereupon writes a sad Relation to the Duke, to move his compassion and favour, and knowing the Baron *Chandais*, (a great man in credit with him) well affected to the Earle by a long and reciprocall affection, he repaired to his house neare Saint Malo, and prevailed with him to use his power with the Duke, for returning the Earle; who posted to *Vanes*, where the Court was then, and tooke the Duke at such an advantage, by suggesting his credulity abused, and cunningly drawne into this contract by the King, that there was a Post dispatcht to stay the Earle. In that interim, *Landois* had not been Idle, to find a way to let the Earle escape into the Abbey Church of St. Malo, where he claimed the benefit of the holy Asyle, which was easily contrived, by corrupting his Keepers. But the Duke to stand cleare of the Kings suspition, sent over *Maurice Brumell* to satisfie him, that the Earle according to promise was sent to Saint Malo, there delivered to his servants deputed, whose negligence let him escape; and that he had demanded him of the Covent; who denyed to render him without security & caution; & that he should be continued a prisoner in *Vanes*, with as much courtesie as formerly. Now being it was falne into those strict and peremptory termes, and within the contumacie of such lawlesse persons, where he could not use power, he yet faithfully protested no suite from the French King, or any other, should draw him from his former promise: All which, he religiously performed, whilst King *Edward* lived, the space of twelve yeares (after *Phillip de Cominés*) in which circle of time, it may with admiration be observed, through what changes and interchanges of hazards, dangers, and difficulties, he was preserved. Soone after King *Edwards* decease, King *Richard* renewed and continued the Treaty by Sir *Thomas Hutton* of Yorkeshire, receiving the same satisfaction in Answer, but was failed in the performance, and so dishonourably, that it then appeared, the Duke had kept in with *Edward*, more for feare, then for love or honour (the name of *Edward*, and the Earle of March, being (indeed) accounted terrible, where his victorious sword was drawne) which breach of the Dukes was not left unpunished (at least as that age then guessed) by a divine revenge; for having married *Margaret*, Daughter and Co-heire of *Francis de Mountford*, Duke of Brittaine, she dying without issue, he married *Margaret*, Daughter of *Gaston de Foix*, King of

K. R. reneweth suit to the D. of B. for the Earle of Richmond.

E. 4. *Fulmen belli, ut Seleuc. Rex inde κεραυνὸς, i. fulmen dictus.*

Claud. Paradin.

of Navarr, by whom he had one only daughter *Anne*, married to the French King, *Charles* 8. Thus Duke *Francis* dyed without issue male, the Dutchy being swallowed up, and drowned in the Lillies or Crapands of France, and with his Family of Brittaine irrecoverably lost and absorpted.

Thus much for the jealousie and feares of those two Kings, now to the progresse of our Story, where the Barons and Commons with one generall dislike, and an universall negative voice, refused the sonnes of King *Edward*, not for any ill will or malice, but for their disabilities and incapacities; the opinions of those times too, held them not legitimate, and the Queene *Elizabeth Gray*, or *Woodvill*, no lawfull Wife, nor yet a Woman worthy to be the Kings Wife, by reason of her extreame unequall quality. For these and other causes, the Barons and Prelates unanimously cast their Election upon the Protector, as the most worthiest, and nearest, by the experience of his owne deservings, and the strength of his Alliance, importuning the Duke of Buckingham to become their Speaker, who accompanied with many of the chiefe Lords, and other grave and learned persons, having Audience granted in the great Chamber at Baynards Castle (then Yorke-house) thus addrest him to the Lord Protector.

B. Mort. Sir Th Moore, Hollingshed, Grafton, Stow, Hall, Virgill, &c. Parliament.

The Duke of Buck. to the L. Protector in the behalfe of the 3 Estates.

SIR, May it please your Grace to be informed, that after much grave Consultation amongst the Noble Barons, and other worthy persons of this Realme, it stands concluded and resolved, that the sons of King *Edward* shall not raigne; for who is not sensible, how miserable a fortune, and dangerous estate that Kingdome must be in, where a childe is King, according to the Wise man, *Væ tibi terra cujus Rex est Puer*. But here, Sir, there is exception of further consequence against them, That they were not borne in lawfull Marriage, the King having than another Wife living, Dame *Elizabeth Butler*. Besides, the great dishonour and reproach he received by disparaging his Royall bloud, with a woman so far unmeet for his bed. These Considerations have resolutely turned all their eyes, and Election towards your Grace, as only worthy of it, by your singular vertues, and that interest in the Crownes of England and of France, with the Rights and Titles, by the high Authority of Parliament, entailed to the Royall bloud, and issue of *Richard* Duke of Yorke, whose lawfull begotten Sonne and heire you are; which by a just course of inheritance, and the Common Lawes of this Land, is divolv'd and come to you. And unwilling that any inferiour Bloud, should have the Dominion of this Land, are fully determined to make your Grace King; to which, with all willingnesse and alacrity, the Lords and people of the Northerne parts concurre. And the Maior, Aldermen, and Commons of this City of London, have all allowed, and gladly embraced this generall Choice of your Grace: and are come hither to beseech you to accept their just Election, of which they have chosen me their unworthy Advocate and Speaker. I must therefore againe crave

The common published stories have *Eliz. Lucy*, but that is false.

leave

leave in the behalfe of all, to desire your Grace will be pleased, in your noble and gracious zeale to the good of this Realme, to cast your eyes upon the growing distresses and decay of our Estate, and to set your happy hand to the redresse thereof; for which, we can conceive no abler remedy, then by your undertaking the Crowne and Government, which we doubt not shall accrew to the laud of God, the profit of this Land, and your Graces happinesse.

This speech of the Duke is recorded by Doctor Morton, *Sir* Thomas Moore, *and other Chronicles and Historians, to which the Protector gave this reply:*

The Answer of the Lord Protector to the 3 Estates.

MY most noble Lords, and my most loving friends, and deare Country-men, Albeit I must confesse, your request most respective and favourable, and the points and necessities alledged and urged, true and certaine; yet for the entire love and reverend respect I owe to my Brother deceased, and to his Children, my Princely Couzens, you must give me leave, more to regard mine honour and fame in other Realmes; for where the truth and certaine proceedings herein are not knowne, it may be thought an ambition in me to seeke what you voluntarily proffer, which would charge so deep a reproach and staine upon my honour and sincerity, that I would not beare for the worlds Diademe, Besides, you must not thinke me ignorant (for I have well observed it) there is more difficulty in the Government of a Kingdome, then pleasure; especially to that Prince, who would use his Authority and Office as he ought. I must therefore desire, that this (and my unfained Protestations) may assure you, the Crowne was never my ayme, nor suits my desire with yours, in this; yet I shall thinke my selfe much beholding unto you all, in this Election of me, and that hearty love I find you beare me, and here protest, that for your sakes it shall be all one, whether I be your King or no; for I will serve my Nephew faithfully and carefully, with my best counsels and endeavours, to defend and preserve him and this Kingdome; nor shall there want readinesse in me, to attempt the recovery of that hereditary right in France, which belongs to the Kings of England, though of late negligently and unhappily lost. There the Protector became silent, and thought it not safe in his discretion, or policy, to open all the disgusts he had of the Soveraignty, for that would have been matter of Exprobation of the Barons, and toucht too neare the quicke, though he had well observed, by sundry experiences of the leading times, and moderne too, the inconstant ebbing and flowing of their dispositions, how variable and apt they were, to take up any occasion of change, pursuing their Kings (if once stirr'd) so implacably, that many times they never left without death or deposing. Examples he had in the Raignes of King *Edward* his Brother, and *Henry* the sixth; not long before that in the time of *Richard* the second, and his Grandfather *Edward* the second; more anciently the extreame troubles,

troubles and distresse of King *Iohn*, and *Henry* the third, all by the Barons, being dreadfull warnings and insolent monuments of their haughtinesse and Levitie; and this was *Altamente repostum* with the wise Prince.

But the Duke of Buckingham, thinking the Protector set too slight a consideration upon so great a Concernment, and the affection tender'd by himselfe and the Nobilitie (and over hearing something, he privately spake to the Lord Maior and Recorder, tending to his mislike) for an Epilogue or close to his former Oration, he thus freely addes.

The bold and round conclusion of the D. of Buck.

SIR, I must now, by the Priviledge of this Imployment, and in the behalfe of those and my Countrey, adde so much freedome unto my dutie, as to tell your Grace, It is immoveably resolved by the Barons and people, that the Children of King *Edward* shall not Reigne over them. Your Grace hath heard some causes, nor need I intimate, how these Estates have entred and proceeded so offensively to other men, and so dangerously to themselves, as is now too late to recall or retire. And therefore, they have fixt this Election upon you, whom they thinke most able and carefull for their safetie. But, if neither the generall good, the earnest Petitions of the Nobility and Commonalty, can move you, wee most humbly desire your Answer, and leave to Elect some other that may be worthy of the Imperiall Charge; in which, (wee hope) wee shall not incurre your displeasure, considering the desperate necessitie of our welfare and Kingdome, urges it. And this is our last Suit and Petition to your Grace.

The Protector toucht by this round and braving farewell, which made him very sensible: For (as Sir *Thomas Moore* disertly confesseth) the Protector was so much moved with these words, that otherwise of likelyhood he would never have inclined to their Suit: And saith, That when he saw there was no remedy, but he must either at that instant take the Crowne, or both he and his heires irrecoverably let it passe to another; paradventure, one that might prove an Enemy to him and his, especially if *Richmont* stept in; betwixt whom, and this Prince, the hatred was equally extreame: Therefore, it behoved the Protector to Collect himselfe; and fixing his Consideration upon the effect of that necessitie they last urged, gave this Reply:

The Protectors Reply to the Dukes last Suit.

MY most Noble good Lords, and most loving and faithfull friends, the better sense of your loves and most eminent inconveniencies insinuated by your Noble Speaker, hath made me more serious to apprehend the benefit of your proffer and Election. And I must confesse, in the meditation thereof, I find an alteration in my selfe, not without some distraction, when I consider all the Realme, so bent against

against the Sonnes of King *Edward*. And therefore being certaine, there is no man to whom the Crowne by just Title can be so due as to our selfe, the rightfull Sonne and Heire of our most deare and Princely Father, *Richard* Duke of Yorke; to which Title of blood and nature, your favours have joyned this of Election, wherein wee hold our selfe to be most strong and safe. And having the lawfull power of both, why should I endure my professed Enemy to usurpe my right, and become a Vassall to my envious Subject? The necessitie of these causes (as admitting no other remedy) urges me to accept your offer, and according to your request, and our owne right, we here assume the Regall Præheminence of the two Kingdoms, England and France, from this day forward, by us and our heires, to Govern and defend the one, and by Gods grace, and your good aydes, to recover and establish the other, to the Ancient Allegeance of England; desiring of God to live no longer then wee intend and endeavour the advancement and flourishing Estate of this Kingdome; at which they all cry'd, *God save King Richard*: And thus he became King. But yet his Detractors stick not to slander and accuse all that was said or done in these proceedings of State for meer dissimulation; by which justice they may as well censure (*At sit Reverentia dictum*) all the Barons, worthy and grave Commons, which had their Votes therein, which would fall a most impudent and intolerable Scandall upon all the High Court of Parliament; for in short time after, all that was alledged and acted in that Treatie and Colloquy was approved, and ratified by the Court of Parliament, so that their Cavills onely discover an extreame malice and envy. For it was not possible, therefore not credible, he could upon such an instant (as it were) by any practice attaine to that power and credit, with all the Barons, Spirituall and Temporall, and Commons, to procure and perswade them from the Sonnes of King *Edward*, so unanimously to become his Subjects, and put the Crowne upon his head with such Solemnitie and publicke Ceremonies. Whilst those matters had their current, the Northerne Gentlemen and his Southerne Friends joyned in a Bill Supplicatory to the Lords Spirituall and Temporall, earnestly expressing their desires for the Election of the Lord Protector, with the former causes urged; Also, that the blood of the young Earle of Warwicke was attainted, and his Title confiscate by Parliament. This Bill was delivered to the Lords, Assembled in the great Hall at Westminster, the Lord Protector sitting in the Chaire of Marble amongst them, upon the 26 of June, some six or seven dayes after he was Proclaimed; the tenor of the Bill was thus written in the Chronicle of the Abbey of Croyland: *Lib. Abb. Croyl.*

P*Rotector eodem die, quo Regimen sub titulo regii nominis sibi vendicavit* (viz) 26° *die Junii*, *Anno Dom.* 1483. *se apud Magnam Aulam Westmonasterii in Cathedram Marmoream*

mi-

Immisit & tum mox omnibus proceribus tam Laicis quam Ecclesiasticis & Cæteris assidentibus, astantibus &c. ostendebatur rotulus quidam, in quo per modum supplicationis in nomine procerum & populi Borealis exhibita sunt, Primum, quod filii Regis Edwardi *erant Bastardi, supponendo, illum præcontraxisse matrimonium cum quadam Domina Elianora Boteler, antequam Reginam* Elizabetham *duxisset in uxorem: deinde quod sanguis alterius Fratris* (Georgii *Scil: Clarensiæ ducis) fuisset Attinctus. Ita quod nullus certus incorruptus sanguis Linealis ex parte* Richardi *Ducis Eboraci poterat inveniri, nisi in persona* Richardi *Protectoris, Ducis Glocestriæ, & jam eidem Duci supplicabant, ut jus suum in Regno Angliæ sibi assumeret & Coronam acciperet.*

But the Barons were all accorded before this Bill came, both sides moving with an equall and contented forwardnesse; And in July next following 1483. was Crown'd and receiv'd, with as generall Magnificence and Acclamations, as any King in England many years before. For as a grave man writeth, (*Fuit dignissimus regno &c. non inter malos sed bonos principes Commemorandus*; That he was most worthy to Reigne, and to be numbred amongst the good, not bad Princes. The Queene his Wife was Crowned with him, and with no lesse State and Greatnesse; Accompanied him from the Tower to Westminster, having in their Traine, (besides the Nobilitie of the South parts) foure thousand Gentlemen of the North. Upon the 19. of June 1483. in the 25. yeare of *Lewis* the French King, he was named King of England, the morrow Proclaimed, and rode with great Solemnitie from London to Westminster, where in the seat Royall, he gave the Judges of the Land a strickt and religious charge for the just executing of the Lawes; then departed towards the Abbey, being met at the Church doore with Procession, and the Scepter of King *Edward* delivered to him by the Abbot; so Ascended to Saint *Edwards* Shrine, where he offered; the Monks in the meane time singing *Te Deum*: From thence he return'd to the Palace, where he lodged untill his Coronation.

Cambden.

Upon the fourth of July he went to the Tower by water with the Queene his Wife, and the next day, Created *Edward* his onely Son, (about ten yeares old) Prince of Wales: He Invested Sir *John Howard* (who was made Lord *Howard*, and Knight of the Garter, 17. *Edward* 4.) in the Dukedome of Norffolke, in a favourable admission of the right of the Lady *Margaret* his Mother, Daughter of Sir *Thomas Mowbray*, Duke of Norffolke, and an heire generall of the *Mowbrayes*, Dukes of Norffolke, and Earles of Surrey, descended from the Lord *Tho. Plantagenet* of Brotherton, a younger Sonne of King

Monstrolet. Comines. Anglici scriptores.

Stile of the D. of Norff. *In rotulis in domo convers.*

King *Edward* the first, and Earle of Norffolke. This King also made him Marshall and Admirall of England; he was as rightfully Lord *Mowbray*, Lord *Segrave*, Lord *Bruce*, as Lord *Howard*, as I have seene him Stiled by Royall Warrant, in a Commission for Treatie of Truce with *Scotland*.

His eldest Sonne, Sir *Thomas Howard*, was at the same time Created Earle of Surrey, and made Knight of the Garter; *Henry Stafford*, Duke of Buckingham, was made Constable of England for terme of life, but he claimed the Office by inheritance.

Sir *Thomas Moore* writes, That Sir *Thomas Howard* Executed the Office of Constable that day; *William* Lord *Berkley* was Created Earle of Nottingham, *Francis Lovel* Viscount *Lovel*, and Chamberlain to the King; the Lord *Stanley* restor'd to liberty and made Steward of the Houshold, *Thomas Rotheram* Chancellour and Arch-Bishop of Canterbury, having beene committed for delivering the Great Seale to the Queene Widow, receiv'd to grace, and many Knights Addubbed of the old Order, and some of the new, or habit of the Bath, whose names I have set downe, to shew what regard was had of their Family, and in those times accused of so much Malignity.

Sir *Edward De-la-Poole*, Sonne to the Duke of Norfolke.
George Gray, Sonne to the Earle of Kent.
William Souch, Sonne to the Lord *Souch*.
Henry Nevil, Sonne to the Lord Abergaveny,

Christopher Willowby.	*Thomas Arundel.*
Henry Bainton.	*Gervoise* of Clifton.
Thomas Bullen.	*Edmond Beddingfield.*
William Sey.	*Tho. Leukenor.*
William Enderby.	*John Browne.*
Thomas of *Vernon.*	*William Berkley.*
William Barkley.	i. Another *Berkley.*

The fift day of July he rode from the Tower through the City in Pompe, with his Sonne the Prince of Wales, three Dukes, and nine Earles, twentie two Viscounts and simple Barons, eighty Knights, Esquires and Gentlemen, not to be numbred, besides great Officers of the Crowne which had speciall service to doe. But the Duke of Buckingham carried the Splendour of that dayes Bravery, his habit and Caparisons of blew Velvet, imbroidered with golden Naves of Carts burning, the trappings supported by Foot-men habited costly and sutable. On the morrow, being the sixt of July, all the Prelates Miter'd in their Pontificalibus, receiv'd him at Westminster-Hall towards the Chappell; the Bishop of Rochester bare the Crosse before him, the Cardinall and the Earle of Huntington followed with a pair of guilt Spurres, and the Earle of Bedford with Saint *Edwards* Staffe for a Relique. After the Precession, the Earle of Northumberland beares a poyntlesse Sword naked, the Lord *Stanley*, the Mace of the Constableship (but waited not for Constable) the Earle of Kent bare the second Sword naked with a poynt, upon the right hand of the King, the Viscount *Lovel* another Sword on the Kings left hand with a poynt. Next came the Duke of Suffolke with the Scepter, the Earl of Lincoln with the Ball and Crosse, then the Earle of Surry with the Sword of State in a rich Scabbard, in place of the Constable of England, the Duke of Norfolke on his right hand with the Crowne: After him immediately, the King in a SurCoat and Robe of Purple, the Canopy borne by the Barons of the five Ports, the King betweene the Bishop of Bath and Durham, the Duke of Buckingham bearing up his Traine, and served with a white Staffe for Seneshall, or High Steward of England.

Signifying mercy.

Signifying Iustice to the Temporalty. Iustice to the Clergy. Peace. Monarchy.

In the Front of the Queenes Traine, the Earle of Huntington bare the Scepter, Viscount *Lisle* the Rod with the Dove, the Earle of Wiltshire her Crowne, and next to him followed the Queene her selfe (in Robes like the King) betweene two Bishops, the Canopy borne by Barons of the Ports, upon her head a Coronet set with precious Stones, the Lady *Margaret* Somerset, Countesse of Richmond, carried up her Traine, followed by the Dutchesse of Suffolke, with many Countesses, Baronesses, and other Ladies. In this manner the whole Procession passed through the Palace, and entred the West doore of the Abbey, the King and Queene taking their seats of State, stayed untill divers holy Hymnes were sung, then ascended to the high Altar shifting their Robes, and putting on other open and voyded in sundry places for their Anoynting; which done, they tooke other Robes of Cloth of Gold, so returned to their seats, where the Cardinall of Canterbury and the other Bishops, Crowned them, the Prelate putting the Scepter in the left hand of the King, the Ball and Crosse in his right, and the Queenes Scepter in her right hand, and the Rod with the Dove in her left; on each hand of the King stood a Duke, before him the Earle of Surrey, with the Sword as aforesaid; on each hand of the Queene stood a Bishop, by them a Lady kneeling, the Cardinall said Masse and gave the Pax; then the King and Queene descending were both housled with one host parted betweene them at the high Altar: This done, they offered at Saint *Edwards* Shrine, where the King layd downe Saint *Edwards* Crowne & put on another, so returned to Westminster-Hal in the same State they came, there dispersed, and retired themselves for a season. In which interim, came the Duke of Norfolke, Marshall of England, mounted upon a brave Horse, trapped with Cloth of Gold downe to the ground, to submove the presse of people and void the Hall. About foure of the clocke the King and Queene sat to Dinner, the King at the middle Table of the Hall, and the Queene on his left

hand

hand; on each side a Countesse attending her, holding a Cloth of Plaisance (or rather of Essuyance) for her Cup: On the Kings right hand sate the Arch-Bishop of Canterbury, and all the Ladies were placed on one side of a long Table in the middle of the hall against them, at another Table, the Lord Chancellour, and all the Nobles; at a Table next to the Cup-board, the Lord Maior of London and the Aldermen.

Behind the Barons of the Kingdome sate the Barons of the Ports; there were other Tables for persons of qualitie. After all were seated, came the Lord Marshall againe, the Earle of Surrey Constable (*Pro illa vice tantum*) the Lord *Stanley* Lord *Steward*, Sir *William Hopton* Treasurer of the Houshold, and Sir *Thomas Piercy* Controler, they served the Kings boord with one dish of Gold and another of Silver. The Queene was served all in guilt Vessells, and the Cardinall Arch-Bishop in Silver Dishes.

As soone as the second course was served in, Sir *Robert Dimock* the Kings Champion makes Proclamation, That whosoever would say, King *Richard* the third was not lawfully King, he would fight with him at all utterance, and for gage thereof threw downe his Gauntlet, then all the people cryed, *King Richard, God save King Richard*; And this he acted in three severall parts of the Hall, then an Officer of the Cellar brought him a guilded Bowle with Wine which he dranke, and carries the Cup away as his ancient Fee. After that, the Heralds cryed *Largesse* thrice, and returned to the Scaffold. Lastly came the Maior of London with the Sheriffs, with a Voyder, serving the King and Queene with sweet Wines, who had each of them a covered Cup of Gold for reward: By which time, the day began to give way to the night, the King and Queene departing to their Lodgings.

And this is a briefe and true Relation of his Coronation, testified by all the best Writers and Chroniclers of our Stories, publicke and allowed, which may confute the boldnesse of that slander that sayes, he was not rightfully, and Authentically Crowned, but obscurely and indirectly crept in at the Window. But all times have Detractors, and all Courts their Parasits, and many that have admired Princes to their graves, even there have turn'd from them, with ingratitude and murmur. Soone after this the King dismissed, and sent home all the Lords, Spirituall and Temporall, with a straight charge and direction to them, the Judges of *Oyer* and *Terminer*, with all other Magistrates and Officers in generall and particular, for the Equitable and just Government of their Jurisdictions and Circuits: And it is observed, those times were under as happy an expectation of Law and Justice, as those, either before or after more flatter'd; which *Iohn Hide* (a Learned man, and Doctor of Physick) implyes in a Manuscript Poesy of his.

Moore. Grafton. Polidore. Hall, Croyland. Hollingshed. Stow, &c.

——Solio juris rectiq; Minister,
Ille sedens alto, tali sermone profatur;
Moses concilio soceri persuasus Iethro,
Solus quod Populi nequijt componere lites,
Constituit populi praefectos atq; tribunos;
Sic cum me praecelsa premant fastigia Regni,
Ardua magnarum teneatis munera rerum;
Et primùm, à vobis pravos secludite motus
Aequis Iustitiae trutinis appendite causas;
Ob paupertatem miseros nè spernite cives,
Nec vota in cassum fundat pupillus in auras,
Deniq; largitio, nè vos Corrumpat iniqua, &c.

All things thus in a happy presage and good order, the King with the Queene departed from London, and makes Windsor the first gist in his Progresse for some few dayes: From thence to his Mannor of Woodstock, then to the Universitie of Oxford, where the Muses Crown'd their browes with fragrant Wreathes for his entertainment. Next he visited the circular Citie of Glocester, and gave the Citizens, (for the love and loyaltie they exprest, in holding the Castle and Towne so constantly against Queene *Margaret* and the forces of *Henry* the sixt, for him and his Brother the King) large Priviledges and Immunities.

And here the Duke of Buckingham takes his leave for Brecknock, constantly disposed and affected in all outward appearance. The King making small stay any where, (save at Coventry) untill he came to the goodly and ancient Citie of Yorke, the scope and goale of his Progresse, which receiv'd him with all honour and Festivitie, and was there the second time Crowned by Dr. *Rotheram* Arch-Bishop of that Sea, in the Cathedrall Church, and his Sonne invested in the Principalitie of Wales, as the Prior of Croyland reporteth; *Eodem die quo* Richardus *Coronatus est Rex in Ecclesia Metropolitana Eboracensi, mox filium* Edwardum *in Principatum Walliae cum insigniis virga aurea &c. evexit & Pomposa & sumptuosa festa & convivia ibi fecit.*

And indeed, it was a day of great state; for (as *Polidore* saith) There was then three Princes in Yorke wearing Crownes, the King, Queene, and Prince; In acclamation whereof, there was Stage-Playes, Turneaments, and other Triumphall Sports, as Sir *Thomas Moore* relates. At this time the King Knighted *Richard* of Glocester his base sonne, who was after Captaine of *Calice*, and many Gentlemen of those parts. But (albeit this was an intermission as it were of all busie and serious agitations) yet the King, still where he travall'd had a just regard to the Administration and Execution of Justice and the more facinerous Malefactors: And surely these respective inclinations of his had their solemn affections and desires Naturalized

Chron. *M.S.* in Quar. *apud.* D. *Ro. Cotton*, and *Rob. Fabian.*
Rich. the Bastard of the D. of Gloc. Captaine of Calice.

ralized in him, witnessed by the scope and integritie of those just Lawes which after followed.

The Progresse thus spent, he returnes to London; and having consulted some matters of State, declares his first resolution for the Tribute detain'd by France, which he had formerly by a friendly Message demanded, but now sends stout menaces and threats for it. The French would not have it cal'd a Tribute, but a Pension, as *Philip de Comines* insinuates, though it had beene rays'd and payd to King *Edward* the fourth, in lieu of the Dutchy and Countries of Aquitaine, Normandy, Poictou, and Maine, &c. whereof the the French had deseis'd the Crowne of England, which King *Edward* the fourth forced *Lewis* to acknowledge, and to Covenant and agree, That he, his heires and Successors, should pay unto the Crowne of England, the summe of fiftie thousand Crowns, with caution and securitie to be payd in the Citie of London, or after *Iean Tillet* and *Iohn Maierus*, seventy five thousand Crowns to be payd into the Tower; with which the French King allso granted, in the name of Annuall Pension, sixteen thousand pounds to some Noblemen and others of speciall credit with the King: As to Sir *Thomas Gray*, Marquesse of Dorset, *William* Lord *Hastings*, Chamberlaine to the King, Doctor *Thomas Rotheram*, Bishop of Lincolne, and Lord Chancellour of England; *Iohn* Lord *Howard*, Sir *Iohn Cheyney*, Master of the Horse; Sir *Thomas Mountgomery*, Master *Challoner*, and to the Master of the Rowles; The chiefest of these had two thousand Crownes apiece *per annum*. Besides which Pensions, he gave rich Presents, and sent rewards to such Lords as stood most for this accord. *Enguerannt de Monstrolet* avoucheth, that the Lord *Howard*, and the Master of the Horse, were the chiefest of the mediators in it; his reason is, that they were the men most in favour with King *Edward*. *Iean Tillet*, with *Philip de Comines*, tells us, the Lord *Howard* in lesse then two yeares had the value of twentie foure thousand Crownes in Plate, Coine and Jewels, over and above his Annuall Pension; the Lord *Hastings* at one time to the value of two thousand markes in Plate, besides his Pension. And if their owne Stories speake truth, *Richard de Nevil*, the great Earle of Warwick, had of the Kings of France much more then any other English Nobleman, which the Chronicle of Brittaine seconds. And doubtlesse, King *Richard* had still compel'd him to continue it, had not eruptions of State and tumultuary practises fatally deterr'd his Sword: For as Kings have vaster limits, they have higher bounds then others. If our vulgar paths be rugged, theirs are slippery, and all their mighty resolutions and ambitions have their fate and circle, hither they must, and no further; yet as envious as fortune shew'd her selfe, he brought King *Lewis* to termes of faire promises and mediation for time of payment, as *Comines* obscurely implyes.

Iohn Maierus. Iean Tillet. du Tillet saith, That this tribute or Pension was 75000 crowns, or, *Escu's & chatun Escu vallant. trois souls.*

This yeare the King kept a very magnificent Christmas at Westminster, and was reconciled to the Queene Dowager, who left Sanctuary, and to congratulate the Kings favour, sent her five daughters to Court,

The Q. Mother & King *Rich.* reconciled.

Court, where they were received with all Princely kindnesse.

On the three and twentieth day of January, in the first yeare of his Raigne, he summon'd a Parliament to be holden at Westminster, in which (after the enacting of many good Lawes) the marriages of King *Edward* were debated, that with the Lady *Gray* adjudged unlawfull, and her children illegitimate, there being proofe of a former Contract and Marriage with the Lady *Elianor Talbot*, daugher of the old Earle of Shrewsbury, and Relict of the Lord *Butler* of Sudely, then and long after living, and all that had been inserred by the Duke of Buckingham, or contained in the Bill supplicatory, demonstrated, was againe consulted, and judgement given against that Marriage, and incapacity of the Children also, of the Earle of Warwicke and his sister, the Lady *Elizabeth Plantagenet*, all decreed and confirmed by Act of Parliament; so that here to taxe so generall an Assent, were to say there was not one honest nor just man in that High Court, and what greater scandall to the whole Kingdome?

The Parliament of *R.3.*

There was likewise notice taken of the Earle of Richmonds pretence to the Crowne, by a Title derived from the House of Lancaster, who was at that time in France, labouring to engage the King and the Duke of Brittaine in the quarrell. Oh the infinite windings, and perplexed sleepes we labour through, to get that we must bid goodnight to to morrow; And yet the true and rightful Lancaster had no finger in it, for this Earle was not then granted to be of the House of Lancaster, untill the Pope by his Bull had given him that stile, and himselfe (after he was King) by his Prerogative assumed it. In this Parliament he was attainted of High Treason, and with him *Iohn* Earle of Oxford, *Thomas* Marquesse of Dorset, *Iasper* Earle of Pembroke, *Lionell* Bishop of Salisbury, *Peirce* Bishop of Excester, the Lady *Margaret* Countesse of Richmond, *Thomas Morton* Bishop of Ely, *Thomas Naudick* by the stile of *Thomas Naudick* of Cambridge Conjurer, *William Knevet* of Buckingham smeared with the same pitch, *George Browne* of Beechworth, *Thomas Lukenor* of Tratton, *Iohn Guilford*, *Iohn Fogg*, *Edward Poinings*, *Thomas Fieries* of Cherstmonceur, *Nicholas Gainsford*, *William Clifford*, *Iohn Darrell*, with others of Kent and the West Countrey. There was further enacted for the approbation and confirming the true and lawfull Title of King *Richard*, this clause or sentence.

The friends & confederates of the E. of Rich.

It is declared, pronounced, decreed, confirmed and established by the Authority of this present Parliament, that King *Richard* the third is the true and undoubted King of this Realme, as well by right of Consanguinitie and Heritage, as by lawfull Election and Coronation, &c. And in a place of the Rowle of this Parliament, there are Arguments to be gathered, that the two sonnes of King *Edward* were living in the time of this Parliament, which was at the least nine moneths after the death of their Father, and sixe moneths after King *Richard*; which will import thus much, That if King *Richard* then, lawfully and quietly possessed of the Crowne, suffered them to live so long,

The sons of K. E. living in Ian. & Febr. after the death of their Father.

long, there is no reason why, he should after make them away, for their lives could not rectifie their Bloud, or Titles, nor their deaths advantage him, neither can Bastards be dangerous, or prejudiciall to the true and titular Lord, or lawfull proprietary, be he Prince or Subject; Witnesse Forraigne Countries, and England it selfe, which holds Bastards uncapable of Heritage, Honour or Offices: In the Month of February, towards the end of this Parliament, the King in his providence to establish the Regall fortune and Succession in the Prince his Sonne, and to fasten the affection of the Nobility and People unto him with the Crowne, procures them to meet him in the Pallace at Westminster, and there (*Interiori Cænaculo*, as mine Author saith) tendred by the Duke of Norfolke unto them, an Oath of Fealty and Allegeance in writing, to be taken to the Prince of Wales; which they tooke and subscribed most willingly; the occasion of this, was his jealousie of that new League struck up between the Earle of Richmond and the Duke of Buckingham, who was now discovered more apparantly, and the rest of the engagement: To oppose and suppresse them therefore, and stifle the Confederacy before it should grow more threatning; The King makes a Commission by Letters Patents, in the name of the Vice Constable of England, unto Sir *Ralph Ashton*, A Coppy whereof (the President being unusuall, and the Office great) I have Transcribed verbatim from the Records in the Chappell of the Convertits.

Vice Constable of England.

Vice-Constabulario Angliæ Constituto.

Patents de anno 1 Rich. 3. part. 1. mem. 2.

REX dilecto & fideli suo, Rudolpho Ashton militi, salutem. Sciatis, quod nos de fidelitate, circumspectione, & probitate, vestrâ plenius confidentes, assignavimus deputavimus & ordinavimus vos hac vice Constabularium nostrum Angliæ, ac Commissionarium nostrum, dantes & concedentes vobis tenore presentium potestatem & authoritatem generalem, & mandatum speciale, ad audiendum & examinandum ac procedendum, contra quascunque personas de crimine læsæ nostræ regiæ majestatis suspectas & culpabiles tam per viam examinationis testium quam aliter prout vobis melius visum fuerit ex officio vestro; nec non in causis illis judicialiter & sententialiter juxta casus exigentiam & delinquentium demerita omni strepitu & futura Iudicij appellatione quacunque remota, quandocunque vobis videbitur procedendum, judicandum et finali executione demandandum cum omnibus etiam clausulis, verbis, et terminis specialibus

cialibus ad executionem istius mandati et authoritatis nostræ de jure vel consuetudine requisitis, quæ etiam omnia hic expressa habemus, assumpto vobiscum aliquo tabellione fide digno, qui singula conscribat unà cum alijs quæ in præmissis vel circa ea necessaria videbuntur seu qualitercunque requisita; mandantes & firmiter vobis injungentes, quod alijs quibuscunque prætermissis circa prædicta quoties & quando opus fuerit intendatis, causasque antedictas audiatis, examinetis, & in eisdem procedatis ac eas judicetis & finali executione ut præfertur demandetis. Damus etiam omnibus & singulis quorum interest in hac parte tenore præsentium firmiter in mandatis, quod vobis in præmissis faciendis pareant, assistant & auxilientur in omnibus diligenter, in cujus, &c. Teste Rege apud Covent. 24. die Octobris, Anno regni primo; per ipsum Regem ore tenus.

What successe this Commission, and new Office had, I find not reported, but it might come too late, or the new Officer forget what he was to execute, for the faction lost none they could corrupt or winne; yet surely, the institution of it was very politicke and important, as a plaine Image and pourtraict, of the Office and Authority of the great or High-Constable of England, which in the execution of a wise and valiant person, is of a high and great use.

Other Officers of King *Richard* 3.

Having made mention of these Offices, it shall not be a Parergue, between these Acts, to interadde the rest of this Kings Officers, both Chiefe and others; at the least such as were of Honour or Dignity: I have before named the High-Constable, the great Marshall, high Admirall, Lord Chamberlaine, the rest were Sir *John Wood* the Elder, L. Treasurer the first yeare, and Sir *Iohn Touchet*, Lord *Audley* during the rest of his Reigne, Doctor *Russell* Bishop of Lincolne had the great Seale, *Thomas Barrow* was Master of the Rowles, (which place *Henry* the seventh continued to him, and made him a Privy Counsellour) *Iohn Kendall* was principall Secretary, Sir *William Hopton* Treasurer of the Houshold, Sir *Thomas Peircy* Controler, after him Sir *Iohn Buck*, *Iohn Gunthorpe* Keeper of the Privy Seale, Sir *William Hussey* Chiefe Justice, *Thomas Tremaine* and *Roger Townsend* the Kings Serjeants, *Morgan Kidwell* Attorney Generall, *Nicholas Fitz-William* Recorder of London.

Treaties for League and commerce with Flanders, &c. *In Thesauro Scaccarij* 1 R. 3.

For matters of Treaty, betwixt this King and Forreigne Princes, I have seen a memoriall of one, for intercourse and commerce, between him and *Philip* Duke of Burgundy, and the Estates of Flanders, who in the Record are called *Membra Flandriæ*: These Princes and States had each of them their Commissioners to treate and determine the Affaires, which I find they dispatcht with approbation of the Princes their Masters.

There was also a Commission about these times, to heare and redresse the complaints made to the King, by the Subjects of the King of France and of Denmarke, which was well expedited. In Rowles *An.* 1. R. 3.

Anno Regni 2. That Treatie of Peace and League with Scotland, (began before) was continued, and finished by Commissioners sent from *Iames* the fourth King of Scotland, and by other Commissioners delegate for the King of England; those for Scotland, were *Coli:* Earl of Argile, Chancellor of Scotland, *N.* Bishop of Aberdene, the Lord *Lisle*, the Lord *Dromonde* of Stobhall, Master *Archibald Quhitlaw*, Arch-Deacon of Lodion, & Secretary to the King, *Lion* King at Arms and *Duncan* of Dundas; they came to Nottingham in September *Anno Domini* 1484, and were honourably receiv'd in the great Chamber of the Castle, the King sitting under his Royall Cloth of State; Master *Archibald Quhitlaw* stepping before the rest, addrest a very Eloquent Oration unto him in Latine, which reflected upon the praise of Martialmen & Art Military, including much to the honour and praise of King *Richard*. This Treatie aimed partly at a Truce and Peace, partly at a Marriage, betweene *Iames* the Prince of Scotland and the Lady *Anne*, Daughter of *Iohn de la Poole*, Duke of Suffolke, and Neice to King *Richard*. *An.Dom.* 1484. *Argile* in Record.

Commissioners for the King of England, were *Iohn* Bishop of Lincolne, *Richard* Bishop of Asaph, *Iohn* Duke of Norfolke, *Henry* Earle of Northumberland, Master *Iohn Gunthorpe custos privati sigilli*, Sir *Thomas Stanley*, Lord *Stanley*, Sir *N.* Lord *Strange*, Sir *N.* Lord *Powis*, Sir *Henry* Lord *Fitz-hugh*, Sir *Humphry* Lord *Dacres*, Master *Thomas Barrow* Master of the Rowles, Sir *Richard Ratcliff*, *William Catesby*, and *Richard Salkeld*: The other for the Treatie of Alliance and Marriage, were *Thomas* Arch-Bishop of Yorke, *Iohn* Bishop of Lincolne, *Iohn* Bishop of Worcester, *Iohn* Duke of Norfolke, *William* Earle of Nottingham, *Iohn Sutton* Lord *Dudley*, *N.* Lord *Scroope* of Upsall, Sir *William Hussey*, Chiefe Justice of the Kings Bench; Sir *Richard Ratcliffe*, and *William Catesby*: But the successe of that, and many other good intendments, were interposed by the inconstancy and contraste of the times. The Lady *Anne de la Poole*, upon the the breach thereof, (resolving to accept no other motion) forthwith tooke a religious habit in the Monastery of Sion. The Lady *Anne de la Poole* a Nun.

There was another Treatie of Peace and Truce in this second yeare, betweene him and the Duke of Brittaine, or at the least given out for peace, yet was indeed but a part and pretext of the Treatie; for the maine negotiations on the Kings side, was, how to get the Earle of Richmond out of his custody into his owne, or be as well secured of him there as his Brother King *Edward* was: And for this Treatie, the chiefe Negotiators, were the Bishop of Lincolne and Sir *Thomas Hutton* for the King, the Bishop of Leon and others for the Duke. The Treatie began *Anno Domini* 1484. and was finished and ratified in the yeare following, but the Duke violated his part immediately by giving ayde to the Kings Enemies. Treaty with the Duke of Brittaine. *Ib. in Scaccar.*

Treatie with the King of France.

In the same yeare there were Letters made (which are yet extant in the Treasury of the Exchequor) that moved a Peace and Truce betweene King *Richard*, and *Charles* the eighth King of France; wherein it must be understood, the tribute before mentioned was Articled.

Treaty of marriage of King *Rich.* with the Lady *Eliz.*

Also in this yeare, and the yeare before, there was a private Treatie, which we must not passe by, for the Marriage of the Lady *Elizabeth* with King *Richard* himselfe: what the successe of it was, and how farre it proceeded, will more aptly present it selfe in another place.

Revolt of the D. of Buck.

Wee are now to take notice of the Duke of Buckinghams revolt, for this was the preparative and fourrier of the rest: And to give it the more taking feature and specious pretence, it must be given out, That the cause was the Reformation of an ill Government and Tyranny, under which species, (for Treason is ever fairely palliated, and seldome wants the forme of some plea, though at the Barre) they must take up Armes against the King. And here (as some Rivers deriv'd from the Sea, cannot suddenly loose their taste of saltnesse) they discovered their ancient taint and inconstancy which the Prince wisely suspected from the first.

The Duke of Buckingham first riseth in Rebellion.

The quarrell of the Duke of Buck. against the King.

For the Duke of Buckingham (how affably soever he trim'd his countenance) it should seeme departed male-content from Court, yet made not that generall publick pretended cause of the Kings Crimes all his quarrell, but challenged him by some private grudges, as denying to give or restore to him the Earledome of Hereford, and Constableship of England, (for they went together a long time) which he alledged belonged to the Partage that fell to his great Grand-mother the Lady *Anne*, Daughter and Heire of *Thomas Plantagenet*, alias *Woodstock*, created by King *Richard* the second Duke of Glocester, and Earle of Buckingham, and of his Wife *Elianor*, daughter and co-heire of *Humphry de Bohun* Earle of Hereford, and Constable of England: Which claime, had he considerately look't upon, could not rightly revolve to him, but rather was for the Kings part;

The Title of the Earldome of Hereford, & of the Constableship of England.

For *Humphry de Bohun*, Earle of Hereford, of Essex and Northampton, Lord of Brecknock, and Constable of England (in the time of King *Edward* the third, and the last Earle of the Family of the *Bohuns*) had by the Lady *Iane* his Wife, Daughter of *Richard Fitz-Allan* Earle of Arundel, two Daughters and Heires, *Elianor* and *Mary*: *Elianor* was Married to the same *Thomas Plantagenet*, alias *de Woodstock*, youngest Sonne of King *Edward* the third, Duke of Glocester and Earle of Buckingham: *Mary* the second Daughter was Married to *Henry Plantagenet* Duke of Lancaster, and after King of England by the name of *Henry* the fourth, and the Earledome of Hereford fell to his Wife: In favour whereof, he was Created Duke of Hereford by King *Richard* the second, and the Earldome (now a Dutchy) and the rights therof, remained in the King, and in the Kings Heires and Successors untill the death of King *Henry* the sixt, who dyed without Issue, & then all the Estate of Lancaster (especially that of the Royall Family of Lancaster) escheated to King *Edward* the fourth, and from him it came to King *Richard*, as Heire to his Brother and all his Ancestors. But the Duke of Buckingham pretended Title to that Earledome by his said Grandmother *Anne*, who was one of the Daughters and Heires of the aforesaid Lady *Elianor* (Wife of *Thomas de Woodstock* Duke of Glocester) and the Wife of *Edmond Stafford* Earle of Stafford, and Grand-father to this *Henry* Duke of Buckingham, who the rather presumed to make this Claime, because the Issue of the other Sister *Mary*, being extinct; he tooke himselfe also to be her Heire.

But King *Richard* relishing something in this, neare the disposition and inclination of Bullingbrooke, answered, That the Earledome of Hereford was of the inheritance of *Henry* the fourth, who was also King of England (though by tort and usurpation) and will you my Lord of Buckingham Claime to be Heire of *Henry* the fourth? You may then also happily Assume his spirits, and lay Claime to the Crowne by the same Titles.

This was as bitter as short, and doubly ill taken: First, because it came with a Repulse: Next, because it seemed to proceed from a suspition, and as a tax of his Loyaltie, and begets another pretence of exception in the Dukes bosome; which he called a breach of promise in the King, for not joyning the Prince his Sonne in Marriage with the Lady *Anne Stafford* his Daughter; but all those Colours were but to give complexion to the face of his defection, the true cause was well devined and found out by the King; his Ambition and aime to be Soveraigne, rays'd by an overweening of that Royall Blood he supposed to be in his descent from the said *Thomas de Woodstock*, &c. Sonne of a King; and yet he was not resolutely determined to make his Claime to the Crowne this way, nor to attempt the Kingdome by Armes, untill those embers which (as it were) lay but luke-warme in his thoughts, were quickned and revived by the animation of Doctor *Morton* Bishop of Ely then a Privie Counsellour though he stood in some umbrage and disgrace in the Court with the King, for his practises against him, and was at this time in the custody of the Duke of Buckingham as a Prisoner; more expressely, for that being a Privie Counsellour, he had given secret advertisement to the Earle of Richmond of what passed in the secret Councells of the King; To this advantage, he applyes that which he had wittily drawne from the Dukes discontent and passionate discourses at times passed. By which, perceiving the glance of his Ambition, and that deriv'd from the great opinion of his Royall Blood, he pregnantly tickles and feeds that humour, untill he had soothed him past his owne strength or retyrement; for his secret drift was, to apt and prepare the Duke to a Rebellion at any hand, though not to set his owne Title on foot, yet layes open the advantage of the present times to it, proposing flat usurpation and tyranny against the King Regnant, and the strong likelyhood of his Deposing. This lifts the Duke something higher in his owne opinion. But comming to a pause, (and perceiving *Richmond* was the man they had aimed at for this great blow (who had conditioned by Oath to marry the Lady *Elizabeth*, (for the Countesse of Richmond, had by the meanes of Doctor *Lewis*, conciliated the friendship of the Queene Mother to that Alliance, and to draw as many of the House of Yorke into the Action as were at her Devotion) that many Potent Lords and some Forraigne Princes had promised their ayds) he began to retreat, and conceive he had taken the wrong path to his journyes end, for his Title and Claime must be nothing, if those of Yorke and Lancaster were united: And that the Earle (who stood betweene him and his Aimes) was not onely resolute to attempt, but strongly ayded for it, himselfe not able upon such an instant to raise a power able to encounter, much lesse give check unto his violent Ambition, therefore concludes all against himselfe, and that it would fall out farre better to side with the times; a consideration which doubtlesse would highly stirre a spirit where so much greatnesse of opinion and ambition was. And the Doctor discerning this disgust, and that he was startl'd in his hope and resolution, to recover him an intire man, & not let him stand by, an idle spectator in so meritorious an action, he opens a private way of honour and satisfaction, suggesting him the first and greatest man, the Kingdome was to know next the King: And finding his particular distasts to King *Richard*, of quickest sense and argument to him, he freshly urges (and as it were) refricates each particle, to the greatnesse of his spirit and discontent; the Duke replyes not much at that time, but busie in his thoughts leaves him, and presently fashions a visite to the Countesse of Richmond, (a Lady of a politick and contriving bosome) to know the credit of his intelligence, which she insinuates with arguments so full of circumstance and honour, besides her Sons indearment to him, their nearnesse of blood, affirming the Dukes Mother a Somerset, the reciprocall affinitie betweene her Father and his, and then the bravery and Religion in the Cause, that the Duke now forsakes himselfe, and fully gives up his resolution and promise to her; thus prepar'd, he finds out the Lord *Stanley*, the Marquesse of *Dorset*, *Edward Courtney* Earle of Devonshire, and his Brother the Bishop of Exeter, Sir *John Bowrchier*, Sir *John Wells*, *Robert Willowby*, *Edward Woodvill*, *Thomas Arundel*, who had severally raised forces, and intended their Rendezvous neere Glocester, so to march for Dorsetshire, there to receive the Earle and the Duke, with his Welchmen: But the King was early in his preparation, to prevent them before they could unite, or the Earle of Richmond arrive there, else they had fastened a most dangerous Blow upon him. And at this full stop, in these progresses (me thinkes) wee may observe, how uncertainely, in our strongest valuations, we are our owne; and that our greatest Confidences, and humane Policies, are but heavie weights hung at trembling Wyers, while our expectations are apt to be flattered, and out-goe themselves, but are over-

taken

Sir *Tho. Moor.*

This *Margaret* Countesse of Richmond, was Daughter and Heire to *John Beaufort* Duke of Somerset, & *Margaret de Beaufort*, Mother of the D. of Buck. was Daughter of *Edmond* D. of Somerset; and thus were the E. of Rich. and the D. of Buck. a Kin. *Rob. Glov. in Catal. &c.*

The Conspirators with the D. of Buck. for the E. of Rich.

taken in their Successe, and Fates, as was this great Mans; for their Forces neither met by Sea nor Land, the English being scatter'd by a suddaine and huge inundation that so dangerously over-flowed all passages, they could not joyne nor passe the River Severne, while the suddainnesse and strangenesse of it stroke the Souldiers with such alteration, that most part of them forsooke the Duke and left him to himselfe: The Earle of Richmond was as unfortunately met at Sea by a great tempest, upon the coasts of England.

The overthrow of the Duke of Buckingham.

The King took the advantage this accident offered, and pursued the Duke, not onlywith a galloping Army, but with Edicts & Proscriptions, that promised a thousand pounds in mony (whereunto some Writers adde, so much Lands as was worth one hundred pounds *per annum*) to any that should bring in the Duke, who was betrayed and brought to the King then at Salisbury, by *Humphry Banister*,) an eternall brand) having lived by this mans service, and now thought treacherously to subsist by his Ruine. The Duke being examined, freely confessed all, and for it lost his head in the field according to Marshall Law used by Armies, in November *An. Dom.* 1484. *An.* 2 *Rich.* 3.

Polidore lib. 25

King *Richard* sharply reprehended *Banister* for betraying his Master, which argued a noble mind.

The D. executed by Marshall Law.

And here, if wee view him in the figure of his Ambition or Fate, wee shall find Doctor *Morton* his *Caput Argoll*, or the malignant Planet of his fortune; who, as Sir *Thomas Moore* confesseth and affirmeth, by his Politick Drifts and Pride, advanced himselfe, and brought the Duke to this ruine. The rest fled, some into Sanctuaries, others into Brittaine to the Earle of Richmond, and some into Flanders, all their Plots being now how to be safe.

And thus farre King *Richard*, in the Voyage of his Affaires had a promising Gale; wee will therefore here cast Anchor a while, and claspe up this first Booke, with the Relation of his better Fortunes.

Explicit Lib. I.

THE

[illegible] and Fate, [illegible] Margaret [illegible] Land, [illegible] being [illegible] that [illegible] flowed [illegible] the King [illegible]

[illegible]

[illegible] his [illegible] Dukes [illegible]. The rest [illegible] Earle of Richmond, [illegible] into Flanders, all [illegible] Plots [illegible] now how to be [illegible].

And thus fare King Richard, in the Voyage of his Affaires had a [illegible] Gales; wee will therefore here cast Anchor awhile, [and cl]ose up this first Booke, with the Relation of his better [fort]unes.

Explicit Lib. I.

THE

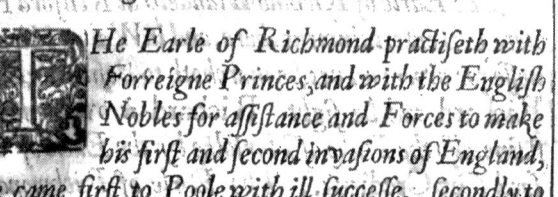

THE
SECOND BOOKE OF THE HISTORY OF KING *RICHARD* THE THIRD.

The Argument of the Second Booke.

THe Earle of Richmond practiseth with Forreigne Princes, and with the English Nobles for assistance and Forces to make his first and second invasions of England, He came first to Poole with ill successe, secondly to Milford cum bonis avibus.

What Bastards are, and whereof they are capable, who be of the House of Lancaster, how Lancaster and Beaufort or Sommerset differ.

Bastards of Kings must not take the Sirnames of the King or Kingdome.

The honourable priviledge of the name of Plantagenet.

Prince Edward, *and Queene* Anne, John de la Poole *proclaimed Heire of the Kingdom by* Richard *the Third.*

Bastards of John *Duke of Lancaster made legi-timate*

timate, and capable of Offices, Honour, and of Heritage by Richard 2, and the Parliament.

What the Legitimation of the Pope is.

Armes and Names of Princes Bastards.

The Nobility of King Henry 7th. *He affied not much in the Titles of Yorke and Lancaster.*

The Pope giveth to him the Title, de jure belli, & de domo Lancastriæ.

The greatnesse of the Title of Yorke, of Counsell, and Counsellours.

The Prerogative of the King in Iudgements and Controversies.

The Earle of Richmond landeth at Milford Haven; His entertainment there, and in Wales; His aptnesse for divers wives; he marcheth to Bosworth; King Richard *and he fight,* Richard *is overcome and slaine, also the Duke of Norfolke by the Earle of Oxford (*ut Creditur.*) The Earle of Richmond is straight Crowned King in the field; The fatall Errour of King* Richard; *Kings loved Combate; The Titles of King* Henry 7th. *Kings go not now to wars; Cruelties committed upon the body of King* Richard; *He was attainted of Treason, though against the Laws of Nature, and of Royall Majesty, with many of his followers and servants; The Earle of Surrey how released out of prison, his Geneology from* Hewardus walter de Buck, *and his Progeny.*

The

The Second Booke.

WE left King *Richard* the Third in the growth of a flourishing and promising Estate, and his fate now, in the rise of a peacefull and prosperous Raigne, of a calme and hopefull presage; But Fortune that lends her smiles as Exactors do mony, to undoe the Debtor, soone cald for the Principall and Interest from this Prince, to whom she was meerly Novercall, and he might well call her with the expert Heros in *Euripides fortuna diurna, i. e.* fortune of a daies life, for in her best mood, she is most slippery in her favours, and tedious in her mischiefes, as was aptly considered by a grave man: *Fortuna adversas res cupido animo inducit, secundas parco*; she is a mother but a little while, a stepdame a long time, and for ever to some; here then, we are aggressing into the turbulent and lustuall times, which were towards the end and period of his Life and Raigne; the formall and finall causes, happening from the invasions attempted by the Earle of Richmond; I will begin the Second Booke there, and may say invasions, because he twice invaded the Kingdome, though by errour or ignorance of our Vulgar Historians, they are confounded and made one, which corruptly maimes the Story, and conceales and pretermits some very remarkeable agitations: particularly, the true cause of the Duke of Buckinghams ill successe and defeate, is misunderstood, or not at all known. To come to it therefore more certainly, we must take notice of the first preparation by the Earle of Richmond, who was resolved to advance his claime that way, and unbosomes himselfe to the Duke of Brittaine, his possibility and advantage by friends, if he could raise but sufficient strength to set him safely in England. The Duke gives him all good wishes to his undertaking, but opposes (against all Arguments of drawing him in) first, his Amity and League with England, which in honour and justice he was not to violate: Then his wants by the long Civill and cruell Warres, with his Barons, that had so exhausted his Coffers, as durst he dispense with

Eurip. in Herc.

Valer. Max. l. 7

the former cause, yet that might render him excused, being unable to furnish him, at least in so short a time as his expedition required; beyond which answer, for the present, the Earle thought not fit to presse him; But having a prompt and strong affiance in his good fortune, makes up to some of the Dukes most honourable and powerfull Friends, to lay siege that way to him by private advantages, for by his ingenious demeanour, he had won the inclinations of many great ones, being Master of a pleasant acute wit, which was well supplied in him by the straine of all Courtly Acts; to those he had the helpe of the French Tongue, which he spoke excellently well, and (to give all the more plausible accesse and influence) hee was (as *Philip de Comines*, who knew him, testifies) a very compleat and well featur'd Gentleman which makes the rule certaine, and well animating

Virgill.

Gratior est pulchro veniens e corpore virtus.

The beauties of the mind more gratious are,
When as the bodies features are more faire.

In the number of those eminent persons he had gained during his faire imprisonment: more fortunately he had applyed himselfe unto the Lady *Margaret*, Dutchesse of Brittaine, Daughter of *Gaston de Foix*, (a great man in the Westerne parts of France, whose Ancestors were well affected to the English) and Madam *de Bevier* the Dutches, so farre countenanced him in his designe, that she became an earnest suitor unto the Duke her husband, and prevailed both for his liberty and aide; for caution and pledge herein, he was only to kneele at the High Altar, before the blessed Sacrament, in the Cathedrall Church of Saint *Vannes*, there to make his religious Vow, justly and truely to observe what restitution he privately had promised to the Duke and Dutches; which protestation made, he had three Ships well rigged and furnished with Men, Armes, and Victuals, as my Author relates.

John Froissard.
Paradin.
Hist. de Brit.
The Duke had by this Lady his daughter and heir *Anne*, who brought the Dutchy of Brittaine to France.

Hist. de Brit.

Au Conte de Richmond furent aux despens du duc trois grosses Navires de Brittannia, charges de gens de Armes, &c. & qui se misent in mer.

But, by the favour of this Brittish Writer, the Earle staid many daies at Saint Malo, to receive and send intelligence, and made it the beginning of October 1484, before he came to Saint Poole in Dorset, where he lay some time at Anchor, to send his Boates a shore as Explorers or Spies, for discovery of the Coasts, where the Kings Armie, or his friends lay, who returned without any particular satisfaction, but that there was many Armed men about the Country. The Earle (who in all things was circumspect, and cautiously timorous) resolved immediately to loose from thence; but the night following, a terrible tempest constrained them with all hast to weigh Anchor, and make into the Maine, the Storme and darkenesse of the night severing and dispersing their Ships, some to the Coasts of Brittaine,

taine, but the Earle himselfe to the Coasts of Normandy. And this was the successe of his first invasion, which, though it bore an inauspicate face, it proved of a friendly event: For had he landed about Poole, or but stayed till the Kings Ships had come in, that lay waiting not far off, he had been a lost man every way, the King being not only active to meet their contrivements, but had some advantage upon them, by the close intelligence of a friend, and knew that the Forces of the Duke of Buckingham, with the Earle of Devon, and others, were to meet neare Gloucester, and march in their full and united strength, towards the sea-Coasts of Dorset, there to receive the Earle: But the King encountred with the Duke of Buckinghams Army, beate him, and cut off his head, before any of the rest could come at him daily putting the ordinary bands of these West Countries in a ready posture for guard of their Coasts; and that if the Earle of Richmond, or any of his French Forces came a shore, they were to be entertained courteously by them pretending themselves of the Duke of Buckinghams Army, who had routed the Kings Party, and were sent thither to receive and conduct the Earle with his men to London. This was the projected end: But it is of rem..rkeable note, to look into the various paths of this Earles fortune, and how they brought him to his journies end, when they appeared most doubtfull and threatning, not only gave him advantage by the good successe of his Enterprises, but made the most adverse accidents serve as prosperous unto them; for was it not happy the storme at Poole drove him from the Coasts of England, and no lesse fortunate, that the Duke of Buckingham was defeated, whereas, had the Duke atcheived that day, the Earle of Richmond not being there, (who was to be present in person, and Generall of the field) we may with reason conjecture his Emulation and Policy, would have accumulated the honour and fortune of the Conquest to his owne pretended Title: such Spirits like the Sea, where they intrude or win, making their advantage their right, and not easily surrender, so much is the engagements of Ambition, too strong for all ties of faith and right.

The example is observable in the Earle of Richmond himselfe; who although he knew the Children of the Duke of Clarence and others, had better right to the Crowne, yet once possest, would not resigne, no not to his owne Sonne, whilst he could hold it; nor did he want his Presidents, as all men know, who know any thing. And to take all Relations in our way, that may be levell with our Story, betwixt this and his second Invasion, some other passages offer themselves, as an interim, and not impertinent to supply the Readers observation.

Amongst other, the Death of the Kings deare and only Sonne (at least Legitimate) who dyed in the Castle of Middleham in Yorkeshire, in the Month of Aprill, *Anno Dom.* 1484. which newes gave such a passionate Charge upon the Nature and Affections of the King and Queene (being then in the Castle of Nottingham) that as mine

The death of *Edw.* Prince of Wales, Sonne of *Rich.* 3. Chron. Croyland.

Ibidem.

Author saith, *Subitis doloribus insanire videbantur.*

Yet the King, being a man of an equall moderation to his courage, puts it into the Scale of his other worldly encounters, and as it was said of *Iulius Cæsar*, that he soone passed the death of his only daughter *Iulia* (most pretious in his affection) *Et tam facile dolorem hunc, quam omnia vicit*; So King *Richard* tempered his griefe and businesse so together, that the one made him not unsensible, nor the other negligent; but as the Prior of Croyland telleth, did all things gravely and discreetly as before.

Seneca.

Rex Richardus nihilominus tamen suam partem defensione vacaverit: although the Queene could not hold so proportioned a temper over her griefe, the tendernesse of her Sexe, letting it breake upon her in a more passionate manner, and with such an Impression, that it became her sickenesse past recovery, languishing in weaknesse and extremity of sorrow, untill she seemed rather to overtake death, than death her; which was not long after the Princes, and added not a little to the Kings sufferings and sorrowes, (though traducing Spirits have charged him with shortning her life by poyson, or some other practice, which are prestigious and blacke Comments, falsly plac't in the Margent of his Story, and may mere nearely touch the credit of the Authors than his, if we judiciously take a view of him and his Actions; and looke upon the indulgent and active care for his Country, which he gave a constant and sincere expression of, instantly after his Sonnes death, when by the deliberation and consent of the Barons, he was industrious to thinke of a Successour, and to nominate such an one whose bloud and worth might make him equally Heire to the Crown and the peoples affection, (with the highest approbation of the Kingdome) and none more neare to either, then Sir *Iohn de la Poole* Earle of Lincolne, Sonne and Heire of *Iohn de la Poole* Duke of Suffolke, and of the Lady *Elizabeth Plantagenet*, Duchesse of Suffolke, the Sister and Heire of this King *Richard*, who was declared and proclaimed Heire apparant to the Kingdome. This was a *Contrecarre* to the Faction of Richmond, and (indeed) what greater affront could thwart them, if those of the House of Lancaster or Beaufort, were next Heire to the Crowne, (as the pretenders affirmed for the Earle of Richmond) who would likewise have him to be *Caput gentis Lancastriæ, & Princeps familiæ*, though they could scarcely prove him (not without question I am sure) *Membrum illius familiæ*, untill he came to be King; for it was a question in those times, and much disputed, whether the Beauforts or Sommersets were of the House of Lancaster, or no: most true it is, the Children of the House of Lancaster being lawfully borne, and after *Henry Plantagenet* Duke of Lancaster, had Conquered and deposed *Richard* the Second, were to be held Princes of the Bloud Royall, and capable of the Crowne in their naturall and due Order. But those of Beaufort or Sommerset, were as the Vulgar hath it, *filij populi*, or as the Imperiall Juris-consults say, *liberi vulgo quæsiti*, who by the old Greeks were termed *Απάτορες*, *i.e. sine Patre*, the Doctors of the Spirituall

Iohn Earle of Lincolne, and after Duke of Suffolke proclaimed Heire Apparant.

tuall Law, drawing the *Originem* of such children, *ab illicito & damnato coitu*, of the polluted adulterous bed (and so those *Beauforts*, three males and one female, begotten by *Iohn* of Gaunt (as he believed) according to the Lawes were to be reputed, the children of Sir *Otho Swinford*, begotten upon *Katherine* his Wife in his life time, who was daughter of Sir *Payen Rovet* a French-man, dwelling in Beauforts, and was Guyen Herald to the Duke of Lancaster. His Dutchesse *Dona Constantia*, (a most noble and vertuous Lady, daughter of *Don Pedro* King of Castile) was living also in the time he kept this *Katherine*, and had those *Beauforts*, who were Sir-named so from the place of their birth, a Town of his own in Aniow. But to note *transitu*, how obnoxious this Duke made his frailties, that (thinking to put a smoother face upon his sin) gave it but the same blush, by making this *Katherine Swinford* his Dutchesse, against the liking of the King & all his noble friends, & direct Tenor of the common Laws, which pronounce marriages between such as have lived in Aldutery unlawfull: Nay, to make him the more marvaile and smiling discourse of the Court, the glasse of his age was turn'd to his last yeare when he sacrific'd these scatterd embers of his desires and passion. But he obtained those children to be legitimated: First, by the Pope *Vrbanus* the sixt; next by the Charter of King *Richard* the second, and had both these indulgences afterward enlarged and confirmed by Parliament. Yet neither these foure legitimate children, *nec qui nascebantur ab illis*, were permitted to the Princely familiar Title of Lancaster, so long as that name flourished, much lesse of *Plantagenet*; for that was the peculiar Sir-name in chiefe of the Kings of England, and Princes of the blood Royall, since the time of the second *Henry*, Sonne of the Empresse *Matilda*, the first founder of that name in the Royall Family of England. Of which honour were partakers, the Princely Family of Wales, of Brotherton, of Yorke, of Lancaster, of Clarence, of Woodstock, of Glocester, &c. And there are yet some Noblemen in Portugall, who descended from *Iohn* Duke of Lancaster, and are called and written *de Lancastro*, others of the like *Origine* and Title may doe as much. Neither would King *Henry* the fourth, *Henry* the fift, nor King *Henry* the sixt, all Kings of the Lancastrian race indure to let the Lineage of *Beaufort* (though they respected them as kinsmen, and advanced them to many honours) Assume the the Sir-name of Lancaster, holding it an Arrogation and Usurpation of Royaltie and Royall Rights, wherein they followed their Ancestors, who devised other names for their base children: As *Fitz-Roy*, *Oxenford*, *Fitz-Herbert*, *Clarendon*, *Fitz-Henry Longuespee Cornwall*; and so they continued the name of *Beaufort* and *Somersets* untill the Earle of *Richmond* came, and this was in imitation of the Kings of France as I conceive. For within the reach of my observation, since the time of *Hugh Capet*, they never vouchsafed any of their base sons to be capable of the Crown of France, or to have the Adven (as they call it) nor the Sir-name of France; but the illegitimate daughters may

take

John Sarisburiensis Ep. 85.

Sir *Tho.Walsin. in Rich.* 2.

Parl. *ann.* 20. *Rich.* 2.

Don Duart de Lancastro a Noble Gen. of Portugall, averred himself descended from the D. of *Lan. Valodolid*.

The peculiar Sir-names of the Bastards of the ancient Kings of England take the Sir-name *France*, or *de France*; because they can make no claime to the Crowne by a pretended permission of the Salik-law, which *Iohn de Tillet* witnesseth.

Armes of Bastards of the Kings of England.

La troisiesme lignèe a du tout rejectè, les Bastards non seulement de la Coronne mais aussi de l'aduen, et Surnom de France, qui Concession est permis aux Bastards de roy &c.

And as the Bastards of the Kings of England had other names, so they tooke differenced Armes; or else were permitted to beare their mothers (if of any Family.) If tolerated to beare the armes of England; then they were diversified in a Checking, Debasing and Rebating manner, with Bastons, Bends, Sinister Barres, Bordures, Marks of Basenesse, Obscuritie and Noveltie, which any new Gentleman might beare, such as the Learned call *filios terræ & novos homines*; and wee vulgarly, upstarts. But to object against the use of this in England, the example of *Hamelin* is brought in; and to credit it, his Armes forged by some weake and negligent Heralds, who call him *Hamelin Plantagenet*, when the truth is, this *Hamelin* (base sonne of *Ieoffry Plantagenet*, Earle of Aniow) was simply called *Hamelin*, and his sonne *William* tooke the Sir-name of his Mother Dame *Isabel de Warren*, daughter and heire of *William de Warren* Earle of Surrey, which their *Posteri* continued, as *Ioannes de Warrena* the first, and *Ioannes de Warrena* the second, both Earles of Surrey; and *Isabella de Warren*, and *Elianor de Warren &c.* mentioned in the Charters and Records, but never *Plantagenet*, which is acknowledged by our best Heralds and Antiquaries; Master *William Campden* hath these words: *Isabella filia sola Gulielmi de Warrena Comitis Surreiæ Hamelinum Nothum Galfredi Plantageneti &c. titulo Comitis Surreiæ maritum exornavit. Hamelinus Gulielmum Surreiæ Comitem genuit, cujus posteri à Scito Warrenorū nomine eundem titulum gesserunt.* And that the base sonne of King *Edward* the fourth, was commonly called *Arthur Plantagenet* proves nothing neither, well considered: For in the times when this *Arthur* lived, the name of *Plantagenet*, being onely left in the house of Yorke (the Lancasterian *Plantagenet* being more extinguished) had not the former honour and reputation, but was darkned and setting, rather drawing a contempt and hate to them that bare it, the White Rose dayly fading and withering; and so malignant was their Planet then, that, as a Learned Gentleman hath further observed, It was not safe in that time to be a *Plantagenet*; therefore the permission of those times can be no warrant for the objections, nor the ignorance of the Poeticall Heralds, who have strain'd this fable of *Hamelin*. Yet farther, not onely giving him and his *Posteri* a false Sir-name, but assign'd him by the like *Fabulous* Art, a shield of familiar Ensignes, the Armes of France border'd with an Orle of Normandy or Guyen: which he, nor yet any of the Antique Lineage of Aniow, or their Progeny ever bare, or could by just Title beare, either simply, or compounded, or the Progenitors of our English Kings the Lillies of Gold in an azure field, untill King *Edward* claimed the Crowne of

Camden Surr.

Tho. Gainsford.

France,

France, and assumed them in the right of Queene *Isabel de Valoys* his Mother, who was the first that bare them quarterly with the Armes of England.

But the Armes of the ancient Earles of Aniow were a Scarboucle, (that is, a Golden Bucle of a military Scarffe or Belt, set with precious Stones) not a Carbuncle or more precious Ruby; for the terme is erroneous and absurd, if considered: The Princes of Aniow bare this Scarboucle in a shield party *per* Chiefe, Argent and Gueules; and the Heires of this *Hamelin* (who tooke the Sir-name of *Warren*) bare also the Armes of the house of *Warren* in their Shields and Caparisons; but bare the Scarboucle of Aniow for their Crest, as they were descended out of that House, as I have seene upon a Seal of *Joannes de Warrena* Earl of Surrey, at a Charter, dated 20. *E. 3. An. Dom.* 1346. *apud Dom. Rob. Cotton*, which hath given me occasion to speake thus much to cure the Blemish that mistake hath thrust into History, such absurdities having their infection, and passing by an Age or two upon the easie and common judgments, after grow up for tall and undeniable truths: For some meerly reading the complexion of things, as they do men by their out-sides, or as boyes Poetry, with a tickled faith; through such wide eares and observations, crept in that Parasitisme on the one side, and Pride and Usurpation on the other side, that made the house of Lancaster and the *Beauforts*, alias *Somersets*, all one; which (whilst the house of York flourished) was held to differ as much as Royall and Feudall, Soveraignty and Suzeraignty; for their modestie at first was very well pleased with that of *Beaufort*, and it seem'd honourable enough untill the children of *John de Beaufort*, the eldest Brother (being Earle of Somerset) assumed the name of their Fathers greatest honour and Earledome for their Sir-name, and the rest following, quite left the name of *Beaufort*, and made the other Hereditary. From this, *John de Beaufort* Earle of Somerset, and Marquesse of Dorset, descended *Henry* Duke of Somerset, Father naturall to *Charles Somerset*, created Earle of Worcester by King *Henry* the eight. And it is worth the noting, that this Duke *Henry* left the Faction of Lancaster to follow *Edward* the fourth. The first *Beauforts* legitimated by the Pope, and *Richard* the second have no other Sir-names, but *Beaufort* in either of the instruments Apostolicall, nor any words to give or emure them to any capicitie of Royall Title, or state of Soveraignty in the Crown, onely purged them by the Popes spirituall power from the foulenesse of Bastardy, allowing them as children legitimate and lawfully born, but gives them no other title then *Joanna de Beaufort miles*, *Henricus de Beaufort Clericus*, *Thomas de Beaufort Domicellus*, *Joannus de Beaufort Domicella*, and more the Pope cannot doe. As the Doctors of Sorbone, and some of the best Canonists hold, who peremptorily affirme, That the Pope cannot make Bastards capable to inherit the Hereditary Lands of their Father; neither can give them power to Constitute Successours or Heires, or hold Offices, Dignities, or Ti-

Scarboucle, falsly called Carbuncle.

Difference betweene the house of Lancaster and Somerset.

The Earles of Worcester, from whom.

The civill and imperiall Law against Bastards.
Sir *Edw. Cook.*

tles, without the Princes speciall dispensation, to which the Civill and Imperiall Lawes agree, and is Authentick in England, as a Learned and eminent Judge reports, though others thinke it of too severe a nature, and moderately agreeable to reason and Law (the Law much observing reason) That Bastards being honest and worthy men (the rather if they be avowed by their Fathers) may be admitted to Honours, Dignities, Titles, Feuds, and other Ornaments of rewards and vertue. Of this indulgence and connivence, wee have examples in England by two worthy and deserving men (flourishing in this Age) who, though Bastards held the greatest Offices in England.

Doctor *Stephen Gardiner.*
Sir *Tho. Eger.* Chancellors of England.

So *Richard* the second, in his Charter for the legitimation of the *Beauforts*, would have men of desert (and avowed by their Fathers) capable of Advancement and Honours. The Tenor of which Charter and Confirmation of it by Parliament I shall exhibite, as it is taken out of the Archives and Tower Records, opening the way by a short advertisement, That in this Act of Parliament there is an Induction to the Charter, made by Doctor *Edmond Stafford*, Brother to the Earle of Stafford, and Bishop of Exeter, Lord Chancellour of England in the twentieth yeare of *Richard* the second; which intimateth, that Pope *Vrbanus* the sixt, at the earnest request of the *King*, vouchsafed to legitimate these *Beauforts*, the base sonnes and the daughter of the Duke of Guyen and Lancaster: That the *King* also, having power to legitimate and enable Bastards in the same kind, and in as ample manner as the Emperour hath or had, for so he pressed and avowed in the Act, was pleased at the humble request and suit of the Duke their Father, to make them not onely legitimate, but also capable of Lands, Heritages, Titles, Honours, Offices, Dignities, &c. And that the *King* for the more authority thereof, crav'd the allowance and favourable assent of the Barons in Parliament, which was granted: The Charter runnes thus.

Charta Legitimationis Spuriorum *Joannis* Ducis Lancastriæ.

RIchardus *dei gratia Rex, Angliæ, Franciæ, Dominus, Hiberniæ, charissimis Consanguineis nostris, Nobilibus viris* Ioanni *de* Beaufort *Militi*, Henrico *de B. Clerico*, Thomæ *de* Beaufort *Domicello & Nobili mulieri* Ioannæ Beaufort *domicellæ præclarissimi patrui nostri Nobilis viri* Ioannis *Ducis Aquitaniæ & Lancastriæ Germanis natis & liegis nostris salutem.*

Nos pro honore & meritis &c. Avunculi nostri, Proprio arbitratu & meritorum suorum intuitu vos, quia magno probitatis

bitatis ingenio, ac vita ac morum Honestate fulgetis, & ex regali estis prosapia propagati, &c. hinc est quod Ioannis *&c. avunculi nostri genitoris vestri precibus inclinati vobis (cum (ut asseritur) defectum natalium patimini) hujusmodi defectum & ejusdem qualitates quascunque abolere præsentes, vos haberi volumus, pro sufficientibus, ad quoscunque honores, dignitatis præeminentias, status, gradus, & officia, publica, & privata, tam perpetua quam temporalia, atque Judicialia & Nobilia, quibuscunq; nominibus nuncupentur, etiam si, Ducatus, Principatus, Comitatus, Baroniæ vel alia feuda fuerint, etiamsi mediate vel immediate, à nobis dependeant seu teneantur præfici, præmoveri, eligi, assumi & admitti, illaq; recipere proinde libere ac licite valeatis, ac si de legitimo thoro nati existeritis, quibuscunque Statutis, seu Consuetudinibus regni nostri Angliæ in contrarium editis seu observatis quæ hic habemus pro totaliter expressis, nequaquam obstantibus, de plenitudine nostræ regalis potestatis & de assensu Parliamenti nostri tenore præsentium dispensamus, vosque & quemlibet vestrum natalibus restituimus & Legitimamus, Die Feb. Anno regni 20. R. 2.*

Here wee find large Graces, Honours, and Priviledges, conferred upon those *Beauforts*; for the *King* calls them *Consanguineos suos*, and not onely confirmes their Legitimation, but makes them (by the helpe of the Parliament) capable of Baronies, Earledomes, Dukedomes, and Principalities, enableth them for all Offices publique and private, temporary and perpetuall, to take hold of and injoy all Feuds, as well noble as other, all Lands and Signiories Hereditary, as lawfully, firmly and rightfully, as if they had beene borne in lawfull matrimony, but yet conferres no Royall Title nor interest in the Crowne, at the least, to the observation of those who allow not the claime of the *Beauforts* and *Somersets*, and say, that to reach that, there must be words of a higher intent, words of Empire, Majesty, and Soveraigntie, such as *Regni summa potestas, Corona, Sceptrum, Diadema, Purpura, Majestas*, and the like: Neither of these, nor any importing their extent, being in this grant, so no Title to the Crowne nor Soveraigntie could passe to them.

To which the other side replyes, That there is a word in the Charter that comprehendeth Empire, Raigne, and Soveraigntie, that is, *Principatus*; whereof the *King* and Parliament make the *Beauforts* capable, *Principatus* being the State of *Princeps*, a Title of the most absolute Soveraigne Power; for the Roman Emperours in their greatest height, were called *Principes*, therefore *Princeps* is thus defined; *Principatus. Princeps.*

Princeps est penes quem summa Reip. potestas est, & qui primus omnium dominatur; And *Principatus*, and *Dominatus* are used, as *Synonomies*. But it is conceiv'd an errour now, to take *Principatus* for *Regnum*, or *Supremus Dominatus*, being the word *Principatus* long before, and in the age of *Richard* the second, also ever since hath beene restrained to the Estate of *Primogenitus* and Heire apparant, not onely of Kings, but also of Dukes and Marquesses, as well Feudall as Soveraigne. And the next King *Henry* the fourth, a wise, discreet, and wary Prince, though he was much inclin'd to those *Beauforts* (as being his naturall Brethren by the Paternall side, and willing to advance them all he could) yet he discovered clearely enough by that certaine Charter in which he entailed the Crowne successively to his foure Sonnes, and to the Heires of their bodies, that he reputed not the *Beauforts* to be Lancastrians, or neare the Crown. Neither is there the least clause or intention to leave any remainder therein to them: First, he intaild the Crowne to his eldest sonne *Henry* Prince of Wales, after him to the Heires of his body; If they faile, then to *Thomas* of Lancaster his second sonne, and to the Heires of his body, so to his third sonne *Iohn* of Lancaster, and to the Heires of his body. Lastly, to the fourth sonne *Humphrey*, and to the Heires of his body, for still, and for every estate: the words are, *Post ipsum successive Heredibus suis de ipsius Corpore legitime procreandis*, which is all, and implicatively an expresse exclusion of the *Beauforts*. This Charter was confirmed by Act of Parliament holden at Westminster the two and twentieth day of December, in the eight yeare of *Henry* the fourth, and sealed with his owne Signet. Upon the Dexter side of that, hung the seales of sundry Lords Spirituall; on the left side, the seales of the Lords Temporall witnesses. And albeit, the Earle of Richmond could not so well and rightly beare the name of *Beaufort* or *Somerset*, being a Tuador by his Father, and so to be Sir-named, or of some other Welch-name (if there were any in his Family) by his Mother he was descended from the *Beauforts*; for the Lady *Margaret*, Countesse of Richmond, was daughter and heire to Sir *Iohn de Beaufort* Duke of Somerset, and Grand-child to *Iohn* of *Gaunt* by *Katherine* the wife of *Otho de Swinford*, which *Iohn de Beaufort*, was created Duke of Somerset by *Henry* the fift, his Wife was the daughter, and at length the heire of Sir *Iohn Beauchamp* of Bletso, and the widow of Sir *Oliver Saint-Iohn* when he married her: But the Earle of Richmond, by his Grand-mother *Katherine* Queene of England, was descended from the Kings of France, and I have seene in a Pedigree (drawne after he was King) derived from the ancient Kings & Princes of Brittaine. *Polidore* saith, he was *Ex fratre Nepos* to King *Henry* the sixt, who cal'd him Nephew, and he the King, *Avunculum nostrum* (our Uncle) insteed of *Patruum*, as it is in the Records of Parliament, *Ann.* 1. of *Henry* the seventh, but not his Nephew, as wee erroneously now take it, that is his German younger Brothers Sonne, for then he had beene a true Masculine Issue of the house of Lancaster and Royall blood of England.

But

The Charter of *H.4* for entayling the Crowne.

I This Charter saw in the hands of Sir *Rob. Cotton*, & from it tooke these Summary notes. The Noblenes and Family of H.E. of Rich. *Glover*.

1413.

Polid. lib. 25. So King *R.* 2. called *Iohn* of *Gaunt Avunculum nostrum*, Rec. in Tower; But that was the fault of the barbarous Latine Clerks, not knowing the difference between *patruos* & *avunculos*.

But he was Nephew to him by his Brother Uterine, *Edmond Teudor* Earle of Richmond, the sonne of *Owen Teudor* or *Meridock*, and of Queene *Katherine*, daughter of *Charles* the sixt King of France, and widow of *Henry* the fift King of England; which the French well knew, and gave him the better esteeme for it, but those Honours were obscure Additions to him that must not goe lesse then for a Prince of the house of Lancaster, and so of England, which passed with such vulgar credit in France, that *Du Tillet* mistooke *Iohn* Duke of Somerset, Father of *Margaret* Countesse of Richmond, for the true and lawfull Sonne of *Iohn de Gaunt, &c.* by his first Wife *Blanch Plantagenet*, Daughter and Heire of the Earle and Earledome of Lancaster. *Philip de Comines* Lord of Argent, had better intelligence of his Pedigree and Title which he gives us thus. In his Booke *Le Recuerl. des Rangs, &c.* Part 2.

Il n'avoit croix, ny pile, ne n'ull droit (Come Ie croy) a la Coronne d'Angleterre: And this expresses, he had no great opinion of either, though he were then King when this was writ. But let us suppose him lawfully from that Duke of Lancaster, his claime must stand excluded whilst the house of Yorke survived, for *Richard Plantagenet*, Duke of Yorke, and King of England designat, by Act of Parliament holden 39 yeare of King *Henry* the sixt, to whom these Titles of Prince of Wales, Duke of Cornwall, Earle of Chester, and Protector of England, were given by the three Estates in that Parliament, descended from the Daughter and Heire of the second Sonne of King *Edward* the third. (For as before, so still I leave the Infant *William* of Hatfield without the Catalogue) and King *Henry* the fourth and his Progeny, descended from the third Sonne; and King *Henry* the sixt, being the best of the house of Lancaster then living, did acknowledge in that Parliament, the Title of *Richard* Duke of Yorke, the onely lawfull and just Title, so consequently next and better then that of Lancaster or any other; and before any *Beaufort* or their Heires, the Issue of the two daughters of *Iohn* Duke of Lancaster, *Philip* and *Katherine* (married to the King of Portugall and Castile) were to be preferr'd if Forraigne Titles be not excluded by Parliament. But the Earle of Richmond, measuring his owne height, by the advantage of a tumultuary and indisposed time, and finding his Lancastrian pretence, began to have a popular retinew, he was now incompatible of any others precedency and propinquity for those great ones that led him by the hand unto the Action, layd the line by their owne corrupted hopes and feares of the successe, therefore would not let the fortune of their expectation faint in him. Bishop *Morton* steered much in the course of their Affaires, and was a great Oracle to the Earle, who was noted too partiall and credulous, especially where he believed the persons of any honesty, vertue, or learning, for which his fame yet beares some staines of *Morton, Dudley, Empson, Bray, Vrswike, Knevett, &c.* for there be two extreames observed in the Councells of Princes, one when the Prince is subject to follow the councells of evill men; the other, when the Prince is

Philip Plant. Lyonel Plant. D. of Clarence

too opinionated to consult with Counsell, such an one as was *Charles*, the hardy Duke of Burgundy, so opinionated and overweening of his owne wisedome and judgement, that he under-thought all mens else, which wide conceit of his hath left this Monument.

Pe. Heuterus. Ioh. Megerus.

Carolus pugnax aliorum consilia & rationes (ne dicam) sequi vix audire volebat, ignominia loco habens ab alijs discere, & judicavit, se proprio cerebro omnia concilia habere recondita.

And to give us yet further character of Bishop *Morton*, Sir *Thomas Moore* (sometimes his Master) tels us, his best inclinations were swaid to the dangerous positions and rules of pollicie, and Doctor *Iohn Hird* in his metricall History of England, brings him in an Ambodexter and observer of fortune, one while yorkeizing another while Lancastrizing, thus delivering himselfe:

Si Fortuna meis fauisset partibus olim,
Et gnato Henrici sexti diadema dedisset,
Edwardi nunquam venissem regis in aulam,
Sed quia supremo stetit hac sententia Regi,
Henrico auferre, ac Edwardo reddere sceptrum,
Tanta mea nunquam lasit dementia mentem,
Vt sequerer partes regis victi atque sepulti,
Adversus vivum, &c.

Which may be thought well said by a meere Politician, But from a friend it wants something of a Christian, for true friendship and piety will owne us in the blackest adversity and silence of the grave, as the divine *Ariosto* hath something neare observed in this elegant *Stanza*.

Ariost. cant. 19.

Nessun puo super du chi sia amato
Quando felice in sula rrota si ede,
Pere ch' hai veri, & ifiniti amici alato,
Chi mostran tuti, una medessima fede,
Se poi si cangia in tristo il he'sto stato,
Volta la turba adulatrice il piede,
Et quel di cu or' ama riman' forte,
Et ama il suo amico doppo la morte.

No man whilst he was happy ever knew
Assuredly of whom he was belov'd,
For then he hath both feigned friends and true,
Whose faith seemes both alike till they be prov'd,
But he is left of all the flattering Crew
When from his happy state he is remov'd,
But he who loves in heart, remaines still one,
And loves his friend when he is dead and gone:

Doctor

Doctor *Mortons* aimes were drawne from other rules which with good *Alacrity*, made him Archbishop, and Lord Chancellour of England, and put him the next list into a Cardinallship, and then he stood on tiptoes by the King, according to the Roman Marshalling of states for in the Popes list of ranges and presence, his holinesse is the first, then the Emperour, next a Cardinall, then a King: and in this, Sir *Tho. Moore* notes the extremity of his pride, to abuse his wisdome and piety, which otherwise might have kept him and his memory unsullyed in these preferments, so much our vices impostumate our fames, hypocrisie leaving the scarre but of a deformed cure upon it at best.

But Doctor *Goodwin* Bishop of Hereford, presents him nearer (as it were) in his Domesticke nature, and reports when Doctor *Morton* was Archbishop of Canterbury, he exacted and extorted a far greater Summe of money from the Clergy of his Diocesse then was ever before, and for his private Commodity (which he covetously sought) brought certaine Leames or bigger Ditches to his owne grounds about Wisbitch, from the River Nine, which was before navigable, and of much publike use, but hath since served for little or none. And *Iohn Stow* saies he was the stirrer up of those great and grieveous taxes which raised the people to Armes and Rebellion: These notes of his naturall dispositions stucke like wennes upon the face of his Religion, and from that mind, where by-affections justle Religion and conscience out, how hazardous may the Power and Counsell of such be, to the inclinations of a wise Prince: but this Prelate made his so Canonicall, and fitted them to the times, and his Mr temper, that they deceived not his expectation, but brought him home to his ends, and to the favor of a provident & wise Prince; that he was so, the world must justly avow, and in all his actions, we may see him, of a safe and contracted wisedome, governed by a most cautelous spirit, as great a husband of those vertues he had, as of his Glory, not too modest, (if I be not much mistaken) to heare of either; of both which he hath left us pious tastes.

Fra. Goodwin in Catalogo *Episcoporum*.

Iohn Stow.

But the most surviving addition of memory, is that great example of Majesty, and her Sexe, Queene *Elizabeth*, who was said to be like this King her Grandfather, as well in composition of qualities, as favour, and lineaments, that she was his lively and perfect Image; and to use an even hand in the extention of himselfe and his power, it must not be denyed, (how far off soever he was at first) after the Crown yeilded to him, he was the true proprietary of all the Rights and Titles which carried it, or had dependency thereon; and to colleague all in a full and perfect strength, the Title of Yorke was confirmed to him by marriage of *Elizabeth Plantagenet* Eldest Daughter of *Edward* 4, Prince or head of that Family, to whom the Title of Lancaster instantly escheated as he was King, which before was in controversie, or in nubibus, or Abeyance (as our Lawyers say) for no man being a Subject, how Capitall and chiefe a Judg, or of what judicatory power soever, could give a definitive Sentence, in any ambiguous cause or Act

Qu. Elizabeth.

of

of the King: but the King himselfe which is an ancient and Authentique paragraph in the Laws of England, as learned Judge *Bracton* affirmeth.

Brac. li. 2. Cap. 16.

De Chartis Regijs, & de factis regum non possunt Iusticiari disputare, nec si disputatio oriatur possunt eam interpretari, sed in dubijs & obscuris, & ubi aliqua dictio contineat duos intellectus domini Regis erit expectanda interpretatio & voluntas, &c.

The reason is given in the Bookes of the Civill and Imperiall Lawes peremptorily, *quia de principali Iudicio non est disputandum.* So that Controversie, whether the Beauforts or Sommersets were of the House of Lancaster, and capable of the Crowne or no, could not be determined untill there came a competent Judge, a King, and King of England, who by that vertue and power decreed to himself, the Title of Lancaster, with all the Royall Apurtenances confirmed by the Pope, as proper to him, and then the Writers both English and French, had some colour to say he was *de la ligne de Lancastre, & caput gentis regalis & Princeps familia Lancastriensis.*

But the Chancellour *Morton*, by a more happy & plausible insinuation, termed the Marriage an union of Yorke and Lancaster, and not improperly, nor without a very favourable acceptance to the King (at least in the beginning of his Raigne,) though after (as may be observed,) he thought those attributions, but small wyers to hold the weight and consequence of his Crowne, nay, so slender was his Affiance, (or rather none at all) in his Titles of Yorke and Lancaster, much lesse of Sommerset, that he seemed tacitly to wave and quit them, and stucke to that of his Sword and Conquest; For the more publike vote and knowledge whereof, there was at his Coronation, Proclamations made with these Titles, *Henricus Rex Anglia jure divino, jure humano, & jure Belli, &c.* which the Barons could not fancy, nor condiscend to, though the King peremptorily avowed and maintained he might justly assume and beare it, having as a Conquerour entred the Land, fought for the Crowne, and wonne it; they answer as peremptorily, that he was beholding to them, both for his Landing and Victory, and by their permission had that faire and prosperous footing upon their Coasts, not by any stroke of his French, which were not so many as the least Legion of the Romans, and had found but bloudy entertainment by the valiant English, if ever they had landed, besides the instigation of a mortall hatred against the Invader, never to be extinguished but with an utter expulsion and destruction, which they humbly prayed might be worthy of his consideration, and not to take from his loving people the just due of their Affections, by ascribing so much of his victory to the French, or his Welsh Sword, Sith, they voluntarily opened their Armes and Country, to receive him and put the Crowne upon his head, that this was their free and voluntary Act they hoped he could not forget: and if so, why would he make such an Atchievement, a Conquest, or a purchase of the Sword, tearmes of a most harsh and disonant sound to the English, who reputed them as Barbarous and Tyrannicall, their ends and events to enslave them,

King *H.* 7. only affected the Title *de jure Belli.*

their Goods and Fortunes, under a Licentious power that might Act and will any thing: *Quicquid Victor audet, aut Victus timet?* The examples of the conquering Gothes and Vandalls, Longobards, in Italy and Spaine, Saxons and Normans in England; and lately the Spaniards in America, with many other cruell Lords estated onely by their unjust Armes and Swords, being fresh and bleeding instances, that when but mentioned, stirre up thoughts of horrour and detestation of the Swords Title. But the more they oppos'd it, the more he is constant to have it assented by the *Pope* with his Title of Lancaster, which he thought would be a stronger bridle to check all murmurs, but yet indeavoured it not directly and disertly, but under a close and borrowed prætext, the out-side of his Embassage being only to obtaine a dispensation and pardon for his marriage, prætending a feare of Incest, his Wife being his Kins-woman; *Et quarto Consanguinitatis & forsan affinitatis gradu*, which Pope *Innocentius* the eight granted the first yeare of his raigne; and afterward (upon what occasion I cannot say) he renewed the same suit to Pope *Alexander* the sixt, who confirmed and ratified the pardon and dispensation made by his Predecessors in the fourth yeare of this Kings Raigne.

Senec.

An. Dom. 1486.

An. Dom. 1490.

But it is observable, that the Pope herein taketh not upon him to confer or give any new Titles; neither did the King publikely solicite the Pope to confirm these two Titles, his Embassador had that particular in his private instructions: So that by this, the Pope seemeth only to make a rehearsall of those Titles as due and proper to him before, and the Titles *de jure Belli*, & *de jure Lancastriæ*, seem'd not as any matters or subject of the Bull, but rather some desire the Pope had, to expresse a love and honour to the King, and that he was pleased, *Ex proprio & mero motu & certa scientia sua*, to make such honourable memoriall of all the Majesticall Titles in the Kings right, as the more stately embroideries to his glorious Letters of Apostolicall indulgence, for the dispensation of the said marriage conveyed, and in these words:

I have seene this Bull in the Cabinet of Sir *Rob. Cotton.*

Hic Rex Angliæ, de domo Lancastriæ originem trahens, ac qui notorio jure, & indubitato proximo successionis titulo & Prælatorum & procerum Angliæ Electione & concessione &c. Etiam de jure Belli est Rex Angliæ.

The Popes Charter for the Title of Lancast. *Et de jure Belli, &c.* for the dispensing with the Kings incestuous marriage.

After, for the more cleare reparing and curing all flawes and defects of Titles, the Pope addeth this gracious clause; *Supplemusq; omnes, & singulos defectus, tam juris, quam facti, si qui intervenerint in regno dicto.*

And then in the end, not in the front, this Bull is intituled, *Pagina confirmationis nostræ, approbationis, pronunciationis, constitutionis, declarationis, suppletionis, monitionis, requisitionis, prohibitionis, Benedictionis, inhibitionis, & excommunicationis, & Anathematizationis in quoscunque, qui presumpserint, infringere, vel ausu temeritatis, contravenire his literis Apostolicis.*

For all this must be held, and thought to be done *Autoritate Apostolica,*

stolica, i. by the Authoritie of the Apostles, Saint *Peter* and Saint *Paul*.

And thus the King received of the Pope the two Titles, *De Domo Lancastriæ*, and *De Iure Belli*, without any seeking or solicitation (as wee are led to credit) for there appeareth not any expresse suit or motion by the King to that purpose, though by circumstances and probabilitie it was preferred under hand, for the other things were but of slight request and no necessitie, nor obnoxious to any danger; when those two Titles were the present markes, his aime was strongly and mainly directed to. Though I must confesse, after a while, he was as lightly satisfied in these (notwithstanding the Popes thunder and lightning, added to them,) as in the Titles of Yorke and Lancaster, which he discovered, and not obscurely, when he moved the Estates in his first Parliament, to grant an Estate Hereditary and entail'd of the Crowne and Kingdome, with all the Appurtenances, to the Heires of his body: beyond this he could not require much, nor they give, which was unanimously condiscended unto, as a gift of a new Title confirmed by their Act; the Copy whereof I have transcribed (where I come to rehearse the Titles of our Soveraigne Lord the *King* that now is.) Nor is the Devination of this peece so darke, but that the cause may be guessed at, why he held himselfe not safe in the Titles of Yorke and Lanacster, of Beaufort and Somerset already toucht at, but may fall more seasonably elsewhere into our Stories, without confounding it with Historologies, and presenting matters out of their time and place; my purpose onely being, to take so much light from the Story of *Henry* the seventh as shall but properly conduce to the true shadowing and proportioning of *King Richards*, being necessarily inforced to inculcate such matters as may seeme of no present conclusion; yet loosing their observation, wee shall want the knowledge of many things much pertinent to the credit and honour of *King Richard* and his Actions: To which, according to the Order and Affaires of time, I am now to come againe.

The second invasion of the E. of Rich.

And here, upon our accompt, wee shall find it neare upon tenne months since the Duke of Buckingham was suppressed, and the Earl of Richmond driven from Poole with the storme, who was now againe very busie raysing fresh preparations in France, and *King Richard* upon the intelligence, as stickling to Levy Souldiers, and reinforce all his Havens and Frontier places. But the Earle of Richmond found it not so easie a matter now as at first, to draw a party and concurrence from France, having sped so ill in his former undertakings, which indeed struck a great discouragement in the expectation of all his Favourers, and made his welcome the colder to the Duke of Brittaine; the rather also, because he had beene with the French *King* before he came to him, which was taken but ill, although the Earle could not otherwise doe, being forc't upon the Coasts of Normandy; And comming into the Road at Deipe landed, to refresh

fresh himselfe and company: From thence he intended to Roan, which being so neare Paris, ingaged him thither to the King, being (as *Philip de Comines* saith, followed in a very honourable Port by 500 Englishmen) In his stay there (to shew us how much interest a provident and active spirit hath in fortune) he so heightned and sweetned his behaviour to the Court, as conciliated the favour and respect of the Greatest and Noblest Persons to him. But most happily, the faire opinion and esteeme of the Princely Lady *Anne de France*, eldest Sister to King *Charles* the eight, who had such an influence upon him in his minoritie, that she out-pitched *Lewis* Duke of Orleance, chiefe Prince of the Blood. In envy or mis-like whereof, he tooke Armes, and raysed a Civill Warre in France (as *Iohn Tillet* and others write) she was wife to *Pierce de Bourbon* Lord of Beaujen, after Duke *de Bourbon*, but Beaujen being his most stately and honourable Signiory, he was called *Mounsieur de Beaujen*; and this Lady had so flexible an inclination to the Earle of Richmonds Cause, that she importuned the King to aide him with a good summe of mony and 3000 men, but odde fellowes. For *Philip de Comines* saith, they were *trois mille hommes les plus meschants que lux peut trouver*, no better then Rogues and Trewans, men of base qualitie and as low courage. Whilst these were Levying, the Earle (thriftie of all opportunities, and as diligent to adde what advantage of time and ayde he could) visits the Duke of Brittaine to the same purpose. The Duke propounds it to his Councell, which *Peter Landois*, his Treasurer and chiefe Counsellour objects against, with this reason, That if the Enterpize succeeded well, yet the event must fall out unhappily and ill to him, the Earle having now interested himselfe to the favour and assistance of *Charles* King of France: And this would be the first linke of so strong an ingagement, that the Earle and his Confederacy must be lost to Brittaine when he came to be King, being respectively tyed to lend the King of France ayde against them, if any cause should happen, which the King of France had a prepared stomack for, and had not beene nice to seeke any provocation that might countenance a Quarrell against the Dutchy of Brittaine, which was beyond his spanne, so long as they continued in League with England; that being untwisted, and France and England Contracted, how easie was it for the French to envade and swallow up both him and his Dukedome. To make the present advantage (therefore) as profitable, as safe, his advice was to stay the Earle; the Duke knowing his Coffers at that time very lanke, and that the King of England would offer well for him, approved the Counsell, and resolved to be led by *Landois* (whose respects (notwithstanding) were very affectionate to the Earle) But whether by the secret caution of some friends, or suggested to him by his Better *genius*, Sure it is, by some unknowne meanes he had knowledge of it; and yet this was determined but at night, and designed for the morning; But before midnight, or the knowledge of their flight, he and twelve Gentlemen his followers, had left Vannes, and recovered

Comines pag. 535.

Aniow (under the French *Kings* protection) from thence to the French Court againe, the *King* being still very pliable and constant to his promise concerning those French forces under his owne charge. The next thing he works at, is how to enlarge the Earl of Oxford out of the Castle of Hammes, committed thither by *Edward* the fourth (and in this he uses, or rather followed indeed) the contrivement of Doctor *Morton*, who held good quarter with the Earle of Oxford, and by his frequent visits had a familiar and easie doore open'd, which the Earl readily tooke the opportunitie of, least it might be shut againe by some miscarriage, for Richmond thought or found the constitution of his Designe not a little strengthned by the Earle of Oxfords con. federacy: nor did he mistake himselfe in his accompt, when he set him downe of speciall use, knowing him a man of an eminent power; wisely and valiantly temper'd: And to give him the stronger presumptions and confidence) one that most mortally hated *Edward* the fourth, and all the house of Yorke: To begin therefore an Obligation, the Earle of Richmond makes a Complementall journey to Hammes, where the Earle of Oxford was then, under the charge of Sir *Iames Blound*; He finds all honourable and respective entertainment with fit libertie, and occasion to propound himselfe unto the Earle, who had beene partly prepar'd by Doctor *Morton*, and therefore met him the nearest way, engaging himselfe solely to the premises, and (by vertue of an indefatigable confidence) sets upon his *Keeper*, winnes him to the Faction, and to Paris with them. By which time, all preparations were in readinesse; and whilst they make this stay in the French Court, the Earle of Richmond receives a faire excuse and protestation from the Duke of Brittaine, with offer of Auxiliary Forces: This supply came very acceptably, and however he resented the Dukes late purpose upon him, his wisedome told him, he must now convert his anger into thanks, which he returns with a reciprocall Protestation and Order, to send the Troopes to Harflew where his Shipping lay, and was the Rendezvous for his Souldiers.

In the end of July 1485. he tooke leave of the *King* and his most Noble Cousin Madam *de Beaujen*, departing for the Port of Harflew in Normandy, where he met with two thousand Brittaines from the Duke honourably accommodated. But by the way he made some stay at Roven, and had newes which much distemper'd him, That the Lady *Elizabeth* was forthwith to be married to *King Richard*, this quickned his hast for England, presuming, his landing would forbid the Banes, otherwise he might sit downe with folded hands, for upon this marriage insisted the maine hope and consequence of his Fortune; without her, all his great prætexts would faint, yet seemed to heare it, as a thing that could not concerne him so much, having so present and provident a wit, that in any chance he wanted not Councell and determination in himselfe for all Fortunes; instantly resolving, to apply his suit to her Sister the Lady *Cecily*:

but ere he could perfectly fashion these intents, they were also counterchecked, by the next packet, which assured him the Lady *Cecily* was lately married: neither did that (after some Collection) seeme much to discompose him, but quickely, varying his disposition to his fortune, he would now fixe himselfe upon some choice in Brittaine; Amongst his nobler friends (for the most part Welsh-men) and treates about a Daughter of Sir *William Herberts*, a Gentleman of a Noble Allyance and principall power in the South part of Wales: who had married the Eldest Daughter not long before to the Earle of Northumberland, to whom the Earle of Pembrooke (by a new created friendship betwixt them) imbosomes the whole designe, and presses his Comprobation in it; for by this meanes it was presumed, the greatest part of Wales would fall under their Command: which had been no small addition to a Banished mans fortune. Whilst those things were in their mould, Doctor *Morton* gave him such assurance (by Letters) of the Countries readinesse to receive him, that it was thought best to take the advantage of landing there, and in the Month of July, they loose from Harfleu, and safely arived at Milford Haven in Pembrookeshire, his native Country: after some refreshing, he Marches to a Town called Haverford West, and was entring amongst his Brittish kindred, who welcomed him as a Prince, descended from their ancient Princes of Wales, (the Country generally very Noble and loving to their friends) whilst he continued amongst them, Sir *Rice ap Thomas*, Sir *Walter Herbert*, Sir *John Savage*, Sir *Gilbert Talbot* (who drew his young Nephew the Earle of Salop into this Action with him) and divers others of all qualities, brought, or sent their Forces; his Army thus strong and united, he passes the Severne, and Marches to Lichfield, purposing to hold on to London, if the King had not interposed it, who though he lay at Nottingham when the Earle landed, and while he marched through Wales, had constant Spies upon him. But as no Policie, or Law can secure their faith, that thinke they may dispense with it, so all Benefits are too narrow, where Ambition and Ingratitude urges merit; and to shew there is not much of our Fate in our own providence, when this King thought the Nobility most firmly cimented to his side, and was to put himself upon their constancy, they make a present and general defluxion to the other; But he had heightned and contracted his Resolution and judgement, to the greatnesse of his Cause, and was not now to be outbid by Chance, or danger: The next day (which was Sunday about Evening) passing through Leicester in open Pompe, the Crowne Royall on his head, with him *John* Duke of Norfolke, Marshall of England, the Earle of Surrey, the Earle of Westmorland, the Viscount *Lovell*, and other of the Nobility and Gentry at Redmore Heath, the Armies came to an Interview, and put themselves in Array; the next morning early, there was some conference held in the Kings Tent, by those Peeres, and others of principall trust, who gave him particular information of all those, secretly revolted; and it much amazed him the

Leicest. inquit, Rex Richardus, cum maxima Pompa portans diadema, in capite. Chron. Croy.

Earle of Northumberland was one, to whom he had ever been most constant and forward in his respects and favours; therefore, where he had conferred so much, he suspected little. But no Obligations are Religious, if not held so: and although in the conflict he stood but as neutrall, yet the suddainesse and example of it, drew many from the King, even at the instant, when he was ready to Arme himselfe, yet this was not of so great and sensible amazement unto him, as the Lord *Stanleys* defection, who in pledge of his faith, had left his Son *George Stanley*, whilst his wife (the Earles mother) had made her subtill perswasions of stronger tye, and subinduced him to the Lancastrian side, which he ayded with 26000, men, if *Phillip de Commines* be not mistaken: for our stories have but five thousand. But it was a very great defection, and made the Earles Army far stronger, so that the chiefest point of Consultation now, was how to preserve him by flight, and the recovery of some strong hold, untill the tempest had scattered, or spent its violence, which they conceived could not be long, if the Campe brake up, and once dissolved. But no Argument could fasten on him, though the benefit of a swift Horse was offered at his Tent doore, nor the fatality and portent of Prodigies, related by his friends, as presaging some inevitable Calamity, and that Propheticall Prediction.

Iack of Norfolke be not too bold,
For Dickon thy Master is bought and sold.

These things aggravated, the weakenesse of his Army objected, Counsels, Perswasions, Terrours, Prodigies, Prophesies, could not make him heare, so fatally resolute he stood in the jealousie and reputation of his Honour and Valour, peremptorily protesting he would rather adventure Life, Crowne, and Fortunes, than his honour to a cowardly and sinister construction; this might taste of a desperate will, if he had not afterwards given an apodixis in the battaile, upon what plat-forme he had projected and raised that hope, which as it had much of danger in it, so of an inconcusse and great resolution, and might have brought the odds of that day to an even bet; for knowing the Earle to be thirsty and Appetent after Glory and Renowne, but of an unpractised skill in Warre, and as inferiour in courage to him, he had projected (in manner of Stratagem) so soone as the Armies approached ready for the Charge, to advance himselfe before his Troopes, and give the Earle, being Generall of his Forces, the signall of a Combate. And to provoke and single him with a more glorious invitation, he wore the Crowne Royall upon his head, the fairest marke for Valour and Ambition; *Polidore* saies he wore it, thinking that day should either be the last of his life, or the first of a better, which may aswell be a reason of his wearing it three daies before at Leicester, when he rode from thence to Bosworth. But doubtlesse, by it he intended chiefly, that the people might see & know him to be their King.

Why K. Rich. wore the Crowne at Bosworth.

King: and those that stood Armed against him, looking upon that Imperiall evidence, where their own hands and voyces had set it, should by the awe and Soveraignty of it, consider how lately they had avowed him their Lawfull King, and by what Pledges of their Faith and Allegeances, they stood solemnly bound to defend him and his Title in it, against all other; what ever was his mystery, it rendred him a valiant and confident Master of his Right; and in the constancy of hope and resolution, he gives order for the Battaile. The Armies confronted, and whilst the Alarme, and every blow, began to be hot and furious, forth breakes King *Richard* towards the Earle, wasting him by a signall, who seemed readily to accept it, and pricking his Horse forward came on very gallantly, as if but one Genius had prompted their Spirits, and Ambition: for a good Author testifieth that *Comes Richmondiæ directè super Regem Ricardum, &c.* But his cariere soone faltred, and *Mars* became Retrograde, it being but a nimble traine, to draw the King on to some disadvantages, or else he liked not his furious approach, for suddenly he makes a halt, and with as much credit as he could (& no harme) recovered the Vanguard of his Army, whither *Richard* pursued him, with so much speed and fiercenesse, that he forc't him to his Standard. And now, high in bloud and anger (to see his Valour deluded by such a politicke Bravery) with his Sword makes way, and with his owne hand slew Sir *Charles Brandon* Standerd-Bearer, thinking to have made the next blow as fatall to the Earle, but the confluence of Souldiers interjecting, rescued him, Sir *Iohn Cheney* being one of the foremost, whom the King stroke from his Horse to the Earth; But Charged and invironed, with multitudes (that like a storme came on him) Valiant *Richard* falls, the Sacrifice of that day, under their cruell Swords, so rabious in their execution, as if his body must suffer more, because they could not kill his better part, mangling and wounding his dead Corps, whilst it lies drentcht in gore.

Chron. *Croy.*

S. *Wil. Brandon* Father to *Charles Brandon*, afterward Duke of *Suff.*

> *Et Lupus, & turpes instant morientibus ursi,*
> *Et quæcunque minor nobilitate fera est.*

Ovid. Trist. l. 2. Eleg. 5.

As Curs in their kenells will bite and teare the skin of those beasts which in the fields they durst not barke at;

> *Occidit in bello miseranda cæde Richardus,*
> *Crinibus attractus, dum ferro sæviat hostis.*

Dr *Iohn Bird. in Hist. Angl.*

And after all (to compleate their barbarisme) threw his body behind one upon a Jade, and so conveyed it to Leicester. A story to be thought incredible, at least to charitable and modest eares, and highly upbraided by the happier and Christian fame of *William* the Conquerour, who severely punished a Souldier, but for hacking the thigh of King *Harold* after he was dead, though an Usurper and his perfidious enemy; with all noblenesse causing the body to be deli-

vered

Mathew Paris
Henry Huntington.

vered to his Mother for an honourable interment, which was solemnly celebrated in his own Abbey at Waltham.

Henry of Richmond Crowned in the Feild.

The Battle thus fought and won, the Victor was Crowned in the field, with that Crown *K. Rich.* wore, which the L. *Stanley* put upon his head, & salutes him *King*, by the stile of *Hen. 7. K.* of England, &c. And *Henry* Earle of Richmond, Son of *Edmund ap Meredith ap Teudor* (alias of Hadham) Earle of Richmond, and of *Margaret* Daughter and Heire of *Iohn Beaufort* Duke of Sommerset, attained to the Crowne, and had the easier ascent by the oversight and remissnesse of *Richard*, in that Catastrophe of his Raign, who gave too much opportunity and scope to the actings of his Enemies, when they were under his power, and arme. And in the Fortune of his judgment (at the closing Scene) that did not better presuppose his Enemy too prudent, and reserved to trust the advantage he had, upon so sharpe and single an hazzard; But *Richard* beleeving he had the odds in courage and monomachie of him, which probably might make him Master of the Combate, and so of the Field, (the straite being so desperate too) resolved rather to trust to the Fate of his owne Valour, then the chance of an uncertaine escape; a resolution not so rash and overweening, as commendable, if we looke upon the very aymes and necessity of it, neither is it new or improper for Princes to demand the tryall of campe fight, or single Combate, personaly in their Armies, and to the Generals in their absence; *William* the Conquerour challenged King *Harold*; Before that, a Combate was fought betweene *Edmund Ironside*, and *Canute* the Danish King, for the whole Kingdome of England; our *Richard* the first, and *Edward* the first, in Palestine proffered the like to some of the Pagan Princes; so did *Edward* the third, *Henry* the fifth, with the Kings of France:

The Challeng of the 5 King of Scots to *Tho.* Duke of Norfolke.

In the last Age, the valiant Prince, *Iames* the fifth of Scotland, in Person challenged *Thomas* Lord *Howard* Duke of Norfolke, Generall for the *King* of England, who accepted it; But the King into his Demands, would have the Country or Lands then in Controversie, to be made *Brabium victoris*, which was without the Generalls power to engage, being the Inheritance of the *King* his Master, but proffers better Lands of his owne upon the Combate, which was not accepted, so that concluded nothing.

The better end of these Challenges and Combates, being at first, levelled from Mercy, and Piety, for by this single adventure, the Innocent bloud of Armies was (more then stanched) preserved; Forraigne Stories brings this home to us, and highly Characters their Kings and Generalls in the like examples, which this Age draws a Curtaine before, as not fit for imitation, making too desperate a wound in a setled State and Succession; the (first who rendred that or some more Politike reason) for Princes not to adventure themselves, was *Phi.* the 2 K. of Spain, (as a late writer ascribeth) but is mistaken: For the more ancient Histories of Syria and Persia, mentions some Kings that refrain'd from Warres long before; as *Herodotus*, *Diodo-*

Princes go not to Campe.

rus, *Trogus Pompeius* tells us: But let us take measure from that, Times, Wisedome, Valour, Policy, &c. to this, and wee shall find them but tottering foundations of States which cannot uphold themselves, or obvert the least Decree of God when he intends to scourge or alter kingdomes; for where such vicissitudes are destin'd, the Councells and faculties of men must be darkned, and there will fall out all concurrences and advantages to further that purpose; So in the extirpation and transferring of Families, the Potter in *Ieremy*, breaking one Jarre to make another, whose fatall commutations should extimulate the pietie of our natures, and make us modest censurers of their events: For as wee see things but through a Cloud, whilst wee measure them by accidents, so wee intrude on Gods providence, judging mens actions in their successe, while wee over-act our owne. Of such a composition was the ill-wishers of King *Richard*, who forgot him not in his grave, but indeavoured to be equally cruell to his memory: And in November following a Parliament was holden, in which he was attainted of High Treason; a straine very high to make him guiltie of that, being a King, he could not commit. By the same figure may others, who were stiled chiefe ayders and assistants of King *Richard* in the Battaile of Bosworth, as Sir *Iohn Howard* Duke of Norfolke, &c. though some would have him retired from the Court all King *Richards* raigne. But Sir *Thomas Moore* affirmes, He was constantly with him and neare his Counsells, Sir *Thomas Howard* Earle of Surrey, Sonne and heire apparent to the Duke; *Francis Lovel*, Viscount *Lovel*, Sir *Walter Devereux*, Lord *Ferrers* of Chartley, Sir *Iohn de la Souch*, Sir *Robert Harrington*, *Richard Charleton*, *Richard Ratcliffe*, *William Berkley*, *William Catesby*, *Thomas Broughton*, *Iohn Buck*, *Humphrey Stafford*, *Robert Midleton*, *Robert Brokenbury*, *Iohn Kendall*, Secretary to the King; *Walter Hopton*, *Ieoffry Saint-German*, *Roger Wake*, *Thomas Billington*, *William Sapcoate*, *William Brampton*, all Knights, and some Heralds at Armes, with divers other; an Act of Parliament being made, to disable and forejudge them of all manner of Honour, State, Dignitie; Also to forfeit all Mannors, Castles, Lordships, Hundreds, Franchises, Liberties, Advowsons, Priviledges, Nominations, Presentations, Tenements, Rents, Suits, Reversions, Portions, Annuities, Pensions, Rights, Hereditaments, Goods, Chattells, and Debts. These be the words of the Act, and if *jus*, then *jus summum* in all extremity.

Cruelties done to the body of King *Richard*. Noble Persons attainted by Parliament.

Sir *Tho. Moor*.

Parliament *ann.* 1. *H.* 7.

Those of note that were taken, lost their heads at Leicester two dayes after, being Saint *Bartholmews* day, and had a glimpse like that *Bartholmew* in France in our time; all such slaughters from thence call'd *Bartelmies*, and *Bartelemies*, simply in a perpetuall Stigma of that Butchery.

It is suggested, the Duke of Norfolke was slaine in the Battaile by the Earle of Oxford, and the Story of *Croyland* seemeth to say as much; *Comes Oxoniæ valentissimus miles in eam alam ubi Dux Norfol-*

The Duke of Norfolk slain by the Earl of Oxenford.

cia

cia constitutus erat in agro (de Redmore) tum Gallicorum tum Anglicorum militum Comitatu stipatus tetendit, &c.

The Earle of Surrey escapeth at Bosworth.

Amongst those that escaped the sad destiny of that day, was the Earle of Surrey, Sir *Thomas Howard*, Viscount *Lovel*, Sir *Thomas Stafford*, and his Brother *N. Stafford*, with many other Nobles and Gentlemen that got into Forraigne Countries and Sanctuaries, obscuring themselves till the storme and smart of that dayes memory were past. But some would maintain *Thomas* Earl of Surrey to be one of them that submitted to the new *King* at Bosworth immediately after the overthrow which must not be believed, if wee understand the composition of those times & affairs: for certaine it is, the Earl Richmond had peremptorily proscribed all those he had cause to feare or hate, whose names are partly in the Rowles, kept in the Chappell of the Convertites in Chancery-Lane, and partly omitted by the Scribes.

Now the Earle of Surrey, of all the rest, was so terrible and distastefull to him, there could be no excuse left for his life. And therefore let no man thinke he was taken or submitted, but tooke an happier season some moneths after. The Relation and truth is (by the warrant of one that well knew him, and the inter-passage of his Fortune) the Earle opportunely left the Field, but so wounded, that faintnesse and night constrain'd him to the house of a Gentleman not farre from Nottingham, and one that bare a faithfull respect to the Earle and his Family untill he was well recovered. In the meane time, that terrible Parliament held in the next November was concluded, and the Kings desires reasonably well appeased, in seeing the execution of his new Lawes past upon some of them. After which, (some small distance of time) followed a gracious pardon to all the offenders in that Cause, which proffered mercy, this Earle layd hold on, hoping to restore himselfe (by his submission) his offence, considered, being but an Act of Loyaltie to his Master. But this confidence sent him to the Tower, for though the violence of the storme appear'd well calm'd, yet the *King* retain'd some heavings of it in his thoughts: And this Imprisonment continued from his first yeare of raigne unto the fourth; and towards the beginning of that, being in the Tower with the Queene *Elizabeth* (to whom he was shortly after to be married) he tooke occasion to call for the Earle, (bearing still a gust of the same tempest in his brow) and challenged him upon the old quarrell, his service to the late Usurper & Tyrant, (as he usually termed *King Richard*) the Earle humbly moved his pardon, and more favourable consideration to the nature of his offence, which thousands more conceived to be but a due effect of their Liege duties, and Allegiance to a Prince so lawfully, and with all generall sufferance Crowned, whose Title he held himselfe bound to defend by the law of God and Nations, and would dye in defence of him and that Crowne, though he should find it upon a Stake: The *King* left him with a sterne and ruffling reply, but in cold blood

better

better acknowledged his integritie, and thought he would come of no lesse value to him, having the advantage to merit him by his pardon, which soone after he granted him; nor did the Earle loose ought of that opinion: Shortly after, being made of the Privie Councell, then Lieutenant or Governour of the North, and Generall against the Scots, whom he overthrew; as fatall was he to them at Flodden field, where he tooke their King in the time of *Henry* the eight, who made him High Marshall and Treasurer of England, and restor'd him to his Fathers Dukedome, the Inheritance of his Grand-mother *Mowbray*, being a man of such a happy direction in his carriage and wisedome, that all his Actions came home with prosperous successe, and accumulated what was sometime spoken of his great Ancestour *Hewardus*, of whom it was questioned, *Vtrum fœlicior an fortior esset*, so Fortunate and Honourable hath that house beene in the Service to this State; and in the infinite Alliance and Cognation, it holds with the most Ancient Families, the Extractions and propagations from *Mowbray*, *Warren*, *Bruce*, *Dalbery*, *Marshall*, *Segrave*, *Plantagenet*, *Brotherton*, *Bigot*, *Fitz-Alan*, *Matraver*, *Buckingham*, *Oxford*, and *Dacres*: The Father of which *Heward*, was *Leofrick* Lord of Burne, and the adjacent Countrey in Lincolneshire; his Mother was the Lady *Edina*, descended from the great *Oslac*, a Duke amongst the Easterlings in King *Edgars* time: In whose Family, I also find a Noble Kins-man of his called *Haward* (to note obiter) This *Haward* was of a Noble and Magnificent note, a goodly Personage, answer'd with an equall Strength and Valour; *Et nimium Bellicosus*, much, or too much devoted to *Mars*. He served in the Warres of Northumberland, Cornewall and Ireland; and after in the lower Germany, where he made up much of his Fame, and married a faire Lady called *Turfrida*, the Daughter of a Noble man in Flanders, where he continued untill the death of his Father called him home. About which time, *William* Duke of Normandy made his Conquest of this Kingdome, and had gratified *Iohannes Talbois* the French Counte, now Earle of Holland, with *Leoffricks* Countrey of Holland, in the Marshand; and the Counte very rudely had expuls'd the Lady his Mother, out of her Possessions and Dower. *Hawardus* set upon him with such forces as he could speedily rayse, tooke, and held him prisoner, in despight of the Conquerour, untill he redeem'd himselfe, and accompted for what he had done with a large summe of money. This drew those of the Nobility to the protection of his sword, which the Conquerour had chased out of their Countrey, who had fortified themselves in the Isle of Ely, and made *Hawardus* their Generall, where he built a Castle that a long time after had his name. But the Normans tooke that advantage to infest his Countrey, and put him againe to the recovery of it, which he so fortunately setled, that the Conquerour was contented to make him his, and hold him in good favour whilst he lived. He was buried in the Abbey of Croyland; Concerning his Issue by the the Lady *Turfrida*, there is mention

Scots overthrown by the E. of Surrey.

Ingulfus.

Lib. Eliensis.

onely of a Daughter named *Turfrida*, married to *Hugo Enermua*, Lord of Deeping: But circumstance will perswade us, he had other Issue, if wee consider him in the likelyhood of his strength and abilitie, and that divers continued of his Sir-name in that Countrey a long time after him, which makes it probable, he had a naturall Son, (at least, bearing his owne name of *Heward*) that next to him was the Originall Ancestor of this house of *Howards*. And let it not be thought any disparagement, for a Noble Family to be raysed from a naturall Issue; for many Princely Families have beene derived and propagated from naturall Sonnes, as was *Eneas*, *Romulus*, the Founders of the Roman Families; so was *Theseus* and *Themistocles*, as *Plutarch* writeth; others say as much of *Hercules*, *&c.*

The honour of Bastards.

Homer.
Livy.

The King of Spaine descended from *Henry de Trastamara*, base sonne of *Alphonsus* the Justicer, King of Castile. And who doth not honour the Princely Race of *William* the Conquerour, Bastard son to the Duke of Normandy? where was a more Heroicall man then *Robert* Earle of Glocester, base sonne of King *Henry* the first? The Earles of Warren descended from *Hamelin*, a base sonne of *Geoffry Plantagenet*, Earle of Aniow: The Noble *Herberts* are also said, to come from a base sonne of *Henry* the first.

And the Duke and Earles of Somerset (which followed the Red Rose) were the Off-spring of the *Beauforts*, naturall sonnes of *Iohn de Gaunt*.

For a further conjecture, why these *Howards* must be descended from *Hewardus* or *Herewardus* (for so some Writers call him; but (*Ingulfus*, who best knew him, constantly calls him *Hewardus*) both names may signifie in the Saxon or old Dutch, a chiefe Captaine of an Army, whom the Romans call'd *Imperator*.) And that the Titles and names of great Offices have given Sir-names to many Noble Families, wee have examples in plentie; Particularly the *Visconti* of Millan, the *Chamberlaines* of Normandy, the *Stewards* of Scotland, the *Butlers* of Ireland, and divers others, who had their Sir-names from the Offices of their Ancestours and Fathers; and the same presumption or argument may be for taking the Sir-name of *Howard*, and the Origine of their Family from *Hewardus*, the *Howards* from the time of *Heward*, dwelling in these Countries of Holland and Marshland, and were Lords of some Lands belonging to him, untill by their matches, with the Daughters and Heires of *Fitton*, *Tendring*, *Mowbray*, *Tillney*, *&c.* they became possessed in Norfolke, Suffolke, and Berkeshire, and were Lords sometime of Sunning-hill neare Windsor, and bore the Sir-name ever since (or with small interruption) the old Sir-name written *Heward*, or *Hereward* in Charters and Records, and *Howard* in Stories. But descend wee through the succession of those times to *William Haward*, Chiefe Justice in the Raigne of *Edward* the first, Grand-father to Sir *Iohn Howard*, Admirall of the North Fleet, in the Navall Warres of *Edward* the third; his Sonne Sir *Robert Howard* married the Daughter of the Lord

Lord *Scales*, and Sir *Iohn Howard* (who lived in the time of *Henry* the fourth, and dyed *Anno* 16. *Henry* the sixt) had two Wives, *Margaret* Daughter and Heire of Sir *Iohn Plaiz* Knight, by whom hee had *Eliza*: an onely Daughter, married to *Iohn de Vere* Earle of Oxford, who brought him a goodly part of the *Howards* Lands: Her Heires were married to *Latimer* and *Winckfield*, very fruitfull Families. His second Wife was the Daughter and heire of Sir *William Tendering* of Stoke-Nayland in Suffolke, by whom he had Sir *Robert Howard* his eldest Sonne; who married *Margaret Mowbray*, Daughter of a *Cadet* of the house of Lancaster, who became Co-heire with her Sister the Lady *Berkely*, Wife to *Thomas Mowbray* Duke of Norfolke, dead in Venice, and left his Sonne *Henry Haward* heire to *Haward* and *Mowbray*; and *Iohn Howard*, the sonne of *Iohn Howard*, was created Earle of Norfolke by King *Richard* the third, in the right of his Mother *Mowbray*, he married the Daughter of the Lord *Moulines*, and by her had *Thomas Howard*, the first *Howard* Earle of Surrey; this is he who survived the danger of Bosworth Field, and became afterwards Duke of Norfolke, from whom all the *Howards* now living are descended, whose Family hath beene so fruitfull to furnish this Kingdome with foure Dukes, many Earles, Viscounts, and Barons, three high Treasurers, six high or great Marshalls, tenne high Admiralls, with some honourable Custos of the Privie Seale, and sundry Chamberlaines of the Kings house; and one lately lived who had borne the Offices of high Constable, Lord Lieutenant, Lord high Steward, Marshall and Admirall of England, Lord Chiefe Justice in *Oyer* of the better part of this Kingdome, and Chamberlaine of the Royall house, a man honourable in his deportments, and fortunate in his undertakings; as at the great Marine Battells against all the Navall powers of Spaine, the Pope, and Princes of Italy, *Anno Domini* 1588. and in the siege of Gadys, *Anno Domini* 1596. *Sir Charles Howard.*

And this is the Grand-child of that *Thomas* Lord *Howard*, who for his better distinction and perpetuall honour is stiled *Triumphator Scotorum*. *Camden in Octad.*

I have strayed into this digression, as a gratefull tender of an acknowledgement I owe to that Illustrious Family, for their Noble Patronage aud Favour to my Ancestors, especially to that unfortunate Bucke and his Children, who withered with the White Rose, (bearing an Ancient and Hereditary love to the House of Yorke, and stood in good Credit and Favour with the King his Master) nor let this remembrance of him, and his obscured Family, seeme ostentation or vaine-glory, whilst I say no more then what other Histories dictate, which give him an able Character. Master *Camden Clarentius* (in his Immortall Brittannia,) deriveth this Sir *Iohn Bucke*, from Sir *Walter de Bucke* of Brabant, and Flanders, who had that Sir-name of great Antiquity from the Castle *de Bucke* in Lisle, a City and Frontire Towne in Flanders, where the Ancient Earles were *Camd. in Octa.*

Lodow. Guicci. du Paes. Baess.
The Ancientry of Buck.

M. Paris. M. Westminst. Radulphus de Cogeshall. Tho. Walsing.

accustomed much to reside, the ruines of this Castle remained in the late time of *Lodwicke Guicciardine*, who saith, he saw the Carcasse thereof: And this *Walter Bucke* was a Cader of the House of Flanders, employed and sent by the Prince (then Duke of Brabant, and Earle of Flanders) to King *Iohn*, with Auxiliary Troopes: *Roger Wondover* saith, *Walter Bucke, Gerard de Scottigni*, and *Godescalius, venerunt in Angliam cum tribus legionibus Flandrensium & Brabantianorum militum, &c.* and he did the King excellent service here (as many of our Historians report, for which the King bountifully rewarded him with Lands in Yorkeshire, and Northampton shire: And in Yorkeshire (where he made his Seat) he found an Ancient Family of the Sirname of *Bucke* of Bucton, in the Wapentake of *Bucrosse*, where that Family had anciently been, (for the name is a Saxon or Dutch word, and signifieth a Beech Tree, or Beech Wood) here *Walter* contracted alliance, and Married *Ralph de Bucke* his Eldest Sonne, to the Daughter and Heire of *Gocelinus de Bucke*, Grandchild to *Radolphus de Bucke*, who was a part Founder and Benefactour, to the Abbey of *Bredlington*, (as is mentioned in the Charter of *Henry* the first, made for the foundation of that Monastery) and from this *Walter*, descended *Iohn Bucke* Knight, who married a *Strelley*, and was so constant in his Affection, that (although she dyed in his best Age) he made a Religious Vow, and became a Knight of the Rhodes, his Armes are yet to be seene in the Ruines of the Hospitall of Saint *Iohns* neare Smithfield, and in the Church of Alhallows at the upper end of Lumbard Street, which was repaired and enlarged with the Stones brought from that demolished Cænoby: he lived, *sub rege Edvardo filio Regis Henrici*: as I have seene by the date of his deed in *Herthill, Anno* 1 *Ed.* 1. & *Anno* 22. *Ed.* 1.

From this Knight of the Rhodes descended Sir *Iohn Bucke*, who for his too much forwardnesse in charging a Fleet of Spaniards (without the leave of the Earle of Arundell Lord Admirall) was committed to the Tower, (testified by the Records there) *Anno* 13. *Richard* the second, *Lawrence Buck* his Son, followed *Edward Plantagenet* Duke of Yorke, and was at the Battel of AginCourt with him, when he was slaine: *Iohn Bucke* Knight, the Sonne of this *Lawrence*, married a Daughter and Heire of the House of *Staveley*, out of which are descended the Barons Parres of Kendall and Rosse, Queene *Katherine* (the last wife of King *Henry* the eighth) the Lord Parre Marquesse of Northampton, and the *Herberts* Earles of Pembrooke and Montgomery.

These *Bucks* residing for the most part at West-Stanton, and Herthill in Yorkeshire, and matched into the Families of *Strelley* or *Stirely* of Woodhall, *Thorpe*, *Tilney*, (then of Lincolnshire) and *Savill*, by which we have much Noble kindred; Sir *Iohn Bucke* for his service to the House of Yorke, especially at Bosworth, lost his head at Leicester, he married the Daughter of *Henry Savill*, by whom he had *Robert Bucke* and other Children, who were brought into the

South-

Southerne parts by *Thomas* Duke of Norfolke, where they have remained ever since; for the Children (being Orphans) were left in miserable estate by the Attainder of their Father; But the Duke bestowed two Daughters in marriage, one with the Heire of Buck, The other, with the Heire of *Fitz-Lewis*, very Ancient Families, from which Matches divers honourable and Noble Persons are descended. The Sonnes were, one a Souldier, the other, a Courtier, the third, a Priest; afterward the Duke bestowed *Robert Bucke*, the Eldest Sonne at Melford Hall in Suffolke, and married him into the Families of *Higham* and *Cotton*, as also did the *Blounds* of Elwaston, the *Talbots* of Grafton, from whom the Barons of Monioy, and the late Earles of Shrewsbury descended; one of the Daughters of this *Bucke* Married to *Fredericke Tilney* of *Shelley* Hall in Suffolke, his nearest Kinsman by the Duchesse his Mothers side) But some perhaps, must call this my vanity, I shall but answer them, that I thinke my selfe bound (by all the bloud and memory I claime from them,) to pay them my best Relations and endeavours, acknowledging with the great Consulare Philosopher, *Parentes charissimos habere debemus, quod ab ijs vita, patrimonium, libertas, Civitas tradita est.* And I should thinke there is none, who hath an interest in the quality of Gentile, or Noble, (for all is one) but lookes backe (which some delight) to their first Commemoration; and finds a strong engagement due to the Vertues and worth of their first Fathers, for that expresse charge, to honour Father and Mother, is not to be understood, only of our Parents superstits, and living here with us, but our forefathers: that is, beyond our great Grandfather, for we have no proper word for them above that degree (but Antecessours, *vulgò* Ancestours) whom the Romans called *Majores*, and comprehendeth all our Progenitours departed sooner or later) for the word *Pater* and *Mater*, as also, *Parens & Parentes*, extend very largely, and reach up to the highest Ancestours. The Ancient Roman Jurisconsults, deliver in their Law for an Axiome, that *Appellatione Parentum omnes in infinitum majores utriusque sexus significantur*; and the word *Parentes* yet spreadeth further, comprehending all Kinsfolkes, and Cosins, of our Bloud and Linage, being used in that sense, by *Ælius Lampridius*, by *Iulius Capitolinus*, and other the best Writers in the times of the declined Empire, as *Isaac Casabonus* hath well observed in his Annotations.

The Italians, Spanish, and French (whose Language is for the most part Romanzi (mongrell Latine) and broken and corrupted Romane Language (use *Parenti*, *Parentes* and *Parents* for all their Kinsfolkes and Gentilitious Cosins.

We English-men (being more precise) follow the Ancient and Classique Latine Writers, holding Parent strictly to the simple signification of *Pater*, and *Mater*, the present and immediate Parents. But the using of the word *Parentes*, as those Imperiall Historians use it; serveth better for our purpose here: And I could

(most

(most willingly) imitate the Pious Gentlemen of *Italy*, *Spaine*, and *France*, in their Religious and Charitable indeavours, to advance the happinesse of their Parents defunct, if those desires could besteed them, But where I should crave pardon, I become more guilty and extravogant, it is time therefore to know good manners, and returne home to our proper taske, which will be, to refell the grosse and blacke Calumnies, throwne unjustly upon the Memory and Person of King RICHARD, And falls within the Circle of the next Booke.

Explicit Liber Secundus.

THE

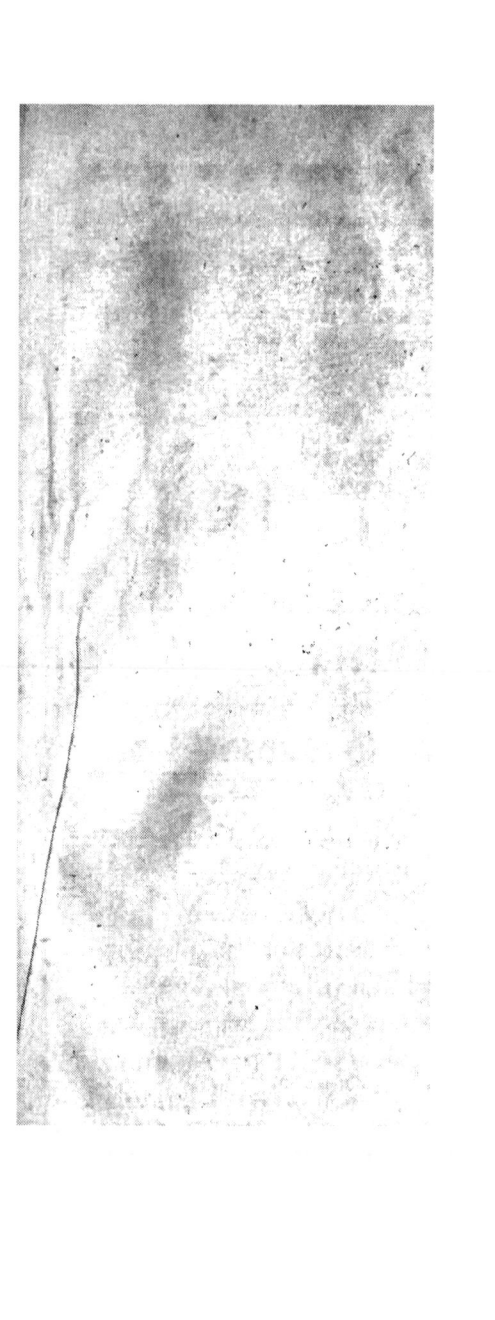

THE

THIRD BOOKE

OF

KING RICHARD THE THIRD.

The Contents of this Booke.

THe Defamations of King Richard *examined and answered.*

Doctor Morton *and Sir* Thomas Moore *malevolent to the House of Yorke, Their frivolous exceptions against his gestures, lookes, teeth, shape and birth, his vertues depraved.*

The death of King Henry *the sixth and his Sonne* Edward *Prince of Wales.*

The Actors therein.

The offence of killing an anointed King.

Valiant men hate treacheries and bloudy acts.

King Richard *not deformed.*

The Slanders of Clarence *translated to King* Richard.

The Cause of Clarences *execution.*

How the Sonnes of King Edward *came by their deaths.*

King Richard *Exculpable thereof.*

The story of Perkin VVarbeck *compared with* Don Sebastian, *King of Portugall, who are Biothanati.*

Counterfeit Prince detected, young Prince marvellously preserved.

Many testimonies for the assertion that Perkin VVarbeck *was* Richard *Duke of Yorke; his honourable entertainment with forraigne Princes vox populi.*

Reasons why it is not credible King Richard *made away his two Nephewes; the force of Confession.*

The evill of Torture, the guilt of attempting to escape out of prison, what an escape is.

The Earle of Oxford severe against Perkin, *and his end.*

The base Sonne of King Richard *the third secretly made away.*

The Sonne of the Duke of Clarence *put to death.*

The power of furies, Demones & Genii. Apollonii Majestas.

Quid tibi non vis alteri ne feceris.

THE

THE THIRD BOOKE OF KING RICHARD THE THIRD.

THere is no story, that shewes the planetary affections and malice of the vulgar more truly then King *Richards*: and what a tickle game Kings have to play with them; though his successor *Henry* the seventh play'd his providently enough (with helpe of the standers by) yet even those times (which had promised the happiest example of a State, and best of a King) both groaned and complained; but had not the sting and infection of King *Richards* adversaries who did not onely as the proverbe saith, *cum larvis luctare*, contend with his immortall parts, but raked his dust, to finde and aggravate exceptions in his grave; having learnt their piety from the Comicall Parasite, *obsequium amicos, veritas odium parit*, and finding it as well guerdonable as gratefull, to publish their Libels and scandalous Pamphlets, (a piece of policy and service too) to the times, (and an offence to resent any thing good of him) they gave their pens more gall and freedome, having a copy set by Doctor *Morton*, who had taken his revenge that way, and written a * Booke in *latine*,

Erasmus in Chiliad.

Terentius in Adelphis

* This Booke was lately in the hands of Mr. *Roper*, of Eltham, as Sir *Edward Hoby* who saw it told me

against King *Richard*, which came afterward to the hands of Mr. *Moore* (sometime his servant) so that here the saying of *Darius*, (which after became a proverbe) hath place

Herodotus.

Hoc Calceamentum consuit Histiæus, induit, autem Aristagoras, Doctor *Morton* (acting the part of *Histiæus*) made the Booke, and Master *Moore* like *Aristagoras* set it forth, amplifying and glossing it, with a purpose to have writ the full story of *Richard* the third (as he intimateth in the title of his Booke;) but it should seeme he found the worke so melancholy and uncharitable, as dul d his disposition to it; for he began it, 1513. when he was Under-Sheriffe, or Clerke to one of the Sheriffes of London, and had the intermission of twenty two yeares (which time he tooke up in studies, more naturall to his inclination, as law and poetry,* for in them lay his greatest fancy) to finish it, before he died, (which was in, 1535. but did not, yet lift himselfe so happily into the opinion of men, that his commendations had more fortune then observation:) and past him under the attributes of learning and religion; though in both he came short of what was ascribed to him; for if he understood the Latine and Greeke, (then held great learning) yet was he so farre under the desert of an excellent Scholler, as the learned censured him a man of slender reading, and *Germanus Brixius*, *Irruditus*, *i.* unlearned; for the sanctity of his life, *John Baleus* who tooke not up his knowledge of him an age off, (as some of his admirers,) but from the originall, thus gives us his draught.

* He wrote many Poems and Epigrams. sundry petty Comedies, and Enterludes, often times personating, with the Actors, as his loving and familiar friend Erasmus reports.

Brixius Antimore.

Ioan. Baleus de scriptoribus Brit. Cent. 8 *cap.* 69.

Hoc nos probe novimus qui eramus eidem Thomæ Moro *viciniores, quod pontificum, & pharisæorum crudelitati ex avaritia subserviens omni tyrāno truculentior ferociebat, imo insaniebat in eos qui aut Papæ primatum, aut purgatorium, aut mortuorum invocationes, aut imaginum cultus aut simile quiddam diabolicarum imposturarum negabant, a vivifica Dei veritate ita edocti, Consentire hic Harpagus noluit ut Rex Christianus in suo Regno primus esset, nec quod ei liceret cum Davide, Salomone, Iosaphato, Ezechia, & Iosia sacerdotes, & Levitas rejectâ Romanensium Nembrodorum tyrannide in proprio ordinare dominio. &c.*

Adding the attribute of *tenebrio*, of *veritatis evangelicæ perversissimus osor*, of *obstinatus Calophanta*, of *impudens Christi adversarius*; and saith of his end that *decollatus fuit in Turre Londinensi sexto die Julij Anno Dom.* 1535. *Capite ad magnum Londini pontem (ut proditoribus fieri solet) stipiti imposito, & nihilominus a Papistis pro novo Martyre colitur.*

Richard Grafton saith he died mocking and scoffing as he lived.

Thus he became a Martyr and a Saint; but we shall finde other cause of his condemnation by his owne testimony; for when he stood at the Barre arraigned, some exceptions having been urg'd against him, for seeming to uphold and maintaine the Popes supremacy in England; his reply was, he could

not

not see *quomodo laicus vel secularis homo possit vel debeat esse caput status spiritualis aut ecclesiastici*; yet insinuated, that this opinion was taken hold off but for a pretext to supplant him; the greatest cause of the Kings displeasure being for his withstanding the divorce, between him and *Katharine* of Castile his wife, and his second marriage with the Lady *Anne* Bullen Marquesset of Pembrooke: And his owne words (spoken to the Judges, as they were set downe by his deare friend, *George Courinus*, in a short discourse upon his death) are, *non me pudet quamobrem a vobis condemnatus sum (videlicet) ob id, quod nunquam voluerim assentiri in negotium novi matrimonij Regis*, which uttered, after sentence of condemnation, (when no evasion or subterfugies would availe) must proceed surely from his conscience; and before this, he wrote a letter to Mr. Secretary *Cromwell*, (which I have seene) wherein he protested, he was not against the King, either for his second marriage, or for the Churches supremacy: But wisheth him good successe in those affaires, &c. which renders him, (well looked upon) not so stout a Champion for the Pope, as many of his partiall friends and Romanists supposed; neither so sound in his Religion; for I have seene amongst the multitude of writings, concerning the conference about the alteration of Religion, and suppressing of Churches and Religious houses, that his connivance and consent was in it; nor could he excuse it, with all his policy and wisdome, neither had the King ever attempted it, had not the Pope and his Agents opposed that second marriage, an error and insolency Rome hath ever since repented. But it prov'd a happy blow of Justice to this Kingdome, cutting of him and his authority, which else had hazarded the best Queene that ever was, the sacred and eternally honoured *Elizabeth*, to whose growing glory and virtue Master *Moore* became an early and cruell adversary, even before she was *in rerum natura*. To know him further, let me referre you to the Ecclesiasticall History of Master *John Fox*, in the raigne of *Henry* the eight, who describes him graphically; for his historicall fragment, it shewes what great paines he tooke to item the faults and sad fortunes of King *Richard* the third; and how industrious he was to be a time observer, it being the most plausible theame his poeticall straine could fall on in those times, and could not want acceptance nor credit, well knowing in what fame he stood, and that the weaker Analysts and Chroniclers, (of meane learning and lesse judgement) would boldly take it upon trust from his pen; who *tanquam ignotum & servum pecus*, have followed him step by step without consideration, or just examination of their occurrents and consequents. And the reputation of him and Doctor *Morton* (being both Lord Chancellours of England) might easily mislead men part blind, who have dealt with King *Richard*, as some triviall claw-

Courinus.

In scrinijs div. Ro: Cotton.

clawing Pamphleters, and Historicall parasites, with the magnificent Prelate, *Thomas Wolsey* Cardinall and Archbishop o Yorke, A man of very excellent ingredients and without Peere in his time; yet his values had the sting of much detraction, and the worth of his many glorious good workes interpreted for vices and excesses; to such it must be said, *quod ab ipso allatum est, id sibi relatum esse putant.* And if their injustice suffer under the same lash, they must know this doome hath the credit of an Oracle, *quale verbum dixisti tale etiam audies.*

Terent. Phorm.

Iliad. 20.

But so much gall and envy is thrown upon King *Richards* story, as cannot possibly fall into the stile of an ingenuous and charitable pen; all his virtue is by a malitious Alchymy substracted into crimes, and where they necessarily fall into mention, either scornefully transmitted or perverted, with injurious constructions, not allowing him the resemblance of goodnesse or merit: If his disposition be affable and curteous, (as generally it was, which their owne relations cannot deny) then he insinuates and dives into the peoples hearts, so where he expresses the bounty and magnificence of his minde; it is a subtle tricke to purchase friendship; let him conceale the knowledge of his injuries, and his patience is deepe hypocrisie; for his mercy and clemency extended to the highest offendors, (as to *Fogge* the Atturney, who had made a Libell against him, besides the counterfeiting of his hand and seale) they were but palliated, and his friendship meerely a Court brow. They have yet a more captious and subtle calumny, reproaching the casting of his eyes, motions of his fingers, manner of his gesture, and his other naturall actions.

The virtues of King Richard malitiously censured.

I confesse with *Cicero* that *status, incessus, sessio, occubatio, vultus, oculi, manuum motio,* have a certaine kind of decorum; but he makes it not a vice to erre in any of them, nor that any errour committed in them was a vice; although in him it must be so defined by the Lawes of Utopia: nay, they will dissect his very sleepes, to finde prodigious dreames and bug-beares, (accidents frequent to themselves) which they dresse in all the fright and horrour fiction and the stage can adde, who would have sung Peans to his glory, had his sword brought victory from Bosworth field: but now, their envy is borne with him, from his mothers wombe, and delivers him into the world with a strange prodigy of Teeth; although (I am perswaded) neither Doctor *Morton*, nor Sir *Thomas Moore* ever spake with the Dutchesse his Mother, or her Midwife about the matter.

Cicero de Offic. lib. 1.

But if true; it importeth no reason why those early and natalatious teeth should presage such horrour and guilt to his birth; when we shall remember those many Noble and worthy men, who have had the like, (without any imputation of crime) as * *Marcus Curius* sirnamed thereupon *Dentatus*,

* *Pliny, Livy, valel. Maximus, Plutarch.*

Cu.

Cn. Papiene, King of the Epirots (a Prince much renowned for his victories and virtues) *Monodas* Sonne of *Prusias* King of Bithynia, borne with an intire semicircular bone in their mouthes, instead of Teeth; then they aggravate the pangs of the Dutchesse in her travaile with him: which had not been sufferable without death, if so extreame and intolerable, as they would have them thought for,

Quod ferri potest leve est; quod non, breve est.

But she overcame them and lived almost fifty yeares after; others have died in that Bed, yet the children not made guilty of murther; *Julia* the daughter of *Julius Cæsar*, Wife to great *Pompey*, *Juliola* the deare daughter of *Marcus Cicero*, Wife of *Dolabella*, and *Junia Claudilla* the Empresse, and Wife of *Caligula*, died all of the difficulties and extremity of their childebearing; so did Queene *Elizabeth* Wife of King *Henry* the seventh; and since the Mother of that most towardly and hopefull Prince *Edward* the sixth in travaile of his birth; with many thousands more, whose deaths (much lesse their paines) were never imputed to their children.

This Dutchesse of Yorke died about the 11 of King Hen. 7. at Barkhamsted and was buried at Fothering. am, *Iohn Stow*. *Senec*.

The next objection is somewhat of more regard, (but as farre without the certainty of a proofe) which is the pretended deformity of his body, controverted by many; some peremptorily asserted he was not deformed, of which opinion was *John Stow*, a man indifferently inquisitive (as in all their other affaires) after the verball relations and persons of Princes, and curious in his description of their features and lineaments, who in all his inquiry could finde no such note of deformitie in this King: but hath acknowledged *vivâ voce*, that he had spoken with some ancient men, who from their owne sight and knowledge affirmed he was of bodily shape comely enough, onely of low stature, which is all the deformity they proportion so monstrously; neither did *Iohn Rouce* who knew him and writ much in his discription, observe any other: and *Archienbald Qhuitlaw*, Ambassador unto this King from Scotland, in his Oration saies, he had *corpus exiguum*; not otherwise; so (to my conceit) *Philip de Comines* and the Prior *de Croyland* (who had seen and knowne this Prince) seeme to cleere him implicatively; for in all their discourses of him they never directly nor indirecty, covertly or apertly, insinuate this deformity which (I suppose) they would not have passed; And by his sundry Pictures which I have seen, there was no such disproportion in his person or lineaments, but all decently compacted to his stature; his face of a warlike aspect, (which Sir *Thomas Moore* calleth a crabled visage) of all the children being said to be most like his Father in favour and composition of shape, who though not tall was of an even and well disposed structure.

King *Richard* not deformed.

*

Rot. in an. 2 R. 2.

And

Sir Thomas Moor apud Harlington.

And Sir *Thomas Moore* himſelfe, doth not certainely affirme the deformity, but rather ſeemes to take it as a malitious report; for ſaith he, King *Richard* was deformed as the fame ranne by thoſe that hated him; *habemus reum confitentem*, and ſurely, it had been a ſtrange kinde of confidence and reaſon in Doctor *Shaw*, to diſclaime a thing which muſt be ſo palpable, openly in the Pulpit at Saint Pauls Croſſe, whilſt the Protector was preſent, before many hundreds of people, (who had ſeen and known him before) and might then better view and note him; In theſe words, the Lord Protector is a very noble Prince, the ſpeciall patterne of Knightly prowesse, as well in all Princely behaviour as in the lineaments of his body and in the favour of his viſage, repreſenting the very face of the Noble Duke his Father; this is the Fathers owne figure, this is his owne countenance, the very ſure and undoubted Image and expreſſe likeneſſe of that Noble Duke.

Doctor *Shaw.*

Socrates. Æſopus, Epictetus. Galba a great and excellent Captain of the Romans, all of deformed ſtature.

Now, what can malice extract out of this, to upbraid or ſtigmatize his honour; if men of blemiſht perſons may containe a wiſe, valiant, learned, liberall and religious ſoule, and be in every part moſt abſolute, exampled to us in many famous men; and at our home (as well in this preſent age, as in the more ancient) we have had men of a harſh fabrick, moſt nobly furniſht in the compoſures of their mindes.

But becauſe theſe cavils could not fetch blood from him, they will make him guilty of other men, and firſt of King *Henry* the ſixth, whoſe murther they ſay (and very favourably) his Brother *Edward* contrived, but wrought him to act it; an accuſation of very harſh credit, that either King *Edward*, ſo truly noble and valiant a Prince, ſhould put a Prince and his owne Brother, upon ſo horrid a thing, or he indure to heare it: Sir *Thomas Moore* holds King *Edward* would not ingage his Brother in ſo butcherly an office, there being many reaſons that he durſt not, neither doe his adverſaries charge him directly by any credible Author of that time, or diſcover by whom this murther was; onely the Prior of *Croyland* maketh it ſomewhat ſuſpitious.

Chron. Croyland.

Hoc tempore inventum eſt corpus regis Henrici ſexti exanime in turre Londinarium. Parcat Deus, & ſpatium pœnitentiæ ei donet quicunque ſacrilegas manus in Chriſtum Domini auſus immittere, unde & agens tyranni & patiens glorioſi martyris titulum mereantur.

Tyrannus in the proper conſtruction, being *Rex*, for whoſoever is *Rex* is *Tyrannus*, according to the ancient ſignification; for amongſt the Greeks Τύραννος was uſed for a King ſimply, good or bad, and this (ſome hold) makes againſt King *Edward*; *Richard* being Duke of Glouceſter then, yet ſo doubtfully

fully as may be refelled by good authority; for it is the opinion of very grave men, *Henry* the sixth was not murthered, but died of naturall sicknesse, and extreame infirmity of body.

Idem Croyland.

Rex Henricus sextus, ab annis jam multis ex accidente sibi ægritudine quandam animi incurreret infirmitatem, & sic æger corpore & impos mentis permansit diutius; this considered with the aggravation of his griefe and sorrow, in the losse of his Crown and liberty (being then a prisoner) the overthrow of all his friends and forces in the Battaile of Teuxbury, but (above all) the death of his Sonne the Prince, might master a stronger heart and constitution then his, in a shorter time; which opinion is received and alleadged by a learned and discreet Gentleman.

Anonymus M.S.

The occasion of the murther of King *Henry* the sixth, hath no other proofe but the malitious affirmation of one man; for many other men more truly did suppose that he died of meere griefe and melancholy, when he heard the overthrow of his cause and friends, with the slaughter of the Prince his Sonne: And *Iohannes Majerus* saith it was reported, King *Henry* the sixth died of griefe and thought. Concerning the slaughter of the Prince his onely Sonne, it is noted to be casuall, and made suddaine by his owne insolence, not out of any pretended malice, or premeditated treachery, and so it cannot be called wilfull murther; for the King demanding him why he invaded his Kingdome, his reply was, he might, and ought to doe it, in defence and preservation of the right, which the King his Father and his heires had in the Crowne, and maintained this lofty answer so peremtorily and boldly, the King in rage strooke him with his fist, (as some say armed with a Gantlet) and instantly the Noblemen attending, as *George* Duke of Clarence, Marquesse Dorset, the Lord Hastings and others, drew their swords upon the Prince and killed him; which they would make the particular fact of Duke *Richard*.

Rex Hen. 6. in custodia ut alij referunt, gladio. & alij merore, &c. perijt. Joan Majerus, Annall Flandr. lib. 17.

The slaughter of the Prince sonne of H. 6.

Polidor. Virgil. lib. 24.

Chron in quarto M.S. apud Dom. Regis. Rob. Cotton.

But to the contrary, I have seene in a faithfull Manuscript Chronicle of those times, that the Duke of Gloucester onely of all the great persons, stood still and drew not his sword; the reasons to credit this are, first it might be in his meere sence of honour, seeing so many drawn upon him, there was no need of his, or in his respects to the Princes Wife, who (as *Johannes Majerus* saith) was in the roome and neare akinne to the Dutchesse of Yorke his Mother, and to whom the Duke was also very affectionate, (though secretly(which he soone after demonstrated in marrying her; nay, this Duke bore such a sence of noble actions in his bosome, that misliking the obscure and meane buriall of *Henry* the sixth, this Princes Father, he caused his corps to be taken from Chertsey,

Anna, uxor Ed. filij reg. H. 6. capta est cum marito. Joan. Majerus in Annal Fland. l. 17.

and to be Honourably conveyed to the Royall and stately Chappell of Windsor, ordained for Kings.

Richard not guilty of the Duke of Clarence.

And Sir *Thomas Moore* saith further, he was suspected to have the contriving part in the Duke of Clarence his Brothers death, yet confesseth it was commonly said *Richard* opposed himselfe against the unnaturall proceedings of the King, both privately and publiquely; and the truth is, it was the Kings owne immoveable and inexplorable doome who thought it justly and necessirily his due; for Clarence stood guilty of many treasons and great ones, and by his ingratidude had so forfeited himselfe to the Kings displeasure, that no friend durst move in his behalfe; this the King did afterward acknowledge with some discontent, when his wrath had cooled, as we may guesse in this expression of his: *O infælicem fratrem, pro cujus salute nemo homo rogavit*; yet *Polidor Virgil* doth not rightly understand here as I conjecture by the sequell; but let us interpret that a little, and take up another accusation which puts into the way.

Polidor. Virgil.

That *Richard* Duke of Gloucester should scandall the birth of the King his Brother with basterdy, and alleadge it for a speciall matter in Doctor *Shawes* Sermon, that he should fame King *Edward* the fourth a bastard, and that the Dutchesse his Mother had wanton familiarity with a certaine Gentleman; this he might erroneously scatter in the Pulpit, and take it upon the like intelligence, by which (in the same Sermon) he called her (to whom King *Edward* was betrothed before his marriage with the Lady *Grey*) *Elizabeth Lucy*, whose name was for a certaine *Ellenor Butler*, *alias Talbot*, so called by King *Richard*, and written in the Records.

Errour of Dr. Shaw.

That the Duke of Gloucester raised not the slander against the Dutchesse his Mother, nor of his Brothers basterdy.

This drift had been too grosse for King *Richard*, to lay an imputation of whoredome upon his owne Mother, (a virtuous and honourable Lady) being it cast also a shame and basterdy upon himselfe; for if she offended in one, she might as likely offend in another, and in the rest.

And to quit him of it, Sir *Thomas Moore*, *Richard Grafton*, Mr. *Hall*, say that King *Richard* was much displeased with the Doctor, when he heard the relation, which the Duke of Buckingham also affirmed in his speech to the Lord Mayor of London. That Doctor *Shaw* had incurred the great displeasure of the Protectour for speaking so dishonourably of the Dutchesse his Mother.

That he was able of his owne knowledge to say, he had done wrong to the Protectour therein, who was ever known to beare a reverend and filiall love unto her: and to cut of all farther doubt and question, it was proved and is testified upon records that *George* Duke of Clarence onely raised this slander in an extreame hatred to the King his Brother, many jarres falling

falling between them) by which the King had a just cause to take notice of his malice.

Visus est dux Clarentiæ magis, ac magis a regis præsentia desubtrahere, in consilio vix verbum proferre, neque libenter bibere aut manducare in domo Regis.

When *Richard* even in that calamitous time *Henry* the sixth had overthrowne King *Edward* in a battaile, * recovered the Kingdome, and proclaimed *Edward* an usurper; so faithfull was his Brother, that (*a*) he was proclaimed traitor for him; and (*b*) when Queene *Margaret* besiedged the City of Gloucester with the Kings power, the Citizens stood at defiance with her Army, and told her it was the Duke of Gloucester his Towne, who was with the King, and for the King, and for him they would hold it; his Loyalty bearing a most constant expression in this motto (*c*) *Loyalte melie*; which I have seen written by his owne hand and subscribed *Richard* Gloucester. The other was as constantly underminiing at him, after confederated with the Earle of Warwicke his Father Allie, who had turn'd faith from the King, and went into France, sollicíting for force against England; which they brought in, fought with the King and overthrew him, and so fiercely pursuing the victory, that the King was forc't to fly out of the Land: Clarence not so satisfied, (unlesse he might utterly supplant him) studied that slander of basterdy, to bring in himselfe an heire to the Crowne, which was proved and given in expresse evidence against him, at his triall and attainder by Parliament, amongst sundry other articles of high Treason.

* *Anno.* 10. *Edward.* 4.

(a) *Lib.M.S. in quarto. apud Dom. Rob.Cotton.*

(b) Chronicle, *Croyland.*

(c) Loyalty bindeth men.

Father allie. *Quod vulgo & corrupte* Father in law *dicitur.*

Videlicet That the said Duke of Clarence had falsly and untruly published King *Edward* a bastard and not legitimate to Raigne, that himselfe therefore was true Heire of the Kingdome, the Royalty and Crowne belonging unto him, and to his Heires; these be the very words of the Record, and enough to tell us who was the Author of that slander, and what important cause the King had to quit himselfe of Clarens: a bitter proofe of the old Proverbe, *fratrum inter se iræ acerbissimæ sunt*; and all the favour Clarence could at his end obtaine, was to choose it, (as *Iohn de Serres* reporteth it) so that it was not the Duke of Gloucester, but the Kings implacable displeasure for his malice and treasons that cut him off, who could not thinke himselfe secure whilst he lived: Witnesse *Polidor Virgil*, *Edvardus Rex post mortem fratris se a cunctis timeri animadvertit, & ipse jam timebat neminem.*

In Parliament, *anno.* 17. *Ed.*4. *Ju. Stow. vidit & legit.*

Erasmus Chiliad.

Joan de Serres. Invent.

Next for the murther of the two sonnes of King *Edward* the fourth, *Edward* the fifth King in hope, and *Richard* of Shrewsbury Duke of Yorke and Norfolke his younger Brother, they alleadge it in this manner.

Who made away the sonnes of King Edward the fourth.

That King *Richard*, being desirous to rid those two Princes his Nephews out of the world; imployed his trusty servant *John Greene* to Sir *Robert Brackenbury* Lieutenant Constable of the Tower, about the executing of this murther; and by reason that plot tooke no effect, (Sir *Robert* not liking it) The Protectour suborned foure desperate Villaines, *John Dighton*, *Miles Forrest*, *James Tyrrell*, and *William Slater* to undertake it, who, (as they further alleadge) smothered them in their beds, which done, they made a deepe hole in the ground, at the foote of the staires of their lodging, and their buried them, hiding the place under an heape of stones, (not after the antient manner of *tumulus testis*;) others vary from this, and say confidently, the young Princes were imbarqued in a Ship at Tower wharfe, and conveyed from thence to Sea, so cast into the Blacke deeps; others averre they were not drowned, but set safe on shore beyond Seas. And thus their stories and relations are scatter'd in various formes, their accusations differing in very many and materiall points, which shakes the credit of their suggestion, and makes it both fabulous and uncertaine, one giving the lie to the other, their malice having too much Tongue for their memories, and is worth the noting how opposite (and as it were) *ex Diametro* repugnant they are.

Poedir.Virgill. l. 2. 6. *In vulgus fama valuit filios* Edwardi *Regis aliquo terrarum partem migrasse, atque ita superstites esse.*

Thus *Pollidor*, with which Dr. *Morton* and Sir *Thomas Moore* agree in one place: The man (say they) commonly called *Perkin Warbeck* was as well with the Princes, as with the people, English and forraigne, held to be the younger Son of *Edward* the fourth, and that the deaths of the young King *Edward* and of *Richard* his brother, had come so far in question, as some are yet in doubt whether they were destroyed or no, in the dayes of King *Richard*; By which it appeares they were thought to be living after his death. And as the act of their death is thus uncertainly disputed, so is the manner of it controverted.

Dr. *Morton*, Sir *Tho. Moore*.

For, Sir *Thomas Moore* affirmeth (as before reported) they were smothered in their beds with Pillowes; but *Pollidor* saith peremptorily it was never known of what kinde of death they dyed.

Another Author and more ancient agreeth with them.

Prior Crayland. *Vulgatum est Regis* Edwardi *pueros concessisse in fata, sed quo genere interitus ignoratur*; one reason of this may be that they who held *Perkin Warbeck* and *Richard* Duke of Yorke to be all one, give another accompt of his death, whereas if it had beene certaine these foure before named for *Assasines* had murdered them, then the place, time and manner had beene easily known upon their strict examination, they living freely and securely, (and without question) long after this murder was said to be done; Therefore there can be no excuse for this neglect of Examination, much lesse for the suffering such to goe unpunished, and at liberty, which me thinks maketh much for the cleering of King *Richard*.

As for the burying of their bodyes in the Tower, if that be brought in question, *certes*, the affirmative will be much more hard to prove then the negative.

For true it is, there was much diligent search made for their bodies in the Tower: all places opened and digged, that was supposed: but not found; Then it was given out a certaine Priest tooke up their bodies and buried them in another secret place not to be found; hereunto (but with bette decorum for the more credit of this assertion) they might have added it was done *sub sigillo confessionis*, which may not be revealed.

Sir *Thomas Moore* seeing the absurdities and contrarieties of these opinions, (as a man puzeled and distracted with the variety and uncertainty thereof) concludeth their bodies were bestowed God wot where, and that it could never come to light what became of them; *Hall*, *Hallingshed*, *Grafton* and the rest, confesse, the very truth hereof was never knowne; And (if there be a stricter inquiry into the mystery) we shall discover, that they were neither buried in the Tower nor swallowed in the Sea; for the testimony and Relation of sundry grave, and discreete persons (and such as knew the young Duke of *Yorke*) will resolve us how he was preserved and secretly conveyed into a foraigne Country; also alive many years after the time of this imaginary murder; to which may be added strong authorities having layd downe some conjectures that may answer the iniquiry after the other. And first whereas it is said the Lord *Protector* before his Coronation procured this murder: To refell and contradict that, there bee certaine proofes that the Princes were both living in the moneth of *February* following the death of their Father, which was ten moneths after; for King *Edward* dyed in *April* before, and this is plaine in the Records of the Parliament of *Anno* 1. *Rich.* 3. where there is mention made of this Prince, as then living; and Sir *Thomas Moore* confesseth that they were living long after that time before said; But I conjecture *Edward* the Eldest brother lived not long after, but died of sicknesse and infirmity, being of a weake and sickly disposition, as also was his Brother, which the Queene their Mother intimated in her speech to the Cardinall *Bourser*; and the weake constitutions and short lives of their sisters may be a naturall proofe to infer it probable enough this Prince dyed in the Tower; which some men of these times are the rather brought to thinke, certaine bones like to the bones of a Child being found lately in a high desolate Turret, supposed to be the bones of one of these Princes; others are of opinion it

Moore, Hallingshed, Grafton, Hall, Stow.

it was the carcasse of an Ape kept in the Tower, that in his old age had happened into that place to die in, and having clamber'd up thither, according to the light and idle manner of those wanton Animals, after when he would have gone down, seeing the way to be steepe and the precipice so terrible, durst not adventure to descend, but for feare stayed and starved himselfe, and although hee might bee soone mist, and long sought for, yet was not easily to be found, that Turret being reckoned a vast and damned place for the hight, and hard accesse, no body in many yeares looking into it.

But it is of no great consequence to our purpose, whether it were the Carcasse of a Child or of an Ape, or whether this young Prince dyed in the Tower, or no: for wheresoever hee dyed, why should it not be as probable hee dyed of a naturall sicknesse and infirmity, as for his young Cozen german the sonne and heire of King *Richard*? many reasons conducing why the qualities and kinde of their death might be the same, and neere one time, being even parallels almost, and in their humane constitutions and corporall habitude sympathizing, of one Linage and Family, of one blood and age, of the same quality and fortune, therefore not unlikely of the same Studies, Affections, Passions, Distemperatures, so consequently subject to the same infirmities, to which may be added equall and common constellations, the same compatient and commorient fates and times, and then there is reason and naturall cause they might both die of like Diseases and infirmity, and were not Βιαθάνατοι, taken away by violence, secret, or overt: for it may with asmuch Argument bee suspected the son of King *Richard*, (being in the like danger of secret violence for the same cause as his Cozen was) might suffer so.

But to open the circumstance a little neerer: what danger could the lives of those two Princes be to *Richard*? who was accepted King by a just title, and his Nephewes declared illegitimate, by the high Court of Parliament, and whilst they were reputed such by so great and generall a conclusion, why should he be lesse secure of them, then *Hen.* 2. was of *Robert* E. of Glocester, base sonne to *Hen.* 1.? or *Richard* the first of his base Brother *Geoffrey Plantagenet*? So although *Iohn* of *Gaunt* left base sonnes, aspiring enough, yet they were of no danger to the *Lancastrian* Kings, neither did *Henry* 7. or *Henry* 8. stand in any jealousy of *Arthur Plantagenet*: and surely *Richard* the third was as valiant, wise and confident, as any of his predecessors, and had as little cause to dread his Nephewes, as they stood adjudged, or be more cruell and bloudy; neither hath my reading found any Bastards of *France* or *Spaine*, who have aspired so publickly, onely except *Don Enrique* E. of *Trastamara*, who was drawne into that action by the violent rages of the people,

people, and by the perswasions of the revolted states of Castile, to put downe a monster of Soveraignty the hatefull tyrant, *Don Pedro* & Cruell. But being Sir *Thomas Moore* and our best Chroniclers make it doubtfull, whether these two Princes were so lost in King *Richards* time, or no, and infer that one of them was thought to be living many years after his death; that might be enough to acquit him; which opinion I like the better, because it mentioneth the survivance but of one of them.

Neither doe our most credible stories mention the transportation of more then one, into Flanders, nor had they reason; it will bee sufficient, if one of them survived him, more, or lesse time; we will follow therefore the examination of his story, under the opinion of those times, and the attestation of grave and credible men, because it will be more conspicuous in the true and simple narration of this one Brother; every story being fraught with reports concerning him, and few or none of his brother finding no mention of the Elder Bothers being in Flanders; but of the youngers much, and of his other adventures: The prudent and honorable care of sending away this younger Brother, by some is ascribed to Sr. *Robert Brakenbury*, by others to the Queene his Mother, and it may well be the projection of them both, though no doubt there was the advise and assent of other well affected friends. And it is the more credible, the Queen wrought in it; for the story of Sr. *Thomas Moore* saith shee was before suspected to have had such a purpose, which was objected to her by some of the Lords; and the Cardinall *Boursier* told her the maine Reason which made the Protector and Nobles so urgeing to have him sent to his Brother (being then in the Tower) was a suspition and feare they had shee would convey Him forth of the Realme.

So then, it may be cleerly supposed: he was sent into a forraine Country, and that Flanders (as all our stories testify) there commended to a liberall education, under the curature of a worthy Gentleman in *Warbeck*, a Towne in Flanders, but kept very privately all the life time of his Uncle, his Friends not daring to make him of the councell. After his death, knowing *Henry Richmond* a cruell enemy to the house of Yorke, for his better safety was committed to the care of *Charles* of Burgundy, and his Dutchesse the Lady *Margaret* Aunt to the Prince, as formerly the Dutchesse of Yorke upon a like cause of feare and jealousy had sent thither her two younger sons *George* and *Richard*.

The Dutchesse being very tender to let this young Duke have all Princely and vertuous education in Tornay in Antwerp and after in the Court of the Duke of Burgundy, as hee had

bin

bin in *Warbeck*, &c. And with the greater circumspection, because the Dutchesse of Burgundy had as jealous an opinion of *Henry* the Seventh, as the Queene Widdow had of *Richard* 3. Therefore, as yet, it was advised to conceale his Name and Quality: being not come to the growth nor age to have experience in his own affaires, much lesse to undertake an attempt so consequent and mighty as the recovery of a Kingdome: neither were the times and opportunity yet ripe, or propitious to fashion such an alteration, as was projected and must be produced, though there was pregnant hope of an induction to a change of Government stir'd by the Kings coveteousnesse, and some acts of Tyrany, Greivance and Rebellions in the North and West parts; not long after (which lent a seasonable hand to these designes) great unkindnesse fell out betwixt *Charles* the *French* King, and *Henry* the 7. who so far provoked the *French*, that he besieged Bulloigne, with a great army by land and Sea, the quarrell was of good advancement to the Dutchesse of Burgondy's Plot, and brought the Duke of Yorke better acquainted with forraigne Princes and their Courts; who was sent into *France*, into *Portugall*, and other places where he was received and entertained like a Prince.

In which time such of the English Nobility as were interessed in the secret, and knew where this Prince resided, found some opportunity to give him assistance, and sent Sr. *Robert Clifford* and Sr. *William Barley* into Flanders, to give him a visit and intelligence of what noble friends he had ready to serve him: though their more particular errant was, to take a strict observance of him, and such private marks as hee had bin knowne by from his Cradle: there had beene some counterfeits, incouraged to take upon them the persons of *Edward* E. of Warwick, and *Richard* Duke of Yorke; But here, the certainty of their knowledge found him they looked for, by his Face, Countenance, Lineaments and all tokens familiarly and privately knowne to them; observing his behaviour, naturaliz'd and heightned with a Princely grace, and in his discourse able to give them a ready accompt of many passages he had heard or seene whilst hee was in England; with such things as had beene done and discourst very privately, speaking English very perfectly, and better then the Dutch, or Wallonish: by which Sr. *Robert Clifford* and the rest, found themselves so well satisfied, and were so confirm'd, That they wrot to the Lord *Fitzwater*, to Sir *Symon Mountford* and others (who had a good opinion towards him;) the full accompt of what they had observ'd *ex certa scientia*, & *supra visum corporis*. About this time (to intermix the Scene with more variety, and fill the Stage) some principall persons, well affecting the E. of Warwick, and hoping to get him forth of the Tower in purpose

purpose to make him King) had inticed a handsome young fellow, one *Lambert Simonell* of Lancashire, bred in the University of Oxford to become his counterfeit, and so instructed him in the royall Genealogy, that hee was able to say as hee was taught; maintained and abetted, cheifly, by the Viscount *Lovell*, the E. of Lincolne, Sir *Thomas Broughton*, and Sir *Symon Preist*, &c. who being presented to the Duke and Dutchesse of Burgondy and by them honorably entertained, drew to him in Flanders one *Martin Swartz* (a Captaine of a very eminent fame) and some forces, with which hee made over into Ireland where they received him as *Edward* Earle of *Warwick*, as hee was of many here at home: and when the deceit was discovered, the excuse was, those Lords but used this counterfet of the Earle for a Colour, whilst they could get him out of the Tower to make him King. But the vaile is easily taken from the face of such impostors, examples giving us light in many; for though some men may, all cannot be deceived: so *Speudo-Agrippa* in the time of *Tiberius* was soone found to bee *Clemens* the servant of *Agrippa*, though very like to him, and *Puesdo-Nero* in *Otho's* time, who tooke upon him to be *Nero* revived, was quickly unmasked.

Dion, Tacitus, Suetonius.

Counterfeit Princes.

Valerius Paterculus telleth of a certaine ambitious counterfet in Macedonia, who called himselfe *Philip*; and would be reputed the next heire of the Crowne, but was discovered and nicknamed *Pesudo-Philippus*; Also in the Raigne of *Commodus* one pretended to be *Sextus Claudianus*, the son of *Maximus*; with many such that are obvious in old stories; and many of the like stampe have beene here convicted in *England*; which bred the greater jealousy of this *Richard*, when hee came first to be heard of, Though those jealosies proceeded not from the detection of any fraud in him, but of the late imposture of the said *Lambert* the Shooemakers son, and the abuse of the Complotters; for the Kingdome having been abused with those *Pseudo-Clarences*, had reason to bee doubtfull of every unknowne person, which assumed the name of greatnesse; in regard whereof, many shrunke in their opinions from this *Perkin*, or *Richard*; many others suspecting their beliefe, were very curious to inform themselves who the further they inquired, were the more confirmed, that hee was no other but the second son of *Edward* the Fourth, against whom those of the harder credulity objected it as an impossibility, that this young Duke could bee conveyed out of the Tower, so long, and so concealed; which the wiser sort could easily answer by many ancient examples, which give us divers

Its written by some of the old Historians that King *Harold* was not slaine at the Battaile of *Hastings*, by the Conquerer; but that he survived & went to Ierusalem, &c. But it not importeth whether He were the true *Harold*, or *Pseudo Harold*, because he never came to claime any thing in England.

vers Relations of Noble Children preserved more admirably: and this young Duke himselfe, in his owne behalfe, when such objections were made against him, did alledge to *James* King of Scotland the History of *Ioab* mentioned in the Booke of the Kings, and that most speciall one of *Moses*: which the Dutches his Aunt Sister German to his Father, was strongly confirmed in, giving him all answerable and honorable accommodation: so did the chiefe Nobility of those parts, and as an heire of the house of Yorke, there was rendred him the Title of *La-Rose-Blanch*, the proper and ancient devise of the house of Yorke; with all, a gallant Guard of Souldiers was allowed him for attendance, and much was hee favored by the Arch-Duke *Maximilian* King of the Romans, by *Philip* his Sonne Duke of Burgondy, *Charles* the *French* King, the King of Portugall and Scotland, by the chiefest of Ireland and many Personages in England, who at extreame perill and hazard avowed him to be the second son of *Edward* the fourth.

The Princes aforementioned readily supplying him with Coyne and assistance, towards his atcheivements. King *Henry* actively apprehends what it threatned, and bestirs himselfe to take of their inclinations, dispatching Doctor *William Warkam* (after Archbishop of Canterbury) with Sr. *Edward Poynings* a grave and worthy Knight, to under-rate his credit with those Princes; and such strong perswasions were used That *Philip* Duke of Burgondy (for his Father *Maximilian* was before returned into Austria) utterly declines himselfe and his subjects from his first ingagement, but excepted the Widdow Dutchesse of Burgondy, over whom hee had no power of command, because shee had all justice and Jurisdiction in those large signories whereof her dowry was composed.

The practice of Hen. 7. with the Duke of Burgondy.

And thus *Richard* was supplanted here; what hope of ayde hee had, or did expect by his voyage into Portugall, I cannot say, though his entertainment there was honorable: but by reason of the distance of the Country it may bee thought hee was to build little upon any from thence; his chiefe confidence and refuge being in England and Ireland, where he had a good party, and sayled with a prety Fleete into Ireland; there hee was welcomed, and received as the the second Sonne of King *Edward*; some of the *Geraldins* and other great Lords in Ireland, purposing to make him their King; To overtake him betimes there too, Doctor *Henry Deane*, Abbot of Lanthory (a very wise, able man) was sent and made Chancellor of Ireland; with him went the said Sr. *Edward Poynings*, who so actively bestirred themselves that

The meanes used by Hen. 7. to prevent the practises of Perkin in Ireland.

that in short time they drew the Irish from *Perkin*, so that now hee must returne home, but by the way was encouraged, to apply himselfe to *Iames* King of Scotland, whither forthwith hee directs his hopes, and found his entertainment answerable to them: the King receiving him very Nobly by his title of Duke of York, calls him Cozen, with promises to give him strong footing in England, and (in earnest of his better intents) bestowed in Marriage upon him, the most Noble and faire Lady *Katharine Gordon* his neere kinswoman, Daughter of *Alexander* Earle of Huntly: This came home very sharpely to King *Henry*, who knew King *James* to bee a Prince so Wise, and Valiant, that no easy delusion could abuse him.

This Lady was so rarely faire and lovely that King *H. 7* wondred at her beauty, and was inamored of her sending her to London to be safely kept till his returne out of the West Countries, where he then was and first saw her.

And true it is, King *Iames* was very precise in his consideration of this young Duke: but very cleerely confirmed before hee would acknowledge him. King *Henry* is very Studious how to thwart the event of this scene, and unfasten the King: but casts his confidence againe, upon the fortune of his judgement, and sends many Protestations with rich promises, to King *Iames* for Perkin (for now wee shall so call him with the times) which tooke small effect at first; but King *Henry* (being a man pregnant to finde any advantage, and one whose providence would not let it die) remembers the stong affinity and friendship betwixt King *James* and *Ferdinando* King of Castile, (one of the most Noble Princes then living.) At that time too, it happened so happily, there was a Treaty and intelligence betwixt *Henry* the Seventh and *Ferdinando*, for proposition of a Marriage of *Arthur* the Prince of Wales, and *Katharine* Daughter of King *Ferdinando*: this occasion no sooner offered it selfe to his consideration, but a Post was dispatcht to Castile, with Letters and Instructions to give the King to know what had passed betweene him and King *James* of Scotland, urging him to use the Power and Credit hee had with him, for the delivery of Perkin to himselfe: which *Ferdinando* undertooke; and sends *Don Pedro Ayala* (not one *Peter Hialas*, or *Peter Hayles*) as our vulgar stories have (a wise and learned man and of a very Noble house) who so ably used his Braine in this imployment, that King *James* passed to him his promise, to dismisse *Perkin* to his own fortunes; But would by no meanes deliver him to the King.

The practice of *H. 7.* to the *King* of Scots, and of Castile to get or supplant *Perkins*.

Don Pedro, Aylau.

Thus *Perkin* was againe supplanted *Virtute vel dolo*, and of necessity driven into Ireland, where hee was formerly received and entertained; whilst they were agitating their first Plot of setling him King, *Charles* the French King

Hall in H. 7.

sends to him *Lois de Laques* and *Estiene Friant*, to offer him his friendship and ayde; with this good newes *Perkin* hasted into France, where hee found his welcome very honorable, as befitting a Prince, a Guard appointed to attend him, of which Monsieur *Congre-Salle* was Captaine; before this King *Henry* had threatned France with an Army, but now upon a better view and deliberation, foreseeing what this had in it, He propounds very faire Conditions for a Peace with the French King, which the French King was as willing to intertaine, and so it was concluded; *Perkin* after this began to thinke the King shortned his respects, and looked upon him (as it were) but *imagine lusca*, with halfe a Countenance, and fearing there might bee some capitulation in this new League, that might concerne his liberty, privately quits Paris, returning to his Aunt of Burgondy. Although *Perkin* was thus shortned in his forraine expectations, hee had those both in *England* and *Jreland*, that much favored him and his cause, making another voyage into *Ireland*, but returned with his first comfort; for though they stood constantly affected and were willing, the Kings Officers curbed them so, they could not stir.

From *Ireland* hee sayled into *England*, landing at Bodmin in Cornewall, the Cornish and Westerne men thereabouts receiving him very gladly, proclayming him King of *England* and of *France*, &c, by the Title of *Richard* the Fourth (as Hee had beene proclaimed before in the North parts of *England*, by the Councell and Countenance of the King of Scots.) Out of Cornewall Hee marches into Devonshire to Exeter, to which Hee layd Siege, having then about five thousand men in his Army; but the Kings being at hand and farre stronger, Hee was forc't to rise from the siege, upon which those few friends Hee had left (finding His want, and the King with greater strength approaching) forsooke him to provide for themselves: thus abandoned, no way before him but flight, and being well mounted, with a traine of some forty or fifty resolute Gentlemen, recovers the Abby of Beanely in Hampshire, where Hee tooke Sanctuary, from which the Kings party who persued Him would violently have surprised Him;

Which the Abbot and Religious persons would not indure as a thing too foule against their Priviledge. The King after sends to him profers of favours and mercy, with promises of such Honour and Condition as drew Him to the Court, where the King looked upon him with a very Gratious and Bountifull usage as a Noble person;

Perkins Entertainment in the Court.

But

But his prompting Jealousies and Feares soone cast a dulnesse over this first favours and promises; Then a Guard must bee set upon *Perkin* and his usuall freedome restrained; these were harsh presages (Hee thought) which so justly moved His suspition and discontent that hee thought Sanctuary againe must bee his best safety, and passing by the Monastery of Shrene, hee suddenly slips into it from his Guard, whither the King sends unto him with perswasions of the first Courtly and Honorable tincture; But *Perkin* that had discerned the Hook, was not easily to be tempted with the bait this second time.

Then the King dealt with the Prior for him, who would not yeeld him, but upon faithfull promise from the King to use him with all favour and grace, which was protested, although *Perkin* no sooner came into his power againe but hee was sent to the Tower, where his imprisonment was made so hard and rude, that it much dejected and troubled him, oftentimes in private and with peircing groanes, having beene heard to wish himselfe borne the Sonne of any Pesant. And indeed, every one could tell hee fared the worse for his Name, it being an observation of those times that there was three men most feared of the King.

Edward Plantagenet Earle of Warwicke, *Perkin*, alias *Richard Plantagenet*, and *Edmond de la Poole* Sonne of King *Edwards* Sister, all of the Family of Yorke, but most of all *Perkin*, being of a more active spirit, so more sensible of his wrongs then the other; and cost the King more Consultation and Treasure in the working him into his hands; Therefore answerably aggravated his miseries and disgraces which now beganne to exceede; for hee was not onely sharpely restrained in the Tower, but the fame was the Question or **Gehenne* was given Him: sometimes he was taken forth, and carried in most ignominious manner abroade, to bee set in the Pillory, otherwhile in the Stockes; after all these bitter and cruell punishments (to pull downe his stomacke) there was sent some unto Him of purpose to perswade his submission to the Kings mercy, and by renowncing His Blood, Birth, and Title, to confesse himselfe no other but *Perkin Warberk* the Sonne of a base Flemming, which Hee scorning and denying, His sufferings were made more rigorous, and Hee lodged poorely and basely, as meanely fedde, worse cladde, untill at length by Torments and Extremities, Hee was forc't to say any thing, and content to unsay what they would have Him, to accuse Himselfe by

* Rack.

by a forc't Recantation of his Family Name, and Royall Parentage; this must bee compell'd too under His hand, then to bee brought by the Officers unto the most publique places of *London* and *Westminster*, to suffer as before related, and with a loud voyce to reade the same, which might passe at present with the multitude for current, who knew not how it was forced from Him, nor had judgement enough to know and consider that Racks and Tortures have made very able men accuse themselves and others unjustly: *Seneca* telleth of a man who being suspected of Theft was inforced by torture to confesse the theft and his fellow Theeves; but haveing none, hee accused the good and just *Cato*, to avoyd the torture; nay (which is a thing of more horror) it maketh men by false Oaths to blaspheme God; Therefore Saint *Augustine* inveigheth sharply against the cruell use of it, and amongst many other sins, which hee findeth in it, this is one,

The force and mischiefe of Torture.

August. in Civitat Dei.

Tortus si diutius nolet sustinere Tormenta, quod non commisit, se commisisse dicit.

The tortured gladly doing this the sooner to exchange those torments with death as the far lesse pain.

And therefore this young Man may bee excusable in what hee did against himselfe; his youth being ignorant of these high points of Honour, and could not yet bee confirmed in any brave and firme resolution, nor happily in Religion, and the worse also by the reason of his long imprisonment and heavy trouble, having no Councell to strengthen him, nor so much as in Charity to comfort Him, but left a miserable desperate forlorne Man, and feared to bee so for ever, and at the best. And if learned grave Men, Men of grace, having large Talents of Spirit and Science, for feare of such punishments have denyed some chiefe points of Christian Faith, yet have beene excused for the torture sake; (of which wee have testimony in the Ecclesiasticall Stories) what may a tender and unexperienced youth doe? For which just causes the best Doctors of the Civill Law, and also of Theology condemne and aborre the use of Torture, as having a further mischiefe in it, and is *Arcanum Gehennæ* a secret of Torture or of Hell.

The French call torture *la Gehenne*.

For when the Prisoners body by exteame toment is brought

brought into any mortall State, or symptome of death, or made incurable and deadly, then to avoyde the imputation of Murder, the prisoner by a short and private processe is condemned of some capitall crime, and presently executed, whilst there is yet some life in him; And to that censure *Perkin* at last came; for nothing could serve but his blood, his confession being onely extorted from him to perswade the People hee was an impostor, and because they could not lay hold of his Life by the Course of Law or Justice (being not attainted nor condemned of any capitall crime.) This scruple being a little considered, there was found out a way to remove that, and matter enough to make him guilty of a capitall offence, for which purpose it was devised there should a practise of escape bee offered him; and because the case of *Edward Plantagenet*, Earle of VVarrwicke, was like unto his, and as well wisht, being not attainted of any crime, hee also must desire to escape, that devise being the onely matter of guilt, or capitall crime, which was wanting, and might bee (as it were) created for them the more colorably to effect their executions; there not wanting instruments for that purpose to betray their innocent confidence, whose inprisonment had layne so heavily and cruelly upon them; that they were easily perswaded to catch at any hope of liberty.

Some say the Earle of Warwicke at his arraignment was charged with perswading the other to make this escape, but sure it is they both gladly hearkened to the motion of it; And were (soone after) accused as guilty of practise and Conspiracy, to escape out of the Tower, so for the same arraigned and condemned to die: though great difference was put in their processe, and execution; for the Earle of Warwick was tryed by his noble Peeres, and had the supplice of a Nobleman, in an honorable place, the Tower of London: *Perkin* alias *Richard*, by a Common Jury, who are men (many times) of little honesty, and to suffer at the common and infamous place, Tyburne; by the name of *Perkin Warbecke*, to confirme the People Hee was what they condemned him for; For this Nick-name was supposed to have utterly disnobled Him, and (as it were) divested Him of all his Noble Blood and Titles, the condition of an impostor serving best for a cloke against that purple shower, which was at the fall and cruell usage of this miserable Prince. Yorke and Warwick, paralels.

It

It may bee thought, the Earle of VVarwicke had as shamefully suffered, if the Wit and Malice of the Cardinall could have reacht to have made him a counterfeit; But all men knew Hee was not onely a true and certaine Prince, but free from all practise, yet Hee was restrained of his liberty, and a prisoner the most part of His life; from the time of his Fathers attainder untill He Suffered; this was after they had survived King *Richard* their Unckle about fifteen years.

Of escape.

Now for their Offence, the learned Judges will tell us of what Nature and Quality, it is called in Law.

The French word escape, is to seeke to be free, and the French men translate escape into the Latine *Salvus*.

Escape what.

Some holding an escape to bee but an errour, a naturall dislike of bondage, or a forfeit of simplicity, proceeding from a naturall and very tolerable desire of liberty, which opinion is contingent to right; And the cause of these two Princes may also bee the better received, if it bee well considered, that this Plot of their escape was not projected by themselves, but cunningly propounded to them by proper instruments (being young and unexperienced) to intangle them in some capitall offence, and so of Death, of which kinde of offences they stood cleere before, not once accused, haveing never beene indicted, or attainted of any thing Capitall. Therefore now their innocence must bee made guilty; And in this I say no more then all our Historians, or others say, who agree in one opinion that The KING could not take away the lives of *Perkin Warbecke* and this Earle of Warwicke, untill this practise of their escape was layde to them, and they made guilty thereof. Therefore they were not Traytors before, neither was *Perkin* now to bee thought a Counterfeit, but a Prince of the Bloud, clayming the Crowne; for otherwayes, Hee was *Perkin* of Flanders, a base fellow and a most culpable and notorious Traitor: then what neede they looke further for a Crime to put him to Death?

And if Hee were not a Traitor, surely it was a Tyranny to make of an Innocent and guiltlesse Man a guilty Felon, and by Traines, and Acts, to forge an offence out of nothing.

For doubtlesse an Innocent and a true man may seeke freedome, and purpose an act of escape, also commit it, and yet be still an honest Man, and a faithfull good subject; for nature and reason teacheth and alloweth all men to eschew injuries and oppression.

Besides

Besides this Practise of those young men, to escape, was found (as *Pollidor* well observeth) *Crimen Alienum*, and not *Crimen proprium*: then how much greater was the wrong, to take away their lives.

But however it may bee laid upon them, it was nothing but a desire of liberty out of durance, in which they were kept for a small, or no offence.

The Civill law holdeth suspition of flight or escape, to bee no crime. *Suspicio fugæ quia, non solet detrimentum, reipublice adferre, non censetur crimen*; so *ulpian*. And by the Lawes of *England*, if a Prisoner doe escape, who is not imprisoned for Treason, or felony, but some lesser fault of trespasse according to the old Law of *England*.

Just: *Stanford*, *in pleas de la Corone*. lib. 1. cap. 26, 27.

Escapæ non adjudicabitur versus eum, qui Commissus est prisonæ, pro transgressione. Escape shall not bee adjudged for Felony, or other crime, in one who is committed for trespasse.

For the offence of the escape is made in the common Law, to be of the same nature and guilt with the crime whereof the Prisoner is attainted; And certainely neither the Earle of *Warwicke*, nor *Richard* alias *Perkin* were attainted of Treason or Felony, &c. before.

But to close this dispute and tragedy, not long after some of the Instruments which betrayed them into this, as *Walter Blunt*, *Thomas Astwood*, servants to the Lieutenant of the Tower, finished at *Tiburn* because they should tell no tales.

And to this succinct relation; there can be no better testimony then the hands of those witnesses, who have sealed their confession and knowledge with their bloods.

Men of all conditions and estates, all maintaining at the last gaspe, that *Perkin* was the true Duke of Yorke, whose Affirmations I will produce, give mee but leave by the way, to answer one Objection or Cavill brought against this Duke called in scorn, *Perkin Warbecke*. A new Writer affirming him to bee an Impostor, whose learning may be as much mistaken in this, as other things, though he laid a great pretence to knowledge, especially in the History of *England* and other Countreyes: indeed his judgement and reading are much exprest alike, in his Pamphlet which he cals the History of *Perkin Warbecke*, wherein he forfeits all his skill, to make him a parallel in advers fortunes, and supposed base quality, to the unhappy *Don Sebastian* late King of *Portugall*, who he also protests an Impostore. And to arrive at this huge knowledge, (he would have us thinke) hee tooke much paines in the sifting of Authors (and indeed I thinke he did sift them) concerning his ignorance in the case of *Don Sebastian* (if he be not too wise to have it informed) I will urge some reasons on *Don Sebastians* side, who was King of *Portugall*: and invading the Kingdom of *Barbary*, *Anno Dom.* 1584. was overthrown in a fierce & bloody Battel in the fields of *Alcazer*, by the King of *Morucco*, where it

Whether *Don Sebastian* of *Portugall* were a Counterfeit or not.

was thought he was slaine, but escaped and fled secretly, traverstite or disguised: travailing in that manner through many parts of *Africa* and *Asia* some 30. yeares, in which time and travaile he suffered much, lived in Captivity and misery, but at last got away into *Europe* with purpose to have got into *Portugall* (if possible) to repossesse the Kingdome.

In this returne he came to *Venice*, there discovered himselfe, and desires aide of the *Venetian* States: they entertained him as a Prince distressed, gave him good words, but durst not lend him Assistance, fearing the King of *Spaine*; Yet the chiefe Senators, and many of the wisest of the Signiory, made no doubt of him.

Among them *Signieur Lorenzo Justiniano* of the Senators Order, (a man of wise and great abilities) was appointed by the States, a Commissioner (with others) to hear and examine this cause of *Don Sebastian*, in which they tooke much paines. And this *Signieur Lorenzo* (being lieger Ambassadour in *England*) affirmed and 162. protested solemnly, he and all the other Commissioners were clear and very confident he was *Don Sebastian* King of *Portugall*, notwithstanding they durst not give him aide, but councelled him for *France*, where the King favoured right, without feare of anothers displeasure. But taking *Florence* in his way, in the habit of a Fryer, he was observ'd and discovered by some spyes which the Grand Duke of *Tuscany* had set upon him from *Venice*: who to insinuate with the King of Spaine, *Philip* the second, and for some other commodious considerations, delivered *Sebastian* to the Governour of *Orbattelli* (a Spanish Port in *Tuscany*) from thence sent him by Sea to the Count *De le Mos*, Vice-roy of *Naples*, who conveyed him into *Spaine*: there for a while his entertainment was no better then in the Gallies; what other welcome hee had I know not; but the fame went certainly he was secretly made away after *Philip* the third was King. The said Vice-roy of *Naples* confessed in secret to a friend of his, he verily believed his prisoner was the true *Sebastian* King of *Portugall*, and was induced to be of that opinion, by the strong Testimonies, and many strange and peculiar markes, which some Honourable *Portugesses* did know him by, all found about the body of this *Sebastian*. And the *French* King, *Henry* the 4th it should seeme, was perswaded no lesse: for when the newes was told him the Duke of *Florence* had sent this *Sebastian* to the King of *Spaine*, he told the Queene what an ill deed her Unckle had done in these words; *Nostre Uncle a faict un act fort indigne de sa Persone.*

Hic legatus hæc Domino Baroni Darcey retulit.

Doctor *Stephen de Sampugo*, in a letter to *Joseph Texere*, Councellour and Almoner to the most Christian King, writes thus. The King *Don Sebastian* is here in *Venice*, &c. So soone as hee arrived here (where he hoped to find support) the Ambassadour of *Castile* persecuted him very cruelly, perswading the Signeury that he was a *Calabrois*, &c. I sweare to your Father-hood by the Passion of

Jesus Christ, this man is truly the King *Don Sebastian*, he hath all the markes on his body, without failing in any one as he had in his infancy, only the wounds excepted which he received in that Battel at *Affricke*, he gives the reason of his life, & account of all his passages, &c. He is knowne and re-known by the Conciergres, by the Judges, by the greater part of the Senate, and by his owne Confessor, &c. and a great deal more of him upon knowledg he justifies: as much witnesses *Jon de Castro*, Sonne to *Don de Alvaro de Castro*, one of the four Governours that ruled the Kingdome Conjunctly with the King *Don Sebastian*; who in his letter the same man sayes thus. The King *Don Sebastian* (whom the enemies call a *Calabrois*) is the very same which is detained here, as certainly as you are Fryer *Joseph*, and my selfe *Don Jon*. He departed alive from the battaile, but very sore wounded: God having so delivered him with some other of his company, amongst whom was the Duke *Zuegro*, *&c.* as for the Exterior marks of his body he wants not one of them; he is wounded on the brow of the right eye and on the head, as many witnessed when they saw him in the *Affrick* Battell. His hand-writing is still the same, observing the very same method, as is very well remembred by divers.

There might much more be instanced in the behalfe of this *Sebastian*, but this may serve for better intelligence, to which I may adde, that men experienced in the Affaires and policy of State, know it a rare thing to find in any History the examples of a Prince being seised and possessed of any *Signiory* or *Principality* (how unlawfull soever) who hath resigned them or any part to the true heires. Have we not instances at home, where the Sonne hath taken the Kingdome from the Father, and would not let it goe againe, but rather endeavoured to hast his Fathers fate? Much after that manner when *Henry* Duke of *Lancaster* had got the Kingdome, he held it and would not resigne to the right Heyr *Richard* the second, nor after his death to the Earle of *March*, though these were no Impostors; neither was *Edward* Earl of *Warwicke*: yet King *Henry* would not let his hold goe: and the Cardinall Favourite, finding he could not compasse his aymes one way, contrived it another. By the *Machivilian* advice he gave to *Ferdinand* King of *Castile*, not to conclude the treaty of the Marriage betweene Prince *Arthur* and his Daughter *Katherine* untill this Earle and *Perkin* were disposed of, which *Ferdidando* followed and urged the King, pretending it the security of his Estate and Issue.

Edward 2. and Edward 3.

In briefe, it is not possible to perswade a private man, though wrongfully possessed to acknowledge the true proprietary hath a better title then he.

How unjustly have the Kings of *Spaine* detain'd sundry Signeuries and Principalities from the lawfull Heirs: yet if the wrong done by such another disseising Lord, be put to this former Usurper, *Mala fide* (as the Imperiall *Jurisconsulti* will terme him) his sentence will be, such a Rapinous Prince doth wrong.

But let us now take a more particular view of those witnesses who stood for *Perkin*. And having formerly mentioned Sir *Robert Clifford*, a Knight of the Noble Family of the Barons *Cliffords*, I will proceed with that which may be the more remarkable in him, because hee was of a Family that long hated the House of Yorke, from the Battaile of *Wakefield*, when and where they resolved an enmity so deadly, as was not to bee reconciled or satisfied whilst one of them remained; yet became followers againe of the White Rose family; and this Sir *Robert Clifford* served King *Edward* very neare, and in good credit, so could not but have an assured knowledge of the Kings Sonnes, and was therefore the more particularly sent to certifie his knowledge, who certainely affirmed him to bee the younger sonne of *Edward* 4. and confirmed many with him, such as had likewise served King *Edward*, and had been acquainted with the Prince his conveying beyond Sea, though much was done to alter Sir *Roberts* opinion: the Lord *Fitz-Walter* was of the same beliefe, and avowed *Perkin* the true Duke of *York*, most constantly unto death; as resolute was Sir *William Stanley*, though he were Lord Chamberlaine to *Henry* the seventh, and in great favour; with Sir *George Nevill* Brother to the Earle of Westmorland, Sir *Symon Mountford*, Sir *William Daubeny*, father to the Lord *Daubeny*, Sir *Thomas Thwaits*, Sir *Robert Ratcliffe* of the house of the Baron *FitzWalter*, Sir *John Taylor*, Sir *Thomas Chaloner*, *Thomas Bagnall* with many other Gentlemen of quality, all maintaining him to be the Duke of Yorke, sonne of *Edward* the fourth, & sundry of the Clergy who had beene Chaplaines to the King his Father, or otherwise occasioned to attend the Court, as Doctor *Rochford*, Doctor *Poynes*, Doctor *Sutton*, Doctor *Worsley* Deane of St. *Pauls*, Doctor *Leyborn*, Doctor *Lesly*, with many other learned Professors of Divinity, who would not endure to heare him called *Perkin*. [a] The Lord *FitzWater*, Sir *William Stanley*, Sir *Simon Mountford*, Sir *Robert Ratcliffe*, Sir *William Daubeny* (as martyrs of state) confirmed their Testimonies with their bloods. So did the Kings Serjant *Ferrier*, who left the Kings service, and applyed himselfe to *Perkin*, for which he was executed as a Traitor; and one *Edwards* who had served this Duke *Richard*, was cut in pieces for the same cause, also *Corbet*, Sir *Quinton Betts*, and *Gage*, Gentlemen of good worth, with 200. more at least, put to death in sundry Cities and Townes, particularly in *Kent*, *Essex*, *Suffolke*, *Norfolke*, and about *London* for their confidence and opinions in this Prince.

There were some great men (though they made noe profession of their knowledge of him,) could whisper it one to another which in generall words, is confessed by all our better writers; who say, that as well the Noblemen, as others, held the said *Perkin* to be

Moor, Hollinsh. Stow, Gainsford.

Moor, Hollinsh. Stow, Grafton, Gainsford, Hal.

Idem Autor.

[a] He was the Noble, Progenitor of the Earles of *York*.

Hollinshed, Grafton, Hall, Stow.

be the younger Sonne of King *Edward* the Fourth.

And Sir Thomas *Moore* after Doctor *Morton*, thus writeth, The man commonly called *Perkin Warbeck*, was as well with the Prince, as with the people, held to be the younger Sonne of King *Edward* the Fourth.

John Morton. *Thomas Moor.* *Grafton.*

Richard *Grafton* affirmeth the same, in Flanders (saith he) and most of all here in England, it was received for an undoubted truth, not onely of the people but of the Nobles, that *Perkin* was the Sonne of King *Edward* the Fourth. And they all swore and affirmed this to be true; The learned and famous Mr. *Cambden* averreth, there were many wise, grave and persons of good intelligence, (who liued in that time and neere it) That affirmed confidently this *Perkin* was second Sonne to King *Edward*, then both the Brothers were not made a way by King *Richard*, and surely it was little reason, or policy, to cut off the one & spare the other, neither indeed was there ever any proofes made, by Testimony, Argument, or Presumption, nor by Reason, Honour, or Policy, that this crime could be his, though many to the contrary; for he not onely preserved his Nephew the young Earle of Warwicke, but in his confidence (a speciall note of his magnanimity) gave him libertie, pleasure, and the commmand of a Statly house of his owne.

Mr. *William Cambden.*

Now if he had beene so Ambitious and bloudy, he would have provided otherwise for him, knowing his Title was to take place, if his bloud had not beene attainted in his Father; in regard whereof King *Richard* when his owne Sonne was dead, caused his Nephew *Iohn de la Poole*, Eldest Sonne of the Duke of *Suffolke*, and of the Dutches his sister, (then the next lawfull heir to the Crowne) to be proclaimed heir apparant, an Argument of respect to his kindred & next title to the Crowne, in whomsoever it was; which other men regarded not so much as the unhappy Sequel shewed: (& there was an impious necessitie in that) for whilst the Prince of Yorke survived, (Especially the males) no other titular Lord, or pretender could be King by his owne right, or by colour of right, nor by any other meanes: unlesse he had married a daughter, and the Eldest Daughter of King *Edward* the Fourth.

Some think he dyed unnaturally.

And although the deathes & manner of taking away these Princes (the Sonnes of King *Edward*) is held by our writers uncertaine and obscure, It is manifest (at least for the generall manner of their death) to be either by the Publicke sword, that is the sword of Iustice, or of Battaile as were King *Richard*, the Children of the Duke of *Clarence* and the Duke of *Suffolke*, &c. or by the private sword, that is, by secret and close slights, treachery (which the *Romans* called *Insidiæ*, *dolus*, by Smothering, Strangling, Poyson, Sorcery, &c. And that the sword was used against the family of Yorke, there is more then conjecture, both by Testimonies of writers, and records King *Edward* himselfe, (as Credible Authors report)

Publike sword. Private sword.

The arts of treachery.

port) dyed of poyson. In the Parliament *Anno. 1. Richardi tertij* there was accused and attainted of sorcerie and such other devilish practices. Doctor *Lewis*, Doctor *Morton*, William *Knevitt*, of *Buckingham*, the Countesse of *Richmont*, Thomas *Nandick*, of Cambridge Conjurer, with others; There was also an Earle accused of the same hellish Art, and an old Manuscript Booke, which I have seene, sayes, that Doctor *Morton* and a certaine Countesse, contriveing the death of King *Edward* and others, resolv'd it by poyson.

Reasons why King *Richard* should not destroy his Nephewes.

Which are conjectures and proofes more positive and strong against them, then any, they have against King *Richard*, but it was a great neglect in their malice, makeing King *Richard* soe politick and treacherous as they did, not to charge him also with these Princes Sisters, For it could not serve his turne, to rid away the Brothers, and not them; who were capable of the Crowne and had their turne royall, before any Collaterall males. Then he had, the children of his elder Brother, George Duke of Clarence, Edward *Plantagenet* Earl of *Warwick*, & the Lady Margaret his sister, after countesse of Salisbury to make away; for they without their Fathers corruption of bloud (which might easily have beene salved by Parliament, the Lords and Commons affecting them) had a Priority of bloud and precedency of Title before the Protector.

I would aske the reason too why King *Richard* might not endure his Nephewes (being by Parliament held and adjudged illegitimate) as well as the Kings *Henry* 7. and *Henry* the eight, endured *Arthur Plantagenet*, the Bastard of the same King *Edward* their natales and cases being alike, or why Sir Thomas *Moore* and Doctor *Morton* should in one place, say it was held in doubt, when or how they were made away, and in another place, to averr that Tiroll and Dighton being examined, confessed plainely, the murmurder of them and all the manner of it.

These be contraries which with a great disadvantage, drawes their allegation into another argument, *Bicorne*, or *Crocodilites*; For in revealing the confession of these men, it is implicatively granted, their fault was not then to be punished, and soe it appeares no fault: or not worth the consideration, the confession of a man being the greatest evidence, can be produced against him. Then in regard the confession of those was such as might not be opened, nor the crime called in question (as the same Authors acknowledge) it was but a fained confession, and they had done better not to have mentioned such a thing, which begot but a jealousie in the falsitie thereof, or privity of some great ones in it; & a just imputation of injustice upon the Magistracy. For if Dighton, Tirroll, Forrest and Slater, confesse the murder in Act and manner, King *Richard* being dead (who was said to subborne and protect them) necessarily and in due course of justice, (especially in the Act of so high a nature, and notice as this was) The pu-

Other great ones privy to the deaths of those Princes, especially of King *Edwards* Sons.

nishment

nishment should have beene expected with all extremity.

But being for some unknowne causes deferred, and after a while quite omitted and pardoned, it may be thought such strange Clemency and impunitie proceeded from a singular high indulgence, or else, those examinations and confessions, werebut Buzes and quaint devises, to amaze the people, and entertaine them with expectation of a justice, to be done in some more convenient time (which was never) This was after the death of King *Richard*. All that was done before, was to make him the Author of that horrible crime and no bodie else; For Dighton and the rest were in security and liberty, yet it stood in good steed with the Lancastrians, to draw the peoples hate upon King *Richard*, not unlike that story of great *Alexander*, and a noble man in his Court, who stood so high in the favour of his Nobles and people, that the King grew jealous, and fearefull of his Popularity, studying how he might decline it and him to contempt, but could finde no colour or apt occasion, because he was soe strongly fixt in the peoples likeing and was a man of so great a desert, that noe crime could bee charged upon him. The King unbosoming himselfe to the councell and care of a freind one *Medius* (of his Country, as I thinke) had this advise.

Sir (quoth hee) let not this mans greatnesse trouble you, cause him to be accused of some hainous crime, (though falsly) and wee will finde meanes to make him guiltie, so formally and firmely, that the brand of it shall sticke upon him ever, which he delivered in these termes, though divers, yet the same in effect. *Medeatur licet vulneri, qui morsus, aut dilaniatus est, remanebit tamen Cicatrix.* And it is truely approved by an Antient Christian Poet, thus,

Paulum distare videntur,
Suspecti vereque rei. *Ausonius.*

The guilty and suspected Innocent,
In mans opinion are little different.

For there is no more dangerous or fatall destiny to greatenesse, then to be intangled in the multitudes contempt, *Odium et Contemptus*, being the two evills that overthrow Kings, and Kingdomes, the one, that is, Contempt, proceeding from the vanity and obstinacy of the Prince, the other from the peoples opinion of him and his vices, And then he must neither raigne, nor live any longer: *Ennius* said with *Cicero, quem oderunt perijsse expetunt:* And soe all that was practised upon the fortune, fame, and person of King *Richard* was by this rule (though in the judgment and equity of the most knowing in those times) their cunning *translatio Criminis* could take noe hold of him, neither appeares it probable, that the Earle of Richmond himselfe (when he had got all justice

Ennius apud Ciceronem offic. lib. 2.

justice and power in his hand) did hold King *Richard* guilty of the murder, and Subornation of those fellowes: nor them the Assasines; for doubtlesse then, being so wise and religious a Prince, he would have done all right to the lawes divine and humane, And that I beleeve in the extreamest and publick'st way of punishment, to make it more satisfactory; and terrible to the people and times: but they freely inioyed their liberty with security to naturall deaths without any question or apprehension, Tirrell excepted, who suffered for treason not long after committed by him, against King *Henry* himselfe. Neither was *John* Greene (named a party in this murder) ever called in question, nor doe the Historians of those times (though meere temporizers) charge him with this practise against his Nephewes, untill after his Coronation (some say they survived King *Richard*) and giveing this respite of time, there was no cause, why after that, he should make them away being then secure in his Throne and Title, and they longe before pronounced uncapable; First by the ecclesiasticall Iudges, then by the Barons and Parliament: and where was the cause of feare? but if King *Richard* had beene of that bloody constitution, the man whose life could be most prejudiciall unto him, was the Erle of Warwicke lawfull Sonne of *George Plantagenet* Duke of Clarence, Elder Brother to King *Richard*: now there was a necessitie for the Lancastrian faction (if they must have a King of that family) to take those Princes away, not to leave King *Richard* or his Sonne, nor yet any legitimate issue of Lancaster, for all those were before any of the house of Beauforts in the true order of Succession, and stood in their way, so did the Progeny of Brotherton, of Woodstocke, of both the Clarencies, Glocester, &c. Though they feared few, or none of those Titulare Lords being modest men, not affecting Soveraignty, but content with their owne private fate and feudall estate, when all was one with the Lancastrians, who were so vehement in their royall approaches, that besides King *Edward* the Fourth and his two Sonnes, King *Richard* and his Son, the Prince of *Wales*, there was afterward (and as occasion served) The Earle of *Warwicke* and Duke of *Suffolke* and others, both male and female, of that princely family, laid in their cold vrnes, and it must be so, else, there could be no place for the *Beauforts* and *Somersets*, their turnes being last (the Kings of *Portugall*, of *Castile*, and other being before them, if not excluded by Act of Parliament.)

Sir *Tho. Moor. Edward Hall. Ralph Hollinshead. John Stow, &c.*

In this Tragedy there was a Scene acted by *John de Vere* Earle of *Oxenford*, which may be worthy of our observation for example sake, and makes not against the cause of *Perkin*.

The Earle of Oxen persecutor of *Perkin*.

This Earle of *Oxenford* much affected and devoted to King *Henry* the Seventh, was a great enemie to this *Richard* (*Alias Perkin*) and I thinke the onely enemie he had of the great Nobility, how this dislike grew I cannot say, whether out of ignorance, or

incredulity

incredulity, or out of malice, hateing King *Edward*, and all that had a neare relation to that family, or else to applyhimselfe to the honour of the King, but he and the *Cardinall* are said to be the cheife vrgers of *Perkins* dispatch and hee being high constable pronounced the sentence against the young Earle of *Warwicke*, (which much distasted the Country) and ne're to *Heveningham* Castle, (that was his cheifest Seate) there lived in the woods an old *Hermit* (a very devoute and holy man as the fame of those times admit him) who seem'd much troubled to heare this newes, for the love he bare to the ancient and Noble family of *Oxenford*, of much anguish of Spirit, saying, the Earle and his house would repent, and rue that guilty and bloody pursuite of the innocent Princes, for the event of which prophesy this hath bine observed.

Not long after the Earle was arrested for an offence so small, that no man (considering his merit and credit with the King) could have thought it worth the question, for which he was fined at thirty thousand pounds (in those dayes a kingly sum,) [a] after this he lived many yeares in great discontent: and dyed without issue, or any child lawfully begotten by him, and in much shorter time then his life time, that great and [b] stately Earldome of *Oxenford*, with the opulent and Princly patrimony, was utterly dissipated, and *como sal in agua* (as the Spaniard saith in the refran) yet this Earle was a very wise, magnificent, learned, and religious man in the estimation of all that knew him, and one more like to raise, and acquire a new Erledome.[c] But it thus fell and was wasted, the Castles and Mannors dilapidated, the Chappell wherein this *John de Vere* and all his Ancestors lay intombed with their monuments quite defaced to the ground, their bones left under the open Aire in the feilds, and all this within lesse then threescore yeares after the death of the said Earle *John*; about the same time these unhappie Gentlemen suffered, there was a base [d] sone of King *Richard* the Third made away, having beene kept long before in Prison. The occasion as it seemeth was the attempt of certaine Irishmen of the *West*, and *South* parts, who would have got him into their power and made him their cheife, being strongly affected to any of the house of Yorke were they legitimate, or naturall, for *Richard* Duke of Yorkes sake sometimes their viceroy, and thus much in breife of that.

[e] Now to resolve a question, why the King deferred so long the death & execution of the Earle of *Warwick* & *Perkin*, and tooke so much deliberation after he had resolved it, one reason and the cheifest brought by some, is, That in regard *Perkin* was an Alien, and in the allegeance of a Forraigne Prince, therefore he could not be condemned, nor executed for felony, nor treason by our lawes: which is a ridiculous evasion, for we have frequent examples in our stories, that the naturall subjects of *France*, of *Scotland*, *Spaine*, *Portugall*, *Germany*, and *Italy*, have had judgement and

[a] This Earle *Iohn*, died *Anno.* 4 *H.* 8. 1512 *Dominus de Arundell viva voce*

[b] I may call it a stately Erledome, for the Earle of *Oxenford*, when he came to the possession of it, was offered by some 12000 pounds *per Annum.* and leave to his occupation all Mannors, Houses, Castles, Parks, Woods, Forrests, & all the Demesn lands thereto belonging, which might be more worth by yearly value then many Erldoms in this age.

[c] The Mathematicians that calculated, the Nativitie of this Earle *Edward*, told the Earle his Father, that the Earledome would fall in his Sons time.

[d] Bastards of King Richard. *Grafton & Chron. M. S. in quarto apud Dn. Rob. Cotton.*

[e] Why the publique justice deferred the death of the Princes.

and execution by our lawes, for felony and treason, as *Peter de Gaoston* a French man, Sir *Andrew Harcley* a *Scot*, and lately Dr. *Lopez* a Portugall, therefore apparantly that was not the cause the King so doubtfully, and (as it were) timerously deferred their Arraignments & Executions. The Heathens perhaps would have defined it some inward awe or concealed scruple, such as they called *Eumenides*, and *Eurinnies*, and beleeved haunted those men that had purposed or acted a wickednesse: upon which the Poet said well:

Dæmones Genij.

——*Patiturque suos mens saucia Manes.* And assigned to every man his protecting Spirit, whom the *Greekes* called *Dæmones*, the *Latines Genios*, concluding, that when the *Genius* of him against whom the mischiefe aimes, is stronger and more active then his who is to act it, there the Plot hardly taketh effect.

Plutarch in Anton.

For example, produce the mortall enmity betweene *Octavianus Cæsar*, and *M. Antonius*, in which *Anthony* could never prevaile by any Attempt: who consulting with his Soothsayers, they give the reason to bee the power of *Octavians* Genius above his. It is reported the great Philosopher *Appollonius* had such a secret protection, and so strong, that the Emperour *Domitian* had no power over his life, though hee studied meanes to take it, *Suidas* adding that this Philosopher in confidence of his *Genius* when he left the Emperour, added this verse,

Philostrat in vita Appollon.

Ου μεν με κτανεεις, επει ου τοι μορσιμος ειμι.

Me non occides quia fataliter protectus sum: which is that *Flaminus Vopiscus* calleth *Majestatem Apollonij* (as I guesse) and with it the Professors of Christian Religion agree in the effects, not in the causes, for those whom the Heathen call Δαιμονες *Dæmones*, &c. *Genios*, the Christian Theologues call Angels or Spirits, whereof they hold good and bad.

Vopiscus in Aureliano.

Angels good and bad.

But to returne to the matters further Allegate & Probate. The industrious Antiquary Master *John Stow*, being required to deliver his opinion concerning the proofes of this murther, affirmed it was never proved by any credible evidence, no not by probable suspitions, or so much as by the Knights of the Post, that King *Richard* was guilty of it. And Sir *Thomas Moore* (being puzzelled with his Equivocations) sayes, that it could never come to light what became of the bodies of these two Princes. *Grafton*, *Hall*, and *Hollinshead* agreeing in the same report, that the trueth hereof was utterly unknowne. Then where is their farre seeing knowledge, that will have them transported into Forraign Countreyes, or drowned, or their giganticke proofes, that say peremptorily, they were both murthered and buryed in the Tower by those foure named before: if so, we need go no further for the

truth.

truth. But these are splenitick reaches, and the *Parachronisme* is too grosse as the *Comædian* said,

Quod dictum, indictum est,
Quod modo ratum, irritum est.

Terentius in Phormio.

Besides, if *Perkin* were not the second Sonne of King *Edward*, he must bee nothing, for the *Flemish*, *French*, and *Wallons* acknowledged no such Noble young man to be borne in *Warbecke*, or in *Tourney*, but make honourable mention of a young Sonne of the King of *England*, who was brought to the Dutchesse of *Burgundy* his Aunt, being then in *Flanders*, and how hee was in *France* and in other Kingdomes. And surely so many Noble and discreet *English*, if they had not knowne him to be the same, by most certaine tokens, and evidence, would not so confidently have laid downe their lives to confirme their knowledge of him, or hazarded their judgements and honours upon an Imposture, or vanity, especially those who had places of Quality and Eminency neare the King then living, and were in favour at Court. Therefore I would be resolv'd from our *Anti-Richards*, what aim those Noble-men could have, in averring him the Son of *Edward* the Fourth by the hazard of their lives and Estates (if the KING pleased) and how could they expect lesse; for though they were enough to justifie it a truth, they were too few to maintaine it against him, there could be no aime or hope to super-induce young *Richard* to be King: but meerly I am perswaded in point of truth and honour, as they thought themselves bound to doe, they freely tendred their lives to make good what their Conscience & knowledge witnessed, for it would be an Imposture of a miraculous Deception, so many worthy and wise persons both of the Nobility and Clergy, some of them having served the King his Father and himselfe, that they all in their particular and generall intelligence and understandings, should be mistaken and cheated. I say it was a strange delusion if it could bee so: but indeede those that would have it, so leave it in question, and know not well what to make of their own relations, or how to resolve his History, and if wee marke Sir *Francis Bacon* in the life of *Henry* the Seventh (though his speculation be tender, and as favourable as hee can that way) touching the History of this young Duke, hee gently slides from it;

Explicit liber tertius.

The

THE FOVRTH BOOKE OF THE HISTORY OF KING RICHARD the Third.

The Contents.

UPon what occasion the sentence of Bastardy was given upon the Children of King Edward *the* 4th *and why.*

The sundry Loves, Wooings, Contracts and Marriages of King Edward *the Fourth.*

His divers Concubines, His device of the Fetterlock, and the Faulcon.

His wooing the Lady Elianor Talbott alias Butler, *the Lady* Bona *of Savoy, and the Lady* Elizabeth Gray *widdow, & his marriage with her.*

His former Marriage or Contract with the said Elianor, *her wrongs and her death. Kings must not marry the daughters of their Vassalls, nor other without the consent of their Barons, Doctor* Stillington *Bishop of* Bath *Imprisoned for speaking of King* Edwards *Marriage with the Lady* Elianor Talbott, Spuria vitulamina.

How King Edward *might have salved those Errors and prevented all the mischiefes following them. The Children of King* Edward *the Fourth declared*

The

The FOVRTH BOOK OF King Richard The Third.

THe Title King *Richard* the Third had to the Crown, accrued to him by the illegitimacie of the Children of King *Edward* the Fourth, and the Attainder of the Duke of Clarence, with the Corruption of his Blood, and forfeiture of the Title in him and in his Heirs, of which there was no question: but of the forfeiture and disheritage of the sons of *Edward* the Fourth there hath been much. The true cause hath not nor cannot be well known, without the Narration of King *Edward's* sundry Loves and Wooings, specially his Contracts and Marriages.

I shall not need to intimate how amorous and wanton this King was, his many Mistrisses or *Amasia's* he kept, in several private places; whereof the most famous was *Katharine de Clarington*, *Elizabeth Wiatt* alias *Lucy*, *Jane Shore*, the Lady *Elianor Talbot*. And it is worth the remembring (in the Concourse of such matters as these) there was another fair Creature so dear unto him, that his too much Affection begat Suspition; of which he gave her a kinde expression, by a quaint device sent unto her in a rich Jewel, fashioned much after the manner of the trivial Hieroglifs used in France, and called *Rebus de Picardy*. The device was, A Faulcon encompassed with a Fetter-lock: The Mott, *Au Faulcon Serrure*. The Caution lying in the ambiguity and double

How extreme his desires were, you may see in the Speech of the Duke of Buckingham, set down by Sir *Thomas Moor*.

sense of Faulcon: which being whole and proper, signifieth a Hawk; but divided, hath an obscene signification, and so Faulcon becometh an *æquivoque*.

The King afterward was so affected with this device, that he would have it carved and painted, in many of his Royal works yet to be seen at Fotheringhay and elsewhere.

Yet although the Kings Jealousie was thus particular to her, his Affection was as general to others; being a frank Gamester, and he that would cast at all, fairly set. Above all, for a time he was much speld with *Elianor Talbot*, daughter of *John Talbot* Earl of Shrewsbury (called in the Act of Parliament 1 *Rich.* 3, The old Earl of Shrewsbury) her mother was the Lady *Katherine Stafford*, daughter of *Humphrey Stafford* Duke of Buckingham, and she the widow of *Thomas* Lord *Butler* Baron of Sudesley. Her beauty and sweetnesse of disposition drew his desire so vehemently, and with such respect, that he was suddenly Contracted, and after Married by Doctor *Thomas Stillington* Bishop of Bath, Councellor of State (one much favoured by the King, and often employed by him in great Affairs.) This is witnessed by our English Writers, and veritable *Philip de Comines*, in these words: *Le Evesque de Bath (lequel avoit este Conseillier du Roy Edward) disoit que le dit Roy avoit promis foy de Mariage a une Dame de Angleterre, & qu'il avoit nommè, & que le Roy avoit fait la promise entre les mains dudict Euesque, & dit aussi c'est Euesque, qu'il avoit apres espousè, & n'y avoit que luy & ceux deux.*

Philip de Comines, in Lud. 11. cap. 112. & 122.

In English thus:

The Bishop of Bath, a Privie Councellor of King *Edward*, said, That the King had plighted his faith to marry a Lady of England, whom the Bishop named the Lady *Elianor Talbot*; and that this Contract was made in the hands of the Bishop, who said that afterwards he married them, no persons being present but they twain and he, the King charging him strictly not to reveal it. Which Contract and Marriage are related in the Act of Parliament aforesaid, where it is disertly called a former Marriage, and the King had a childe by her. But where desires are unlawful, they will be unlimited. We are ever young enough to sin; never old enough to repent: never constant, never satisfied in our neerest desires. Though to morrow shew us the sting of to day, the third shall betray us again; and we are taken (like children in a shop of trinkets) by the eye, liking all things, from one to another, until pleasure dull pleasure, and we grow weary of them. As in the dotages of this King, who had now received others into the bosome of his fancy; especially the fame (which was then in every Courtiers ear and mouth) of an excellent Lady in the Court of France, with the Queen *Chareltte*, wife of King *Lewis* 11, and sister to this Lady whose name was *Bona* the daughter of *Lewis* Duke of Savoy. And so suddenly and strongly had he

taken

taken fire and apprehension of her report (the bent of his affection being meerly wanton to every new object, thinking Love a cold Composition, without the priviledge of Variety) that he straight falls into terms of engagement and capitulation of Marriage; to which purpose the great and renowned *Richard Nevil* Earl of Warwick and Salisbury, and Captain of Calais (then in the esteem of his best and most trusty friend) had a Commission of Treaty, and with all speed was sent Ambassadour into France; who, with all honour and magnificence to his wish effects it; with the more noble and easie dispatch; the Earl of Warwick being a man eminent thorow all the parts of Europe, for his Valour, Wisedom, and Heroical vertues. Expecting a welcome at his return, answerable to the period of his employment, but findes an alteration not onely of the Kings affection, but of his countenance: for in the interim he had (in an instant or particle of time as it were) wooed and wedded the Lady *Elizabeth Gray*, Relict of Sir *John Gray*, daughter of Sir *Richard Woodville*, and of *Jaquetta*, sometime Dutchesse of Bedford and daughter of the Earl of *St. Poole*. Her husband was one *Gray* a Knight of Grooby, who became a very vehement Lancastrian, revolting from the House of York, and therefore the more hateful to those of that Family, and the well-wishers thereof (so to the Earl of Warwick.) He was slain at the Battel of St Albans: Of whom, and of this Lady his wife, as of this Marriage, *Philip de Comines* relates something, which I shall leave to the interpretation of the better knowing, and desire not to understand it in the words: *Or de puis le dict Roy Eduart espousè la fille d'un Chevallier de Angleterre femme vefue, qui avoit deux filz & aussi per Amorrettes.*

The great Earl of Warwick.

The Lady *Bona* was afterward married to *John Galeazo Sforza*, Duke of *Millain el Ruèseur*.

But neither the despised state of widowhood, nor the meannesse of her quality and condition, the earnest disswasion of the Dutchesse his mother and best friends, could make him withdraw his affection, so deeply and obstinately he was surprised with her beauty: yet if he could have enjoyed his longings otherwise, he had not married her. But she was of so pregnant and reserved a wit, (seconded by the caution and counsel of the Dutchesse her mother) that his highest temptations and sweetest batteries could not win upon her; protesting never to yeeld to any dishonorable parley or unchaste motion, although it might warrant the safety of her life; and humbly implored his Grace not to think her so exorbitantly and vainly ambitious, to wish her self a Queen, or to have the hope and presumption to be any thing higher then what she was; His poor and humble vassal: nor was she of so lowe and lost a minde, as to violate her Chastity, or be a Concubine to the greatest King.

When the King perceived there was no other remedy but that he must shift his sail to that scantling of winde, he complies with her,

her, and protests it was his desire and suit to marry her, notwithstanding her inequality: for in his esteem, her love, her beauty, and her vertue, made her Fortunes and Dowry great, and high enough for any King. Nor did he defer it any longer then there was necessity; but marry her he did, and with such dispatch, that he stayed not for the advice of any, either Councellor, Kinsman, or other whatsoever.

Nay, his speed admitted not the approved Ceremony of the Banes asking. And such was the want of Reverend Bishops then, that he was fain to take an ordinary Priest to marry them, in a Chamber too, in stead of a Church, and that in a Lodge or Forest-house; no body being present but the Dutchesse, and some few of her company. So where he first saw her (and by chance) there at the next interview he married her; an act of as high exception as improvidence. For his Barony thought it a most unworthy and unequal Match, distasting it the more, as done without their consent, which they assever'd the King ought to have by their ancient priviledges: and were the more exasperated, considering the great inequality between her condition and the Imperial Majestie of *England*, being the Relict but of a poor Knight, his mortal enemy too. Above all, the Earl of Warwick took it for an high indignity and scandal to his Honour, which stood so far engaged in France to the Lady *Bona* and her Princely friends; knowing the French would be as sensible of the scorn, besides the great charge he had been at, to manage the employment. In the heat of these disgraces (for transcendent spirits have their answerable passions; and it is as dangerous to stand in their way, as in the reaches of an angry Tyde) he forsook the King, and soon after takes up Arms against him; an Induction to those succeeding evils which pursued that inconsiderate Marriage: of which the judicious *Polidor* (*lib.* 24.) maketh this Censure.

This Marriage was in the Forest of Which-wood.

Rex Edwardus *mutato Concilio de ducenda in uxorem* Bona, *filia Ducis Sabaudiæ*, Elizabetham *viduam* Johannis Gray *Militis*, *in Matrimonium duxit*; *&* *de eo Matrimonio ob mulieris humilitatem non modo necessarios Principes, verum etiam* Richardum Woodvillum *Patrem mulieris celat: qua causa cognita cuncti protinus mirari, Principes fremere, Passimque voces emittere indignationis, & Regem non ex sua dignitate fecisse, easque nuptias se crimini dare & dedecori assignare, quod cæco amore non ratione ductus esset; sed inde initium profectum est simultatis ortæ inter Regem* Edwardum *&* Richardum *Comitem Warwici, &c.*

L'indignite de ce Marriage du Roy Edw. *avec un simple gentile femme, displaisant au Conte Warwick, & aux principaux Seigneurs de Angleterre, & offensa tellement le Roy* Lewis 11. *qu'ils font confederacon, contre le Roy* Eduart, *&c.* Jean de Tillet, Part 2.

But if you will not give credit to him, you shall hear an English Prelate living in those times.

Edwardus *Rex fretus propria electione cujusdam Militis relictam nomine* Elizabeth, *inconsultis Regni proceribus clandestino sibi destinavit Matrimonio; postea ipsam in reginam Coronari fecit: quod*

quidem

quidem Regni optimates ægrè tulerunt, quia de tam mediocri stirpe fœminam procreatam ad Regni Consortium secum præpropere sublimaret.

Thus this amorous King lost his honour, with many of his best and great friends: yet escaped well, that he had no more real and present feeling of the errour; being the first King of *England* that ever mingled his Royal Blood and Majestie in the Alliance of so private and mean a family.

The Story of Arragon mentions a King deposed for marrying the daughter of his subject. And King *Edward* was somewhat neer it: for soon after, he was expulsed his Kingdom. But being a man that kept an industrious and invincible Courage above his troubles, he happily recovered that losse, never his honour and friends, which he might have preserved, and prevented all those Calamities that overtook him in his issue, by the advice of the Dutchesse his mother, who upon the secret advertisement of his love to this Lady *Gray*, used all the perswasions and authority of a mother, to return him to the Lady *Elianor Talbot* his former love and wife (at least his contracted) to finish and consummate what he was bound to, by publike Solemnity of Marriage; and prest it with such ingenious engagements, that for the Arguments sake, I have transcribed the passage out of Sir *Thomas Moor* and the rest of our English Writers. Thus she disswades him.

The Speech of the Dutchesse of York, to King *Edw.* 4.

MY Liege Lord, and my dear Son, It is very commonly reported you are purposed to marry the Lady Gray*, a widow, and a mean Gentlewoman; which you cannot but conceive will redound to your disparagement and dishonour; all the wise, great and noblest persons of your Kingdom, thinking it far more to the advantage of your Honour, profit and Safety, to seek the Alliance of a Noble Progeny, and rather in a forraign Countrey then your own, as well in regard thereupon may depend great strength to your Estate, and great possibility to enlarge your possessions by such Affinity. Also (if well considered) you may not safely marry any other then the Lady* Bona*, the Earl of Warwick having proceeded so far in the Current of that Match already, that it is likely he will not sit down contented, if his troublesome and costly negotiation should be so slightly blown off and frustrated.*

Besides (Sir) consider it is not Princely for a King to marry his own Subject, (at least no great and important occasion leading him thereunto, nor possessions or other commodity depending thereupon) but will be lesse tolerable to all opinion, then if a rich man should marry his maid, onely for a little wanton dotage upon her person; in which kinde of Marriages, many men commend more the maids fortune, then the masters discretion. Yet there must needs be more honesty in such a Marriage, then can be honour in this which you af-

fect: for the difference is not so great betwixt a rich Merchant and his servant, as you must think between the King and the widow Gray; *in whose person (albeit there be nothing to be misliked) there is nothing so excellent, but it may be found in divers other women, much more noble and many ways exceeding her, and more comparatively to your Estate (those also Virgins, who must be thought of a much more honourable estimation then widows;) wherefore the Widowhood onely of* Elizabeth Gray *(though in all other things she were convenient for you) were enough to restrain you, being a King, and so great a King.*

And it must needs stick as a foul disparagement to the sacred Majestie of a Prince (who ought as nearly to approach the Priesthood in Purenesse and Cleannesse, as he doth in Dignity (to be defiled with Bigamy, in his first Marriage.

Thus far the King could with attention hear the Dutchesse: But being extremly far gone in love, or rather in the hot passion of Love, he was resolute to marry her; and partly in earnest, and partly in play (as one that well wist he was out of the check of a mother) yet reverently thus replied.

The Answer of King *E.* 4. to the Dutchesse of *York* his mother.

MADAM,

A*Lthough Marriage, being a Spiritual thing, ought rather to be made according to the Will and Ordinance of Almighty God, where he by his grace inclineth, either parties to love mutually and vertuously (as I hope and trust he doth work in ours) and not for the regard of any temporal advantage: yet neverthelesse this Marriage (as it seemeth to me, being considered even after the worlds account) is not unprofitable, nor without fruits: for I reckon not the Alliance and Amity of any earthly Nation or forraign Prince so necessary for me, as the friendship and love of mine own Subjects; who, as I hope, will be the more induced to love me, and acknowledge mine to them, seeing I disdain not to marry one of my own Land. When (if a forraign Alliance were thought so requisite) I could finde the means of that much better by other of my kin (where all those parties would be content) but to marry my self to one whom I should (peradventure) never love, and for the possibility of more possessions, lose the fruit and pleasure of this which I have already: For small pleasure taketh a man of all he hath, or can have, if he be wived against his appetite.*

And I doubt not but there be (as you say, Madam) other women in every point comparable to the Lady Gray; *therefore I lett not other men to wed them, no more then have they reason to mislike where it liketh me.*

Nor doubt I my Cousin of Warwick's love can be so slightly setled to me, as to grudge at that which I affect; nor so unreasonable, to look that in my choice of a wife I should rather be ruled by his eye then mine

mine own, that were to make me a Ward; and binde me to marry by the appointment of a Guardian; with which servile and hard condition I would not be King.

As for the possibility you urge of more inheritance by new Affinity in strange Lands, that is not always certain; but contrariwise, it is oftentimes the occasion of more trouble then profit. Besides, we have already a Title and Seisine so good and great, as may suffice to be gotten, and so to be kept, by one man, and in one mans days.

For your Objection that the Lady Gray *hath been a wife, and is now a widow, and hath already Children: Why (by Gods blessed Lady) I that am a Batchelor have some Children too; and so, for our better comfort, there is proof that neither of us are like to be barren. And I trust in God (Madam) you shall live to see her bring forth a young Prince, and your pretty Son, that shall be a joy and pleasure to you.*

For the Bigamy objected; let the Bishop lay it hardly in my way, when I come to take Orders of Priesthood: for I confesse, I understand Bigamy is forbidden to a Priest, but I never wist it yet forbidden to a Prince: Therefore I pray you, good Madam, trouble your self and me no further in this matter.

Then she urged his Contract with the Lady *Elizabeth Lucie*, and his having had a childe by her, (as she said;) and thought her self bound in conscience to charge him with. Master *Moor*, *Grafton*, *Stow* and the rest, say, the King utterly denied that Contract, and protested it a slander; which well and justly he might do, and these Authors may retract what they have written.

For the truth is, he was never contracted to her, though he loved her well, being of an affable and witty temper; nor did she ever alleadge the King was betrothed to her, but that he had entangled her by sweet and tempting language; And who knoweth not *Credula res amor est*? But true it is, he had a childe by her, which was the Bastard *Arthur*, called commonly (but unduly) *Arthur Plantagenet*, afterward made Viscount *Lisle*, by *H.* 8.

In this Relation, the Historians have much and foully erred, not onely corrupting the story, but have injured the Dutchesse of *York* in her judgement and knowledge of these matters, and the tenour of her former Speech, making her to charge the King as contracted to this *Elizabeth Lucy* (of birth and quality much meaner then the Lady *Gray*, whom she conceived so basely of; for *Elizabeth Lucy* was the daughter of one *Wyat* of Southampton, a mean Gentleman (if he were one) and the wife of one *Lucy*, as mean a man as *Wyat*. True it is, the King kept her as his Concubine, and she was one of those most famous three who had peculiar Epithets, being called his Witty Leman.) For that they would have her say, the King was never betrothed to her, it importeth nothing, and therefore I conceive it was never extracted from her. But truely to salve the story, and errour of these Writers, we must know, That

Elizabeth Lucy.

Lady to whom the King was first betrothed and married, was *Elinor Talbot*, daughter of a great Peer of this Realm, of a most noble and illustrious Family, the Earl of Shrewsbury, who is also called in authentick Writings the Lady *Butler*, because she was then the widow of the Lord *Butler* (a Lady of a very eminent beauty, and answerable vertue) to whom the King was contracted, married, and had a childe by her. This is that Lady (not *Elizabeth Lucy*) the Queen spake of to her son; and (to note *Obiter*) the Kings breach with this Lady, was a cause the subtil widow would not listen unto him before Marriage, having learned, *Credulitas damno solet esse puellæ.* This Marriage cast the Lady *Elianor Butler* into so perplext a Melancholy, that she spent her self in a solitary life ever after: and how she died, is not certainly known; but out of doubt kindnesse was not the cause, he having a heart for every new face, and was so become exceedingly fancied to his new wife the Lady *Gray*, no Court or pleasure now, but where she is. In this continuance of his amorous Indulgence (which was many yeers, and rendred a fruitful issue to him) no question that party of her kinred made their best advantage from it. Yet the remembrance of that Pre-contract after a time, moved him by such sensible apprehensions, he could not brook to have it mentioned, which was the cause of his displeasure against his ancient Chaplain Doctor *Stillington* of Bath, because he did what his conscience urged, to God and the Kingdom, in discovering the Marriage, occasioned by the Ladies sudden indisposition and pressing sorrow; who not able to contain her self, had open'd it to a Lady her sister, or (as some say) to her mother the Countesse of Shrewsbury; she to the Earl her husband; he consults it with his noblest kinsfolks and friends, as it was a general scandal to them all: they, to inform themselves the better, had conference with Dr *Stillington*, who affirmed the Contract and Marriage: with whom they advise, that as he was a Bishop and a Privie Councellor, it behoved him to prepare it to the Kings consideration, for some redresse and satisfaction. But the Bishop (though willing) durst not deal with the King in that manner; rather wisht they would apply it to the Duke of *Glocester*, as the man most inward with the King; whereof *Philip de Comines* thus writeth. *Cestuy Euesque d'Bath, mit en avant a ce Dux de Glocester, que le dit Roy* Edouart *estoit fort amoreux, d'un Dame, d'Angleterre, & luy promise de l'espouser pour veu qu'il couchat avec illa, ells s'y consentit: & dit ceste Euesque, qu'il les avoit Espouses, & n'y avoit que luy & eux deux.*

Ovid. — Philip de Comines.

The Duke of Gloucester, as they desired, prest it to the King, who became more incens'd against the Bishop, saying he had not onely betraid his trust, but his children; and upon that heat puts him from the Councel Table, under a strict imprisonment for a long time, which at length he redeemed himself from, by a heavy fine, as

is

1620

is testified by Doctor *Goodwin* Bishop of Hereford, in his *Catalogus Episcoporum*, who writeth thus: *Philip de Comines, le Roy Edw. de supposé l'Evesque, & le tient in prison, & le Ranson d'un bon summe d'Argent.* Which was taken for a piece of more passion then justice; the Bishop not deserving so to suffer in this case, where his conscience might very well excuse what he did.

Not long after, King *Edward* died; of what disease, it is doubtfully suggested: Some thought, of an Apoplexy, or dead Palsie. *Polidor Virgil* saith, of a disease utterly unknown to all the Physitians; which leaves it to a further construction. The Author of the History of Britain delivers plainly, that King *Edward* was killed by poison (as the common report in France went.)

How King *Edward* died.

Lib.4. in Hist. de Britaigne.

Aucuns disopent que le Roy de Angleterre Edovart, *avoit esté Empoisonné au mois d'Avrill en l'an.* 1463. And *Enguerrant de Moustrelet* writeth, that some said he died of an Apoplexy: others, he was poisoned in Wine of *Creu*, which King *Lewis* the eleventh sent to him. *Philip de Comines* (to that purpose) says, *Aucuns disent que le Roy* Eduart, *mourut d'un Catarhe.* That is, Some say that King *Edward* died of a *Catarhe*: for that is their phrase in France, when a great man is made away by Poison. Of such a venemous *Catarhe* died the young King *Edward* the Sixth. But by whose hand King *Edward* the fourth had his death, it is not said. Certain it is, he was generally beloved of all his Subjects, except those of the Lancastrian faction. As soon as he was dead, the silence brake into a general muttering against his Marriage; then into loud and publike inveighing against it. All tongues were at liberty, and Pardons were hoped for all offences; the general and common opinion being quite against it, and the Children. And Doctor *Morton* affirmed, The Duke of Buckingham, with other noble Lords, saw and read certain authentick Instruments made and signed by learned Doctors, Proctors, and Notaries, with the Depositions of sundy credible persons, importing and testifying the Children of *Edward* the fourth were Bastards: with which opinion the City of London was also possessed; and Doctor *Shaw*, Frier *Pinke*, and other Preachers in the Pulpits declared them *Spuria vitulamina.* To this consented all the people of the North parts in their Supplicatory Scroll before mentioned; which the Court of Parliament adjudged and decreed to be so. A fault of Improvidence in their Father, who might have prevented all quarrels and questions about that and future claims, repaired all flaws and defects of Titles; also have taken away the errour and inconveniency of the post-Contract, or later Marriage, that gave the imputation of Bastards to his Children; and so have avoided all the insuing mischiefs and calamities. If first he had procured a Divorce of the former Contract with the Lady *Elianor*, from the Pope, who was then held to have all power both of heaven and earth.

Moustrolet, part 3. de ce Chron.

Doctor *Morton.* Sir *Tho. Moore, Grafton, Holinshead, Stow.*

How King *Edward* might have prevented all after-questions.

Or if after the second Marriage (and while he flourished, which was by the space of Fourteen yeers) he had either by a due consideration, or counsel of his best friends, wrought the Popes Pardon for breach of the Pre-contract with the Lady *Elianor*; then, his Apostolical Bull of Dispensation, for his Post-Contract, or Matrimony superinducted (as they call it) which might easily have been obtained at *Rome*, for money. And after that, to have summoned a Parliament, requiring the three Estates to have ratified and confirmed these Bulls, for the approbation of the said Marriage with the Lady *Gray*, and the Legitimation of his Children, and made them lawful by Act of Parliament (according to the Popes Indulgence (which was then a sacred and most inviolable thing.) Lastly, to have Declared, Pronounced and Decreed in Parliament, That the said Children of the King, being so made legitimate, were also capable of all Honours, Dignities, Estates Publike and Private, of which the King stood seised, or which were any ways appertaining and proper to the Kingdom of *England*, and of *France*. I say, If he had done this, he had composed all defects, and prevented all succeeding dangers of Claims and Practices, which might have been done with small or no trouble. A course by another afterward opportunely thought on.

And surely (it may be conjectured) if this King had not been too secure, and lost in his sensualities, he would by the like Parliamentary power have rectified those errours, these great, high, and difficult works, being (indeed) proper to Parliaments, and pregnant and strong proofs of their great and transcendent power, holding in themselves a just desert and claim of such power and authority (if assembled and held as they ought) being a General Assembly and Convocation of the most wise, honourable, just, and religious persons of the Kingdom. Therefore the word Parliament (saith one) is compounded of *Parium* and *lamentum*, because (as he thinketh) the Peers of the Countrey did at these Meetings complain each to other of the enormities of their Countrey. But the better opinion is, That Parliament is simply from the French word *parler* (and that from the Greek παραλαλεῖν, both signifying to speak) and so by adding the termination, *ment* (which is common in the French Tongue, as well to many Nouns as Adverbs) do make up *Parliament*; meaning thereby an Assembly of men called together to speak or confer, *&c.*

The Authority of Parliaments.

Parliament, how so called and derived.

And it may not unfitly be called Parliament, for that each man should *parler*, *lament*, speak his minde. But *Laurence Valla* misliketh that Etymologie.

Lawrence Valla.

It may be ghessed the word *Parliament* (being transported out of *France*) began shortly after the Norman Conquest. One of the first authentical reports of that name, is found in the Statute 3 *E.* 1. commonly called *Westminster Parliament*; that Assembly being said to be *Primier generall apres Coronament le Roy*. But that is not the first word: for in the Statutes called *Articuli Cleri*, published 9 *E.* 2, these words are read: *Temporibus progenitorum nostrorum quondam Regum Angliæ Parliamentis suis, &c.* Which words *Progenitorum & quondam*, must needs reach higher then *E.* 1. that was but father to him that spake it.

But at what time soever after the Conquest this Court began to be called a Parliament, the same was before known to the *Saxons* or English men, by the word *Sinoth*, and *Micell Sinoth*, of the Greek συνοδος, now appropriated to Ecclesiastical meetings onely; and sometimes by these terms, *Micell, Gemote, Witengemott*, and *Calca Witengemott*; that is, the meeting of wisemen, or of all the wise men: for *witena* signifieth wise men, *Calca*, all, and *Gemott*, a meeting: of which last words the names *Shire-motts, Eolmotts*, and *Halymotts*; that is, the meeting or assembling of the men of a Shire, of a Town, and of the Tenants of a Hall or Mannor, had their beginning also.

Now as *Sinoth* is more used in the Parliaments themselves; so *Gemott* is more familiar to the Historians.

And this Parliament of *Anno* 1 *Rich.* 3. could be of no lesse power and vertue; witnesse the many and good Laws made in it, (albeit the second Marriage of King *Edward* was adjudged unlawful, and the Acts of that Parliament for the most part repealed and abrogated afterward) yet the evidence is clear enough, that the Judges and Law-makers of that Parliament, were wise and religious men, and their Laws upright and just.

Therefore whatsoever was adjudged by them, was to be received and held as authentick and inviolable (how roughly soever it was afterward handled.) And in this case of the disabling of King *Edwards* sons, there is least reason to suspect them, the cause being so new, so plain, and notoriously known, that no man could be ignorant therein: Therefore to have given any other Judgement, but according to the truth of evidence, and certainty of knowledge, it might justly have been censured an act of errour and ignorance, or partiality and injustice.

For it was not the opinion of a few, nor raised out of a weak judgement and perverted knowledge; but a strong and general evidence, by the ablest and best knowing.

If it be objected, The case was obscure and doubtful: That cannot be; for the Estates had all substantial and ready means to inform themselves of the truth, and every circumstance whereby they might be fully satisfied and cleared in all the niceties and doubts: for all the witnesses and dealers in that cause, and such persons as were acquainted with it, were then living; and they must and would have truely and certainly informed the Court of Parliament: For the special and reverend care of this Court is, The advancing of Justice and Right. Therefore all Subjects (by nature or grace) are bound in their Allegeance, to give pious and religious credit to Parliaments, and to believe in their Authority and Power, as the former times did in Oracles. We must also confidently hold the high and transcendent quality and vertue of that Court, to have all power and authority: And no question to repeal a good and just Law made in Parliament, is a wrong and scandal to that General Councel, and to the universal wisedom, providence, justice and piety of the Kingdom.

In the Parliament 1 *H. 7.* there is an Act, attainting the King *R. 3.* of high Treason, for bearing Arms against the Earl of Richmond, intituled The Soveraign Lord (this was at his proceeding from Milford-haven into Leicester:) But when he came to fight the Battel, he was then no King, nor Soveraign, but a Chief of such as made head against their Soveraign. In which Paragraph there appears three grosse faults.

First, Certain it is, *Richard* during his Raign was a Soveraign, therefore no Subject.

Next, there was no enemy in the field who was then a Soveraign, but all liege Subjects to the Crown.

And *Richard* being the King and Soveraign, could not be adjudged a Traitor, nor lawfully attainted of High Treason. Then let it be considered whether a person of sacred Majestie (that is, an Anointed Soveraign) may commit the Crime of Treason. Also in this Parliament, all the Barons, Knights and Gentlemen that bore Arms in the field for the King, were attainted of Treason, their goods and lands confiscate: and one *Thomas Nandick*, (a Necromancer and Sorcerer, who with others had been condemned to die, for using that hellish Art) was in this Parliament pardoned the horrible things he had committed. And it seemed he had not then left his black trade: for he hath in that Act of Parliament still the style of Conjurer: *viz.*

Thomas Nandick of Cambridge, Conjurer: which had been a fitter style for his Gibbet then his Pardon; although he had not by his Sorcery or Inchantment hurt or destroyed any humane, yet for his renouncing and abjuration of Almighty God: for it is the opinion of a learned and religious Doctor:

Magos & Incantores (saith he) *hominum genus indignum, quod vel ob solam Dei, O.M. abjurationem capitali suplicio afficiatur.*

Other such things there be in that Parliament, which detract it in the opinion of some; those of the best and wisest repute.

The Treaty of Marriage between K. *R. 3.* and his Neece the Lady *Elizabeth Plantagenet.*

Now let us come to examine that Treaty the King had about marrying the Lady *Plantagenet*; which is censured to be a thing not onely detestable, but much more cruel and abominable to be put in agitation.

Item, *That all men, and the Maid her self most of all, detested this unlawful Copulation.*

Item, *That he made away the Queen his wife, to make way for this*

this Marriage; and that he propounded not the Treaty of Marriage, until the Queen his wife was dead.

That there was such a motion for the marriage of this Lady to the King, is true; and (which is more, and most certain) it was entertained, and well liked by the King and his friends, a good while; also by the Lady *Elizabeth*, and by the Queen her mother; who received it with so much content and liking, that presently she sent into France for her son the Marquesse of Dorset, that was there with the Earl of Richmond, earnestly solliciting him to renounce the Faction, and return home to the Kings favour and advancement, which she assured him: and sends the Lady *Elizabeth* to attend the Queen at Court, or to place her more in the eye, so in the heart of the King. The Christmas following (which was kept in Westminster-Hall) for the better colour of sending her eldest daughter, she sends her other four thither, who were received with all honourable courtesie by the King and Queen Regent; especially the Lady *Elizabeth* was ranked most familiarly in the Queens favour, and with as little distinction as Sisters. But society, nor all the Pomp and Festivity of those times, could cure that sad wound and languor in the Queens brest, which the death of her onely son had left. The addresse of those Ladies to Court (albeit the feigned wooing of the King was in a politick and close way) gave cause of suspition to the Earl of Richmonds intelligencing friends, that the King had a purpose to marry the Lady *Elizabeth*; which must prevent the Earl both of his hope to her, and to the Crown by her Title: a clause that made them mutter very broadly against it (for indeed, what more concern'd them?) therefore the King treats it more privately and coldly; but the Queen-widow and the Lady stood constant in their desires and expectation; onely the Objection was, The King had a wife; as though he could not marry another whilst she lived; not remembring how usual it was, not onely for Kings, but private men to put away one wife and marry another, for venial crimes, as well as Adultery and Treason.

Chronicle Croyland.

The Romanes might repudiate their wives, for conversing with men that were not of their kinred, and for going to see Playes and Cirque Spectacles (their husbands not being with them) or if the wife were unquiet or curst of her tongue, *&c.* *Henry* the Eighth put away Queen *Katharine* of Castile, and Queen *Anne* of Cleve; the one, because she was too old and cold for pleasure; the other, because she was not fruitful or wanton enough. Sometimes men have put away their wives for being Sluts, for having unsavoury breaths, or some infectious disease, without a necessity of taking away their lives; and it was lawful for either of them to marry when they would.

Pope

Pope *Clement* the Seventh so ratified the Divorce of King *Henry* the Eighth against *Katherine* of Castile, as he defied all Laws (Divine and Humane) that should contradict and impugn his Power and Dispensation, in these words:

Bulla Papæ Clementis 5. apud D. Ro. Coton.

Non obstante Jure Divino nec Humano, nec quibuscunque Constitutionibus repugnantibus, aut in contrarium Edictis.

Ther was a formal Bill or Libel of Separation prescribed by *Moses*, with the manner of Divorces and Repudiations, in this tenour, as *Andreas Osiander* (who translated it out of Hebrew into Latin) affirmeth: which for the rarity I have here transcribed.

Osiander *in Annotation. in 4 Evang. Harmon. Evang.*

Die tertia Hebdomadis, 29 die mensis Octobris,
Anno ab orbe condito, 4349.

EGo Joachim cognominatus N. filius Nathanis, qui consisto hodie in urbe N. in Regno N. Te. N. uxorem meam, cognominatam N. filiam N. quæ fuisti uxor mea ante hac nunc demisi, & liberavi, & repudiavi te tibi, ut sis tui juris & domina animæ tuæ, & ad abeundum, ut ducaris abs quolibet viro, quem volueris, & ne vir quisquam prohibeat, quo minus sis in manu tua, ito hoc die & in æternum. Et ecce, permissa es unicuique viro, & hic esto tibi a me datus Libellus repudii, & Epistola dimissoria, & Instrumentum libertatis juxta Legem Mosis & Israelis.

But the Answer which was made in the name of the King to the Lady *Elizabeth* concerning his Queen, was, That she could be no impediment of long continuance, being a very weak woman in a Consumption, and past hopes of recovery; her Physitians giving their opinions, she could not live past the middle of *February* next following: nor ghessed they much amisse; for she died in the next month, *March*. When the midst and last of *February* was past, the Lady *Elizabeth* being more impatient and jealous of the successe then every one knew or conceived, writes a Letter to the Duke of Norfolk, intimating first, that he was the man in whom she most affied, in respect of that love her Father had ever bore him, *&c.* Then she congratulates his many courtesies, in continuance of which, she desires him to be a mediator for her to the King, in the behalf of the Marriage propounded between them, who, as she wrote, was her onely joy and maker in this world, and that she was his in heart and thought: withall insinuating, that the better part of *February* was past, and that she feared the Queen would never die.

The credit of the Duke of Norfolk with King *Richard*, and with the Lady *Elizabeth*; and her Letter to him.

All these be her own words, written with her own hand; and this is the sum of her Letter, which remains in the Autograph, or Original Draft, under her own hand, in the magnificent Cabinet of *Thomas* Earl of Arundel and Surrey: by which it may be observed,

served, that this young Lady was ignorant that a man having a wife living, might marry another, and suffer her to live. But the truth is, the King had no real intent to make her his wife, from the beginning; onely in policy entertained this Treaty, as it appeared afterward, when his Queen was dead, and he had all fit accesses without any impediment to marry her, yet did not; professing he wooed her not to that end, but for some other causes; and made Protestation (in the great Hall at Saint *Jones* neer Smithfield, before all the Knights of Malta, and a great Assembly of Noble-men; the Lord Maior, Aldermen, and many Citizens being present) that he had no purpose nor intent to marry the Lady *Elizabeth*: avowing, *Quod ea res (viz.) Voluntas contrahendi Matrimonium: cum Consanguinea Germana sua nunquam ei venerat in mentem*: for so it is testified by the Prior of Croyland. Yet it may not be denied, he pretended love to her, and a proffer of Marriage; which he projected in policy, to divert her affection from *Richmond* (whose party the King apprehended privately wrought that way; of which the said Author thus saith, *Non aliter videbat* Richardus *Rex regnum sibi confirmari, neque spem competitoris sui aufferri posse, nisi in Matrimonio, cum dicta* Elizabeth, *contrahendo vel simulando*. And it is most likely the King had no other aim but meerly of Prevention: neither was there any cause (had he been so wicked) to do it by blood, nor any just reason to frame so hard an argument against him, being always so affectionately inclined to his wife, that he was rather thought uxorious then otherwise; which appeared unfeignedly at her death, in the expression of sorrow and magnificent Exequies for her. *Non eum immorte honore quam Reginam dicunt*, as the Prior of Croyland testifieth. Let us look therefore with clearer consideration upon the motion or pretence of this Marriage: to call it detestable and cruel, is ignorant and malicious (though she were so neer of kin to him) for Marriages between Uncles and Neeces, have been very frequent and allowed in other Countreys by the Church. In our time, the daughter and heir of Duke *Infantasgo* in Spain, was married to his brother *Don Alde Mendoza*: and more lately, the Earl of Miranda married his brothers daughter.

The Cabinet of the Earl of Arundel, now Earl of Surrey too.

Chronicle of Croyland.

Chronicle of Croyland.

The Queen died 11. March, 1484.

Prior of Croyland.

In the House of Austria, Marriages in this kinde have been very usual, and thought lawful, the Pope dispensing with them: for they say in Spain, *Que el padre santo quiere Dios loquire*: Therefore how could it be so highly unlawful in King *Richard*? Or if his intents had been so forward, where was the Bar, when his wife was dead, and he absolute, unlesse the Ladies aversenesse? But that suggestion is answered by her own Letter, and other testimonies. So the Account will be (if rightly summed by what hath been produced) that he had never any serious determination of Marriage; onely took the advantage of his gain, by looking into her hand; then no cause to make away his Queen; which his accusers themselves directly and peremptorily charge him not with; but doubtfully say, The Queen (however it fortuned) departed out of this life the 16 of *March*, in the Lent season. But although he had the commendations of a loving and indulgent husband; I say not he lived always continently; for I finde he had some bastards, two of them I have mentioned: yet peradventure he might have them before his Marriage, and then the fault was lesse. So then, let them that affect not blinde and traditory opinion, more then justice and reason, but equally examine his slanders, they shall finde, Malice and ignorance have been the Kings greatest accusers, which can onely lay Suspition to his charge: and Suspition in Law is no more guilt then Imagination: for, though Suspition many times lay a great blame upon a man (men holding him to be guilty whom men suspect to be so, though injuriously) yet the Law holds it not a Crime, because Suspition many times supposeth those to be culpable which are not: for an Instrument may as easily be condemned, as a Malefactor, being an evil grown from the errour of men. Wherefore Suspition of it self bringeth no sentence by Law Natural or Moral, Civil or Divine, according to that of the old *Minographus*; *Suspitio grave est hominibus malum.* And the Divine *Chrysostome* saith, A good man hardly suspecteth another to be evil; but an evil man scarcely supposeth any to be good; far from the counsel of this Epigram.

Sir Tho. Moor. Hollinshead.

Suspitio est opinio mali ex levibus signis. B. Th Aquinas. *Suspitio est actus per quem in dubitationem trahimur.*

Culparem quoquam, quæ non sunt nota malignum est;
Presertim si quam cognita sint bona sunt.
Non pateant faciles duris rumoribus aures
Quæ nescire juvat, credere non libeat.
Linquuntur secreta Deo, qui quicquid opertum est
Inspicit, & nullis indiget indicibus.

Accuse no man of faults to thee unknown,
And much lesse him from whom good fruits have grown:
Lend not thine ears to scandalous reports;
Believe not that, which known, nought thee imports.
Leave secret things to God, who knows all hearts,
And hath no need of the Promoters arts.

But as *Julius Cæsar* (who had many excellent Observations) was wont to say, *Vir bonus tam suspicione quam crimine carere oportet:* That a good man must be as well without suspition as crime. Yet none so innocent, but may fall under the lash of the malicious; for such, like the *Polypus*, will take any colour, or make any tincture of a Crime, to serve their ends. Of such a vertue is the never-understanding Vulgar, that like Kytes and Daws can digest nought but stench and filth; their Ignorance being their Faith, and that drawn from loose Pamphlets, and the vomits of mercinary and mimick pens; to which, and their uncurable fits, I leave them.

Meos tam suspicione quam crimine judico carere oportere. Suet. in vitâ J. Cæs.

Explicit Liber quartus.

THE

THE FIFTH BOOK OF THE HISTORY OF KING RICHARD the Third.

The Contents.

THE

THE
FIFTH BOOK
OF
King Richard The Third.

WE will next endeavour to understand that Vocable, or term *Tyrannus* (that is, a Tyrant, or an evil King) cast upon King *Richard*; which indeed comprehendeth all scandals and impieties whatsoever.

What a Tyrant is.

Tyrannus est qui suis propriis Commodis studet, & publicis adversatur. And, *Tyrannus est qui dominatu crudeliter abutitur.*

Aristot. in E-thic. idem.

A Tyrant is by another wise man compared to a Dragon, who becometh not a Dragon, until he hath devoured many Serpents: of which Conceit this Epigram was wittily framed.

Post plures Coluber Serpentes Draco fit esos,
Gustatâ humanâ carne fit homo Lupus.
The Dragon which doth many Serpents eat,
Becomes a Dragon of huge shape and strength,
And so the man which makes his flesh mans meat,
Transformed is unto a Wolf at length.

Another Philopher differeth not much from these, who saith, that of all tame beasts, the flatterer is most pernicious; and of all wilde, the Tyrant, who forbeareth not for any respect of good or

Bias apud Plut. Libell. de adulat. c. 37.

or ill, but studies Oppressions, Wrongs, Exactions, Robberies, Sacriledges, Blood-shed, Murder, Adultery, Incest, Rape, Riot, Gluttony, Luxuriousnesse, Prodigality, and all manner of Excesses: These be his arts of raigning, and these be his vertues.

Lucan. *Invident Tyranni claris fortesq; trucidant.*

Another saith,

Seneca. Hercules. Furens. *Tyrannus miserum vetat perire, fœlicem jubet.*

So it was truely said by the famous Orator of Athens:

Demosthenes. *Liberalitas Tyranni nihil aliud est quam translatio pecuniarum a justis Dominis, ad alienos idque indignos.*

His thirst and covetousnesse, for his largitious riots and lusts, are so inordinate, that nothing can quench it.

Claudian in Ruff.

Non Tartessiaris illum satiaret arenis
Tempestas pretiosa Tagi, non stagna rubentis,
Aurea Pactoli, totumque exhauserit Hermum,
Arde bit majore siti, &c.

Juvenal Satyre 4.

Quicquid conspicuum pulchrumque ex Equore toto,
Res fisci est, &c.

These may serve for the notions of a Tyrant: to any of which Impieties, our King *Richard* was very little or not at all obnoxious.

Parliam. An. 1 Rich. 3.

For first, Whereas a Tyrant imposeth many grievous Taxes and Oppressions upon his Subjects, he took away such grievances, and particularly by Act of Parliament, a hateful Tax (though disguised with the name of a Benevolence) forbearing to impose any upon the people.

The Duke of Buckingham said, that the name of Benevolence, as it was taken in the time of K. Edw. 4. signified, that every man should pay not what he of his own good will list, but what the King of his good will list to take. Duke Buck. apud Thomam Moor.

Then, A Tyrant doth not onely rapine his Subjects, but spoils and robs Churches and Church-men. But King *Richard* did many good things both for the publike good, advancing Gods service, and maintenance of his Ministers and Church-men.

Tyrannum pium esse non est facile (as *Sophocles* well observed.) And the Oracle pronounced, *Portæ fœlicitatis ad Tyrannidem clausæ.* Tyrants be cruel and bloody: but this King, by the testimony of his enemies, was very merciful and milde; who confesse he was of himself gentle, and affably disposed. These be their own words.

Therefore, where tyrannical acts be objected against him, they must be conceived done by other men, or by their practice, or else before he was King; and what he did then, was not, nor could be properly called Tyranny.

Amongst those they impute to him when he was King, which are called Tyrannies, the beheading *Henry Stafford* Duke of Buckingham was the chiefest: yet that act, the cause and just motives of it being well perused, cannot be censured Tyranny; rather, due and necessary Justice: for if the King had not put down the Duke, the Duke would have put down the King.

Then it is objected, He bare a tyrannical hand over his nephew

Edward

Edward Earl of Warwick. True it is, he sent him to Shery-Hutton, a goodly and pleasant house of his own, in York-shire, where he had liberty, large diet, all pleasure and safety; and if that were imprisonment, it was a prison Curtoise (as *John Froisard* saith) yet this must not be lesse then Tyranny, according to the style of Sir *Thomas Moore*. When King *Henry* the Seventh, as soon as he had got the Crown, sent this young Prince to the Tower, afterwards cut off his head; yet that was no Tyranny, after Sir *Thomas Moore*. But our King *James* (of ever happie memory) hath thought it an act of so much detestation, that particularly he protested against it, and shewed another temper of Justice and Power in his Royal Clemencie, to certain Noble persons in one of his Kingdoms, who being Regal Titulars, and pretending title to the Crown there (as descended from some King of that Countrey) his gracious and pious inclination was so far from seeking their ruine (or so much as the restraining them) that he suffered their liberty, with possession of what they had. *Comes Arund. vi. voce.* King *James*.

Then they call the punishment of *Jane Shore* a Tyrannie: A common and notorious Adulteresse (as the Duke of Buckingham, who knew her very well, censured her) which she deserved so justly, that it was rather favourable, then severe or tyrannous. *Jane Shore.*

Next, the death of *William Collingborn* is made one of his Tyrannies; who (as some trivial Romancers say) was hanged for making a Satyrical Rhyme; when the truth is, he had committed Treason, and was arraigned and condemned of High Treason, as may be yet seen in the Record; and then it was Justice, and not Tyrannie. *Anonimus Juris peritus in Apologia K. R. 3.*

Another proof against their grosse Paralogisms, take from this observation made by *Demosthenes*: *Tyrannus res est inimica Civibus, legibus contraria.* But King *Richard* was ever indulgent to his people, careful to have the Laws duely observed; his making so many good ones, being an evident argument of his love to Law and Justice. It is further observed, that Tyrants contemn good counsel, are opinionated of their own wisedoms, and obstinate to determine all matters by themselves.

These Plaintiffs being called by the Greeks αὐτοβούλοι, that is, self-Councellors, who say they are *natura plerumque occulti & insidiosi, & Arte, & Astu, ea Tagere, & dissimulare conantur, quæ agunt, non communicantes quicquid de suis Conciliis, aut rebus cum aliis, nec ab aliis Concilium petentes, neque admittentes, sed tantum sua Concilia sequuntur.* *Axiom. polit. cap. 219.* *Sententia Arabica.*

Also *Erasmus* hath this Axiome: *Nullo Concilio quicquam magnæ rei aggredi, tyrannicum est.*

But King *Richard* not did nor would do any thing of importance, without consultation with the wisest and noblest. And if in any matters he had delivered his judgement, yet his manner

(as

(as his detractors confesse) was, to say in the end and conclusion, *My Lords, this is my minde; if any of you know what may else be better, I shall be ready to change it: for I am not wedded to my own will.* Thus Sir *Thomas Moor.*

Lastly, Largition and excessive expences, are thought vices proper to Tyrants; the rather, because the Romane Tyrants, for their extreme excesses, were called *Monstra & prodigia, & lues Imperii, pestes reipublicæ, &c.* As *Caligula, Nero, Vitellius, Domitian, Commodus, Heliogabolus, Caracalla,* &c.

Caligula spent 230 millions of Crowns in lesse then a yeer. *Nero* said that there was no use of money but for riots and prodigal expences.

King *Richard* was ever held to be frugal, with the preservation of his honour; nor can they tax him with Palliardise, Luxury, Epicurism, nor Gluttony, vices following many Tyrants; but moderate and temperate in all his actions and appetites; which is confessed, and therefore needeth no further proof. Indeed it had been advantage and safety to him, in the event, if he had been a Tyrant a while; for then he might have preserved his life and kingdom, and given a timely check to the practice of Bishop *Morton*, the Marquesse Dorset, Earl of Devon, and his brother the Bishop, the Lord *Talbot*, the Lord *Stanley*, and his brother Sir *William Stanley*, with the Countesse of Richmond his wife, and the rest. But his remisnesse and patience bred his ruine, not his tyranny; that had been his protection.

King *Richard* in this was like *Julius Cæsar*, who knowing by certain intelligence the conspiracy and conspirators against his life, also the time and place of execution, yet he seemed to slight and not regard it.

King *Richards* vertues.

And now the black curtain of malice and detraction is drawn, let us see this King in his proper Royalty and vertues casting up the general and particular notions of A good King and happie Government; then peruse what was wanting in him.

First then, There is necessarily required proper to Empire, Wisedom, Justice, Fortitude, Beauty, Magnificence, Temperance, and Piety.

That he had Wisedom and Prudence, need no other witnesse, then his wise and provident managing both of his own private affairs, and Government of the Publike. Also in the Military actions, in which he was tried, both as a Subject, and a King; his adversaries can allow him to be a wise, prudent, politick and heroical Prince; his Wisedom appearing, with his Justice, very clearly in the good Laws he made; acknowledged and honourably predicated by our Reverend and most learned Professors of the Laws.

Justice *Shelly* commendeth the Laws of K. *R.* 3. to Card. *Wolsey. Vide Joh. Stow in H.8. pag.* 882. *Chronic. M.S. in quarto, apud D. Rob. Cotton.*

For his further knowledge and love of Justice, there can be no fairer argument, then his desire and custome to sit in Courts of Justice, hearing and distributing Justice indifferently to all men.

And when he made his Progresse into York-shire, being informed there of some extortioners and foul offenders, who were apprehended, not tried, he caused the Law to take the just current, giving strict charge and commandment to all Officers of Justice, for just administration to all men, without partiality or private respects.

The

The Fortitude and Magnanimity of this Prince (though of lowe stature) were so great and famous, as they need no Trumpet or Præcony, being bred from his youth in Martial actions: and the Battels of Barnet, Exham, Doncaster, the second of St Albans, and of Tewksbury, will give him the reputation of a Souldier and Captain.

Being made General of the Kings Armies into Scotland, he prevailed happily in his Expedition, and particularly recovered that famous and strong Hold of Berwick, which King *Henry* the Sixth had so weakly let go.

And in this you shall hear the Elogie of one that was loth to speak much in his favour, yet occasion forced him to speak his knowledge, though coldly and sparingly. *King* Richard *was no ill Captain in the War: he had sundry Victories, and sometimes overthrows; but never by his own default, for want of hardinesse or politick order.* Whereunto he addeth concerning his Bounty; *Free was he called of dispence, and liberal somewhat above his power.* To which I will adde one Elogie more, above all for Credit and Authority, recorded in an Act of Parliament, and addressed to him in the name of the whole high Court of Parliament, in these words. *We consider your great Wit, Prudence, Justice, and Courage; and we know by experience the memorable and laudable acts done by you in several Battels for the salvation and defence of this Realm.*

Sir *Tho. Moor.* Doctor *Morton.*

Parl. anno R. 3.

Here followeth another general and memorable testimony of him, and of more regard and honour, because it is averred by one that knew him from his youth, the Duke of Buckingham, who (after *Richard* was made King, and this Duke became ill affected) acknowledged to Bishop *Morton* in private speeches between them, That he thought King *Richard*, from his first knowledge even to that time, a man clean without dissimulation, tractable, and without injury; and that for these respects, he was very desirous to advance him, and laboured earnestly to make him Protector. Therefore whatsoever the Duke said after, in reproach of the King, it may justly be thought to proceed from spleen and malice.

Morton. Moor apud Stow, p. 774.

There is to this the commendation of his Eloquence and pleasing speech; which though no Regal vertue, yet it is an ornament to the greatest Princes, and commendable. The Prior of Croyland repeating the dispute of a Controversie between the two brothers, *George* Duke of Clarence, and this *Richard* of Gloucester, at the Councel-Table, before the King their brother, sitting in his Chair of State, relates it thus:

Eloquentia Principibus maxime est ornamento. Cic. de finibus, l. 4.

Post suscitatas, inter Duces fratres, discordias, tot utrinque rationes acutissimæ allegatæ sunt in presentia Regis (sedentis pro Tribunali in Camera Concilii) quod omnes circumstantes, etiam periti Legum eam orationis abundantiam ipsis principibus in suis propriis causis adesse mirabantur; &c. Then speaking of the excellent wits,

The praise of the three princely brothers.

extraordinary knowledge and gifts of these three brothers, maketh this honourable Præcony: *Hi tres Germani, Rex, & duo Duces, tam excellenti ingenio valebant, ut si discordare non voluissent funiculus ille triplex difficilime rumperetur.*

The good works of King *Richard*. *John Stow, Annal.*

Let us look upon his charitable, religious and magnificent works.

He founded a Collegiate Church of Priests in Middleham in York-shire; another College of Priests in London in Tower-street, neer to the Church called Our Lady *Berking.* He built a Church or Chappel in Towton in Gloucester-shire; a Monument of his thankfulnesse to Almighty God, for the happie and great Victory his brother had upon the partisans of the family of Lancaster, and the sons of *Henry* the Sixth, who before slew *Richard* Duke of York, King designate, and father of these two Kings.

Polidor, lib. 25.

He founded a Colledge in York, convenient for the entertainment of an hundred Priests.

Richard loved not Wich-wood for his brothers unhappie Marriage.

He disforrested a great part of the Forrest of Wich-wood, and other vast Woods between Woodstock and Bristow, for the good and benefit of the people of Oxford-shire and the places adjacent.

He built the high stone Tower at Westminster (which at this day is a work of good use.) And when he had repaired and fortified the Castle of Carlisle, he founded and built the Castle of Penrith in Cumberland.

He manumissed many Bond-men.

In Rot. in domo Conversorum, An. 1 *R.* 3.

For the better encouragement of the Easterling-hanses (their Trade being beneficial and profitable to this Kingdom) he granted them some good Priviledges, as *Polidor* writeth.

Charles the Great instituted the Colledge and Society of Armorists, calling them Heralds of *Ehr & Halten*, (Dutch or Franchish words) and not of Heroes.

He also first founded the Colledge and Society of Heralds, and made them a Corporation: and (as the words in the Charter are) he ordained it, *Vt sint in perpetuum Corpus Corporatum in re & nomine, habeant Successionem perpetuam,* &c. (A taste of his love to Honour, and his Noble care for the conservation of Nobility, Chevalry and Gentry.) Which Corporation, this King established by his Royal Charter; and placed the Heralds in an ancient fair house, which was called Yorkime, sometimes; after commonly Cole-harbour, situate upon the Thames: ordaining Four Kings at Arms, by the names and Titles of *John Writh*, Garter; *Thomas Holme*, Clarentius; *John Moore*, Norway; and *Richard Champney*, Gloucester.

For Wales, I have seen the Charter wherewith the King created first *Richard Champney* Esquire, King at Arms, by the Title and name of Gloucester, dated *Anno* 1 *R.* 3. at Westminster, in the month of *March*, when the Charter of the Foundation was granted.

He further established, That these four Kings at Arms, and the rest of the Heralds, who are in the Charter called *Heraldi &*

Pro-

Prosecutores sive Pursevandi, should lodge, live and common together, in that house, where the Rolls, Monuments and Writings (appertaining to the Office and Art of Heraldry and Armory) should be kept; giving also Lands and Tenements for the perpetual maintaining of a Chaplain or Chantry Priest, to say and sing Service every day, and to pray for the King, Queen and Prince, and for their souls when they were dead.

Lastly, he gave sundry good Priviledges and Immunities to the said Corporation: which Charter was kept continually in the Office until within these few yeers; but now is in another place: the want of it importeth nothing, being the Duplicate is upon Record in the Archives, kept in the Convert-house, now called the Rolls. It was confirmed by the Parliament, and dated 2 *die Martii, anno regni primo, apud Westmonasterium*, Baron: and underneath was written, *Per Breve de privato Sigillo, de datu predicto, autoritati Parliamenti*.

He also built or repaired some part of the Tower of London towards the Thames: in memory whereof, there be yet his arms impaled with those of the Queen his wife, standing upon the Arch adjoyning to the Sluce-gate.

He began many other good works, which his sudden fate prevented; as *Polidor* thus witnesseth.

Richardus Tertius multa opera publica & privata inchoavit, quæ immaturâ morte præreptus non perfecit. Which works and monuments of Piety shew not the acts of a Tyrant. *Polidor Virgil*, being neither Yorkist nor Lancastrian, speaks much in commendation of his pious and charitable disposition; to which I refer the Readers, and put it to their indifferent judgements, How many of those called Good Kings, have exceeded him in their longer and prosperous time, being in quiet possession too of their Crown and Kingdoms? Let me adde for a Corollary, what that of the worthy Prelate *Archebald Quhitlaw* (chief Secretary, and a Privie Councellor of Scotland) in his Oration, when he was one of the Commissioners for a conclusion of a Peace and Marriage between Prince *James*, eldest son to the King of Scotland, and the Lady *Anne*, daughter to *John de la Pool*: from whence I have collected these.

Serenissime Princeps,

Una me res consolatur, & juvat, tua (scil.) in omni virtutis genere celeberrima fama per omnem Orbis terrarum ambitum dissеminata, tuæ etiam innatæ benignitatis clarissima præstansque humanitas, tua mansuetudo, liberalitas, fides, summa justitia, incredibilis animi magnitudo, tua non humana, sed pene divina sapientia, te non modo singulis facilem, verum vulgo & popularibus affabilem præbes & quibus virtutibus altâque prudentiâ cuncta & pronunciata & dicta in meliora commutas. Serenissimus Princeps Rex Scotorum, *Pacem & uxorem neptem Regis petit.*

rum, Dominus meus, qui te alto amore prosequitur, te desiderat, tuam, Amicitiam & Affinitatem affectat, suprà captum cogitationis meæ; si quid a me erratum erit, tuis & divinis virtutibus, quibus Commercium cum Cœlestibus numinibus & societatem contraxeris, tribuendum putato.

Richardus fuit Statura parva.

Faciem tuam summo Imperio & Principatu dignam inspicit, quam moralis & Heroica virtus illustrat, de te dici prædicarique potest quod Thebanorum Principi inclytissimo statui Poeta his verbis attribuit.

Nunquam tantum animum natura minori corpore, nec tantas visa est includere vires. Major in exiguo regnabat corpore virtus. In te enim sunt rei militaris, virtus, peritia, fœlicitas, & autoritas, quæ omnia in optimo exercitus principe Cicero *requirit.*

In te (Serenissime Princeps) præclari Regis & Imperatoris præcepta ità concurrunt, ut nihil ad tuam Bellicam, aut domesticam virtutem cujusquam oratoris verbis apponi possit.

Tu igitur (Serenissime Domine & Princeps) de ineunda inter te & nostrum Principem charitate & amicitia, sic age, ut Angli & Scoti dilectionis respectu nullum penitus discrimen habeatur, sed in unum amoris & benevolentiæ vinculum videantur esse connexi, sic numerabiles commoditates ex tui, & nostri populi dilectione, dulci connubio, unione, Matrimonio, & Affinitate consurgent.

In freta dum fluvii current, dum montibus umbræ
Lustrabunt, connexa polus dum sidera pascet.
Dum juga montis aper, fluvios dum piscis amabit,
Dumque Thymo pascentur apes, dum rore cicadæ,
Semper honos nomenque tuum, laudesque manebunt.

But what is this, or more, to malice and detraction, that haunt him to his death; and after that, making the Catastrophe, or last Tragical act of his life at Bosworth-field, an immediate stroke of the divine vengeance, for such offences as they please to particular from women or superstitious Clerks, whose natures startle at the noise of War and Martial trial, to whose fears and weaknesse, such reasons would sound tolerable. But if Bishop *Morton* and Sir *Thomas Moor* (although they were men of the long Robe) had considered with whom they conversed, and where they most lived; how could they forget, That to die valiantly in the field, for Countrey, life and friends, was always held a glorious farewel to the world; or what infinite numbers of vertuous and most noble Captains have fallen so by the Sword and fate of War.

To be slain in War, is no evil or unhappie death.

Lampridius affirmeth, that all the best men have died violent deaths: and what higher Quarrel could call any Heroical spirit, then King *Richard*'s, fighting for a Crown, kingdom, and all his happie Fortunes here. God hath many times taken away Princes, and changed the Government of kingdoms for the iniquities of the people; why then should not King *Richard*'s fate be held in a modest Scale, until we can better know or judge it? Nor can it be

Optimos quosq; violenta morte consumptos esse affirmat Lam. Alexander.

safe to enquire, or peremptorily to determine further after Gods proceedings in such cases. He that owes him no malice (things looked upon thorow judgement and charity) may with more justice say he died valiantly, and in a just quarrel, when many of his enemies fell by deaths more vile, and shameful Executions.

But he that hath but a reasonable pittance of Humanity, will censure no mans life by the manner of his death: for many good and holy men have suffered by violent deaths; though it be this Princes fortune to fall under the ill affections of envious pens, more then many that committed more publike and proved crimes then he, which wanted much of his vertues and desert.

King *Richard* was slain, Aug. 22. 1493. when he had raigned 2 yeers and 5 months, accounting his Protectorship; and about the 37th year of his age.

Examine him with *Henry* the First, the good Clerk, and learned Prince, but so covetous and ambitious, that he could not be content to usurp in this Kingdom the Right and Primogeniture of his elder brother, *Robert Courthose*; but by force took the Dukedom of Normandy from him: and to make his injuries more exact and monstrous, cast him into the Castle of Gloucester, there kept him in cruel durance, and caused his eyes to be put out; so wearied him to most miserable death.

King *Henry* 1.

King *John*, by the general voice, is charged with the murder of *Arthur Plantagenet* the son of his eldest brother, and so the next Prince in right of blood to King *Richard* the First.

King *John*.

And it is written by good Authors, that *Edward* the Third was not onely privie and consenting to the deposing the King his father (a King anointed) but also to his Massacre. And because *Edward Plantagenet* Earl of Kent, Protector, and his Uncle, moved him to restore the Crown to his father *Edward* the Second, he called him Traitor, and cut off his head at Westminster.

King *Edw*. 3.

How King *Henry* the Fourth caused King *Richard* the Second (the true and anointed King) to be cruelly butchered at Pomfret, is too notorious: and this was *Scelera sceleribus tueri*.

King *Hen*. 4.

King *Edward* the Fourth is accused of the murder and death of the King Saint *Henry*, and of *Edward* Prince of Wales his son. (*Ut supra*.)

King *Edw*. 4. *Seneca de Clementia*.

King *Henry* the Seventh (although amongst the best Kings in his general character) is not thought guiltlesse of that *Crimen sacrum vel regale*, in cutting off *Edward Plantagenet* Earl of Warwick, an innocent.

King *Hen*. 7.

Edwardum, filium Ducis Clarenciæ, puerum & infantem, in suam, & suorum securitatem capite plexit.

Gul. Campden in Britan. & Corn.

And to secure his Estate, had more then learnt other smart rules of Policie. That reach of State upon *Philip* of Austrich, Duke of Burgundy, King of Castile and Arragon, is not the least memorable.

This Prince *Philip* was by crosse Fortune put into the Kings hands: purposing out of Flanders to go into Spain, with the Queen his wife, took shipping at Sluce, and passing by the coasts

Grafton. Hollinshead.

of England, was by a tempest forced for his safety to put into the Port of Weymouth in Dorset-shire: the Queen being ill, and distempered much with the storm, was compelled to make some stay there.

Sir *John Carew*, and Sir *Thomas Trenchard* (principal men in those parts) gave speedy intelligence of this to the King, who was glad of the accident, and purposed to make good use of it, as speedily returning his command to give them all honourable entertainment; but not suffer them to depart, until he had seen and saluted them.

The Duke ignorant of this, as soon as the Queen and the rest had recover'd and refresht themselves, thought he was onely to give those Knights thanks, and take his leave; which they by way of courtesie and request interpose, in behalf of the Kings vehement desire to salute him and the Queen: a motion the Duke much prest to be excused from, as the necessity of his journey stood: but the intreaty was so imperious, he must stay, and alter his journey for Windsor, to meet the King, who received him there in a magnificent manner; and at the height of a Feast, propounds a suit to the Duke for *Edmund de la Pool* (then in his Dominions) a pretender to the Crown of England, and not so soundly affected to him: a suit of a harsh exposition, as the Duke apprehended it, and to the blemish of his honour and piety, as he nobly urged: but no argument had vertue, nor no vertue argument enough to excuse it; the King must have him, or the Duke must stay. Cast upon this extreme (and foreseeing what disadvantages were upon him, some honourable conditions granted, that he should neither lay punishment nor death upon him) he gave his promise to send him, and the King strictly and religiously bound himself to the exceptions.

The Duke accordingly sent this *de la Pool* into England; who upon his arrival was delivered to the Tower; but his life not toucht until the King lay a dying; then he equivocated his Vow by a Mental Reservation, enjoyning his son after his death to cut off his head; which was done when he came to be King, and was held some taint to them both; though the son held himself acquit & warranted by the example of King *Solomon*, who was made the instrument of such another subtil slaughter by his father *David*, that thought he kept himself by equivocation: examples not to be imitated by any Christian Prince, being a sin; and sins are to be avoided, not imitated.

The eldest brother of these *de la Pools*, *John de la Pool*, heir to the Duke of Suffolk, and Head of this Family, was slain casually at the Battel of Stoke; and is he who, as neerest kinsman to King *Richard* the Third, was proclaimed heir apparant. The sister of these Princely *de la Pools*, the Lady *Katherine*, was kept close prisoner in the Tower, until grief and sorrow bowed her to the grave.

Nor

Nor is it much from our purpose to note, that the chief *Plantagenets*, namely, the children of King *Edward* the Fourth, had but cold influences then: for the Lady *Bridget* was thrust into a Nunnery at Dartford, chiefly (as it was thought) that she should live sterile, and die without issue. The Lady *Cecily* was married to a base fellow, that so her issue might be ignoble and contemptible; the wrong being the greater, in regard she was offered Matches to her quality; the King of Scotland propounding Prince *James* unto her; and the French King *Lewis* demanded her for the Dolphin *Charles* of France.

Grafton.

Polidor. lib. 4.

It was observed too, that this King was but an unkinde and severe husband to his Queen (indeed!) they had all but short lives; and our Stories report he picked a quarrel with the Queen-Dowager-Mother, for an old and venial errour, because she delivered her son *Richard* to the Protector; for which there was a Confiscation upon all her Goods, Chattels and Revenues, and she confined to Bermondsey Abbey, where she lived not long, care and grief untwisting the threed of her sad fate. And when death had seized him from all the glories and policies of this world, his son succeeds; and then, *Residuum Locustæ, Bruchus comedit; & residuum Bruchi comedit Rubigo*: for, what remained of the House of York, he gave the last blowe to; and after the dispatch of the aforesaid *Edmund de la Pool*, caused the Lady *Margaret Plantagenet* Countesse of Salisbury, then daughter and heir of *George* Duke of Clarence, to be attainted of Treason by Act of Parliament, and condemned unheard, being dragged to the Block barbarously by the hair of her head, though above Threescore yeers in age, *Anno* 33 *Henr.* 8. Not long after, Sir *Henry Pool* her eldest son was put to death, and her son *Reynold Pool* was attainted of Treason with her (no man knowing what the Treason was) but got suddenly out of the Kingdom into Italy, where he became much favoured by the Princes there, and by the Popes afterward made Cardinal, and highly renowned) in those times) for his Learning, Piety and other noble merits. *Richard Pool*, another son of the Countesse of Salisbury, fled, and lived a banished man in forraign Countreys; yet at the height of a good reputation, until he was slain at the Battel of Pavia.

Although the Lady *Anne* and the Lady *Katherine* were well married, that may not be alleadged here; for they were bestowed in the time of *Rich.* 3. the one to the Lord *Haward* after Duke of Norfolk, the other to the Earl of Devon.

Robert Glover. Joel, cap. 1.

Dominus Joh. Baro de Lumley, viva voce.

These be sad pauses, which my Pen but touches at, to note the Partiality of some on one side, and the malignity of some on the other side, who have made King *Richard* the worst of all Princes; when other of our own, have had as great an appetite of Empire, whose fames and sacred names we gratulate with honour.

Nor let my just and plain meaning be mistaken, which urges nothing in dislike or exprobation that King *Henry* the Seventh had the Crown, whom our age must acknowledge a wise, provident

dent and religious Prince, The restorer of the ancient Line of the British Kings to their Raign and Kingdom, Nephew of King *Henry* the Sixth by his Grandmother Queen *Katherine*, widow of King *Henry* the Fifth, and mother of King *Henry* the Sixth, and of his brother Uterine *Edmund Teudor* Earl of Richmond, the father of this King *Henry* the Seventh; and so he was Nephew also to *Charles* the Seventh King of France. I onely conceive he took it by too violent a hand, not staying *tempus bene placiti*.

And here I may fitly take occasion to make up a Defect or Brack covertly imputed to the Titles of the Normans, and Princes of York, by our vulgar Historians and Chroniclers.

The sundry great Titles of our King to the Crown of England.

And first, we are to suppose, If there be, it grew by the errour of King *Edwards* Marriage, by which they hold that Title was weakned (at the least blemished) but that could have no continuance, being made sound again as soon as King *Richard* came to raign, and after cured and confirmed by the mighty power of sundry Parliaments, by which it was made as strong and firm as ever; besides the aid of the Dispensations Apostolical (in those times sacred and authentick.) And without that (if need were) our King now raigning hath other Royal Rights, more then *funiculus Triplex*; some more ancient, authentick and just, therefore more secured, and of more prosperous hopes then that Norman Title, which was a violent acquest of the Sword, and a purchase made by blood, so consequently none of the best; which was well conceived by that great *Macedon*, when he said, *Non est diuturna possessio in quam gladio inducimus*. Neither would it avail in this behalf to cite or avouch the Donation of this Kingdom, which the Confessor is said to have made to *William* the Conquerour, being to no purpose, because that gift or Legacy was disclaimed and disallowed by the Barons of this Land, and found to be void.

Alex. apud Curtium, lib. 8.

Yet time now, and prescription, have also made that Title good: for prescription hath power to ratifie and confirm the Titles both of Princes and of private men.

But our King is the immediate and sole lawful Heir of King *Egbert* (who first gave the name of *England* to this Land, and was absolute Lord of it) from him, by the glorious Kings, *Edgar*, *Edmund*, *Athelstan*, *Alfred*, and many others, as well Saxons and Angles, as Anglo-Saxons, the Right and Title of this Kingdom is duely descended and devolved to *Edmund Ironside* King of England, who was father to the most Noble *Clyto*, *Edward* sirnamed *Exul*, whose fair daughter and heir (a religious Lady) the Princesse *Margaret* of England, was married to *Malcom Canmoire* King of Scotland; from which ancient and happie Alliance, the King our Soveraign Lord is directly and certainly descended, and is the true and onely Heir to the Rights and Titles which were without flaw; so the most ancient and

Clyto, that is, A Prince of the blood.

famous Title, and Right of the first Kings of Britain are in him, being the next Heir of our last British King *Henry Teudor*, wose Genealogie I have seen derived from the antique Kings of Britain, and from divers other British Princes. And this *Henry Teudor* (or the Seventh) to confirm all the Titles of this Kingdom unto his claim, by the strongest and greatest autority, procured them decreed to him and to his issue (so established in himself, and his posterity for ever) by Act of Parliament, in this manner and words.

TO the Pleasure of Almighty God, and for the Wealth, and Prosperity, and Surety of this Realm of England, to the singular Comfort of all the Subjects of the same, and for avoyding all Ambiguities and Questions: *Anno* 1. H. 7. in Parliament, in Novemb.

Be it Ordained, Established and Enacted by the Authority of this present Parliament, That the Inheritance of the Crown of the Realm of England, and also of France, with all the Pre-eminencies and Dignities Royal to the same appertaining, and all Liegances to the King belonging beyond the Seas, with the appurtenances thereunto in any wise due or appertaining, To be, rest, remain and abide in the most Royal person of our Soveraign Lord King *Henry* the Seventh, and in the Heirs of his body lawfully comming perpetually, with the Grace of God, and so to endure, and in no other.

Which is also another Title to our King, Heir to *Henry* the Seventh.

And this Act was renewed and firmly established, for our Soveraign Lord King *James*, *Anno regni prima*.

Yet King *Henry* the Seventh obtained of the Pope another Title, *Jure Belli*.

All which Titles and Rights (which ever were appertaining to this Kingdom, and to the Empire of Britain) are coalesced and met in our Soveraign King; for he hath not onely the claims of the ancient Kings of Britain, of the Saxons, and Anglo-Saxons Kings, and of the Norman Race; but also the Titles and Rights of the Royal Families of York, of Lancaster, and of *Wales*, &c.

And (not as the least, in reference with these) he hath in

possession also, those singular and particular Monuments of Empire and Raign, by some called *Fata Regni*, and *Instrumenta & Monumenta Regno, & Imperio destinata*.

The wedding Ring of England.

Edwardus Ethelredus á Rivallis.

One being the Ring of the accounted holy King *Edward*, the son of King *Etheldred*, which was consecrated and extraordinarily blessed by Saint *John Baptist* in Palestine, and sent back by the King (as old Writers tell) which hath been religiously kept in the Abbey of Westminster, and is (as Tradition goes) the Ring which the Archbishop of Canterbury at the Inauguration and Consecration of the Kings, puts upon their finger; called in our Stories, *The Wedding Ring of England*.

The fatall stone.

The other Monument of the British Empire, is the Marble-stone whereupon *Jacob* laid his head, when he had those cælestial and mystical Visions mentioned in holy Writ; which stone was brought out of Palestine into Ireland, and from thence carried into Scotland by King *Keneth*; after translated to the City of Scone, and used for the Chaire wherin the Kings sate at their Coronation; brought out of Scotland by *Edward* the First into England, as the best Historians of Scotland and England relate.

Hector, Boetius lib. 4. Et Geo. Buchan Gul. Cambden.

Cathedram Marmoream Regibus Scotorum fatalem (in qua insidentes Scotorum Reges Coronare consueverant.)

Rex Edwardus primus è Scona Londinum transtulit, & in Westmonasterio (ubi hodie visitur) deposuit.

It is set or born in a Chaire of Wood, and for a perpetual honour (upon a Table hanging in the Chappel at Westminster) this is writ:

——Si quid habet ueri vel Chronica cana, fidesve
Clauditu hac Cathedra, Nobilis ille lapis,
——Ad caput, eximius Jacob *quondam Patriarcha,*
Quem posuit cernens numina mirifica;
Quem tulit a Scotis Edwardus *primus*, &c.

George Buchanus saith, The people are seriously perswaded that in this stone (which he calleth *Lapidem Marmoreum rudem*) the state of the kingdom is contained, and that *fatum Regni* is thus understood; *viz.* What King of Scotland soever is Lord of that Stone, & Soveraignly possessed thereof, shall be King and raign in the Countrey where he findeth that stone: thus told in a prophetical Distich.

In hoc lapide fatum regni Scotiæ continetur. Geor. Buchan.

Ni fallat fatum, Scotus quocunque locatum
Inveniet lapidem, regnare tenetur ibidem.

Which

Which Prophecie was accomplished in King *James*, when he came first into England: for his Titles were not onely *funiculus triplex qui difficile rumpitur*; but also *funiculus multiplex qui nunquam rumpitur.* And may those Titles for ever be establisht in his Loins, according to that of the heavenly Messenger, *Regnum perpetuum. & cujus non est finis.* Amen.

Scotus primus Rex Scotie, ut Anglus Gallus Hispanus &c. pro Rex Angliæ Galliæ Hispan. &c.

Thus I have led you thorow the various Relations, and Tragical Interchanges of this Princes Life, to his last act and place, where, after Revenge and Rage had satiated their barbarous cruelties upon his dead body) they gave his Royal earth a bed of earth, honourably, appointed by the Order of King *Henry* the Seventh, in the chief Church of Leicester, called Saint *Maries*, belonging to the Order and Society of the Gray Friers; the King in short time after causing a fair Tomb of mingled colour'd Marble, adorned with his Statue, to be erected thereupon, to which some grateful pen had also destined an Epitaph, the Copie whereof (never fixt to his stone) I have seen in a recorded Manuscript-Book chained to a Table in a Chamber in the Guild-hall of London: which (the faults and corruptions being amended) is thus represented, together with the Title thereunto prefixed as I found it.

Octob. 9. 1646.
Imprimatur, *Na: Brent.*

TO give you him in his equal Draught and Composition: He was of a mean or lowe compact, but without disproportiō & unevenesse either in lineaments or parts (as his severall Pictures present him.) His aspect had most of the Souldier in it; so his natural inclination (Complexions not uncertainely expounding our Dispositions) but what wants of the Court-Planet, effeminate Censurers think must needs be harsh and crabbed (and Envie will pick quarrels with an hair, rather then want Subject.) The Judgement and Courage of his Sword-actions, rendred him of a full Honour and Experience, which Fortune gratified with many Victories; never any Overthrows through his own default, for lack of Valour or Policie. At Court, and in his general deportment, of an affable respect and tractable cleernesse. In his dispence, of a magnificent liberal hand, somewhat above his power (as Sir *Tho. Moor* sets down.) And surely the many Churches, with other good works he founded, (more then any one former King did in so short a time) must commend him charitable and religious, as the excellent Laws he made, do his wisedom and strain of Government, which all men confesse of the best. So having (even from those his bitterest times) the esteem of a valiant, wise, noble, charitable and religious Prince, why should ours deprave him so much upon trust, & deny works their character and place? Epi-

Sir *Tho. Moor.* Duke *Buckingh.* in his speech to Mr. *Morton.*

EPITAPHIUM

Regis Richardi tertii,

Sepulti ad Leicestriam, jussu, & sumptibus Sti Regis Henrici Septimi.

Hic ego, quem vario Tellus sub Marmore claudit,
Tertius a justa voce Richardus *eram;*
Tutor eram Patriæ, Patrius pro jure Nepotis;
Dirupta, tenui regna Britanna, fide.
Sexaginta dies binis duntaxat ademptis
Ætatesque, tuli tunc mea Sceptra, duas. Annos 2. & 51. dies.
Fortiter in Bello certans desertus ab Anglis,
Rex Henrice, *tibi, septime, succubui.*
At sumptu, pius ipse, tuo, sic ossa decoras,
Regem olimque facis Regis honore Coli.
Quatuor exceptis jam tantum, quinq; bis annis
Acta trecenta quidem, lustra salutis erant, Anno Dominie 1484.
Antique Septembris undena luce Kalendas, Die 21. Aug.
Redideram rubræ jura petita Rosæ.
At mea, quisquis eris, propter commissa precarem
Sit Minor ut precibus pœna levata tuis.

Deo O. M. Trino & Uno,
sit laus & gloria æterna.
Amen.

EPIGRAMMA

In Richardos Angliæ Reges, ex vet. lib. M. S. transcriptum.

TRes *sunt* Richardi *quorum fortuna erat æqua,*
In tribus æscariis sua cujus propria sors est,
Nam Concors horum finis sine posteritate
Corporis, atque rapax vitæ modus, & violentus
Interitus fuerat; sed major gloria primi,
Prælia terrarum qui gesserat & redeuntem
Tela Balistarum feriunt apud extera regna.
Alter depositus regno, qui carcere Clausus,
Mensibus extiterat certis, fame velle perire
Elegit potius, quam famæ probra videre.
Tertius exhausto statim amplo divitiarum
Edwardi *cumulo, proscribens auxiliares*
Henrici *partes, post annos denique binos*
Suscepti regni, Bello confectus eisdem
Mundanam vitam, tum perdidit atque Coronam:
Anno milleno; Centum quater octuageno,
Adjunctis quinque, & cum lux Sextilis adest
Vndena duplex, dentes apri stupuerunt,
Et vindex albæ Rosa Rubra refloret in orbe.

FINIS.

TO THE

FAVOURABLE ACCEPTANCE

Of the Right Honourable

PHILIP Earle of *Pembrooke* and *Mountgomery, &c.*

Sir,

HAving collected these papers out of their dust, I was bold to hope, there might be somthing in them of a better fate (if mine obscure pen darken not that too.) Please your Lordshipp to let your name, make them another witnesse of your noblenesse, it may redeeme and improve them, to a clearer opinion and acknowlegedment of these times, in which I am to meet every Critick, at his owne weapon, who will challenge the Book at the very Title: The Malicious and Malevolent, with their blotted Coments; the Captious & Incredulous, with their jealous præcisianismes, whose inclinations shewes them of envious perplexed natures, to looke at other mens actions and memory by the wrong end of the perspective, and (me thinks) I fancy them to our shaddowes, which at noone creepe behind like Dwarfes, at evening, stalke by like Gyants; they will haunte the noblest merits and endeavors to their Sun-set, then they monster it: but to the Common-rout, they are another kind of Genius, or ignis fatuus; *leades them into darke, strange, wanderings, there they stick: for to perswade the opinionated vulgar out of their ignorant selves, is of as high a beliefe to me, as to transpeciate a Beast into a man; I (therefore) shall crave favour, to protest these papers beyond their Censure, and humour: But to those they are wished (I hope) their weak accesses may be the more pardonable since they are the kindlings and scintillations of a modest Ambition, to truth and gratitude, which gives me the encouragement to assure your Lordship, that if mine Authors be sincere and faithfull, my pen is free and innocent, having learned, that a story (as it ought) must be a just, perspicuous Narration of things memorable, spoken, and don. The Historiographer, veritable; free from all Prosopolepsyes, or partiall respects, and surely his pen should tast with a great deal of Conscience, for there is nothing leaves so an infected a sting, or scandall, as History, it rankles to all posterity, wounds our good names, to all memory & places, by an Authentick kind of preiudice: I am with his opinion, in his excellent* Religio Medici, *who holds it an offence to Charity, and as bloody a thought one way, as* Nero's *in another; My Lord, under these humble addresses, this sues to your honoured hand, Presented by the unfained wishes of your*

Honours avowed

and humble Servant,

GEO: BUCK.

A Table of the Heads contained in this Booke.

*

Sove-

War

The Table.

An Explication of some dark words and Sentences.

SObriquets *or Sobriquets; Nickenams*, 4.

Angeume, of or belonging to Anjou.

Naturall son; i. a Bastard, also a naturall Father.

Rodomantade, *p.* 12. *a brag or bravado.*

Cloth *of assuyance*, 27. *Towel or napkin that wait on the cup.*

Contrast, *withstanding or repugnance.*

Parergum, 32. *Something added that is not of the principall matter.*

Tort, 35. *wrong, injury, and violeuce.*

Vmbrage *or* Ombrage, 35. *Suspition, also disgrace.*

Disgust, 36. *Distaste.*

Contrecar, 44. *A counter-strength, &c.*

Filij populi, 44. *Bastards so called, being children of common women, & in respect of the Father of uncertaine Parentage.*

Ne Croix ny Pile, 51. *Neither cross nor pile, not one title or jot of right, &c.*

Ambidexter, *a Jack on both sides.*

Brother *uterine*, 51. (1) *by the mothers side.*

Abbayance. 53. *In delay or dispute, such as Lawyers use, a term borrowed from another creature.*

Apodixis, 60. *Plain demonstration of a thing.*

Inconcuss, *that cannot be shaken, undaunted.*

Bartlemies, 63. *Meant of the great and generall massacre of above* 100000. *Protestants in* France, *chiefly in* Paris, *and the Countrey adjoyning on Saint* Bartholmews *Eve*, Anno 72. *whereupon* St. *Bartholmews teares*,

Bartholomæus flet, quia Gallicus occubat Atlas.

Como

Authors quoted in this History.

AUgustine.
Aristotle.
Baleus.
Boetius.
Buchan.
Cambden.
Cicero.
Cambrensis.
Claudian.
Croyland Pryor
Comineus
Cooke
Demosthines
Dion.
Æsopus.
Euripides
Ennius
Erasmus
Epictetus
Fabian
Fuchius
Froisard
Grafton
Glover
Gainsford
Goodwin
Du Hailon
Hall
Hollinshead
Hyrd
De-le-Hay
Harding
Hist. de Brit.
Homer
Julius Capitol
Juvenall
Justus Vulterius
Lib. Manuscr.
Apud D. Rob. Cotton.
Lampridius
Lucan
Maximus.
Moore
Monstrolet
Newbrigensis
Nycrus
Ovid
Osiander
Pliny
Paradin
Polidor Virg.
Plutarch
Seneca
Sarisburiensis
Stow
Strabo
Socrates
Stanford
Suetonius
De Serres
Tacitus
Terence
Tillet
Virgill
Valla
Walsingham

With many Parliament Roules and Records.

FINIS.

Ingram Content Group UK Ltd.
Milton Keynes UK
UKHW051315040723
424506UK00005BA/109

9 781015 701656